P9-CRT-407

Wings
of
Change

Wings of Change

A Dutch Immigrant's Journey

Titia Bozuwa

TRIPLE TULIP PRESS
Sanbornville, NH

Pulished by Triple Tulip Press
2717 Wakefield Road
Sanbornville, NH 03872

Copyright © 2007 by Titia Bozuwa

All rights reserved. No part of this book may be reproduced or transmitted
in any form or by any means, electronic or mechanical, including
photocopying, recording, or by any information storage and retrieval system,
without permission in writing from the copyright owner.

ISBN: 0-9754825-2-1 (10 digits)
        978-0-9754825-2-0 (13 digits)

Library of Congress Control Number: 2006907814

Editor: Sue Wheeler
Printer: The Sheridan Press, Hanover, PA 17331
Cover design and interior design: Jo Higgins
Pictures: By the author and taken from private collections

For Gijs
who taught me to fly

Also by Titia Bozuwa:

Joan, A Mother's Memoir (2000)

In the Shadow of the Cathedral (2004)

Acknowledgements

In the first place, I want to thank Gijs, who allowed me to write this memoir from my own perspective and without restrictions. His support and encouragement have been generous and indispensable.

My son Paul has been equally supportive. His experience in publishing provided crucial help. His wife, Colleen, read and critiqued the manuscript in the very early stages and made valuable suggestions. I thank both of them for their time and efforts.

In the fall of 1992, I started taking creative writing classes with Martha Barrett at the University of New Hampshire. She inspired me. The Molasses Pond Writers Workshops were the next step on my path to become a writer, and soon I found myself within a circle of aspiring writers. Teachers like Sue Wheeler, Rebecca Rule and Maren Tirabassi have contributed greatly to my understanding of writing techniques, as have my fellow work-shoppers, too numerous to mention by name.

I am indebted to my editor, Sue Wheeler, for giving generously of her time and talent. Her insights helped shape my memories into a manageable format. Both she and Martha Barrett have greatly inspired me, and I am proud to call them my friends.

Elizabeth Barrett did a fine job of line editing. She has a keen eye for the many details I tend to overlook.

Jane Howe was instrumental in giving me the final push to write this book. Her literary insight, honest comments, and enduring friendship are precious to me.

Last but not least, I want to praise and thank Jo Higgins. Always ready to solve my computer problems, she gave of herself generously. Her talent for graphic design is outstanding. The cover and the interior layout greatly benefited from her artist's eye, and I am in awe of the untold hours she spent behind her computer to give this book a special feel.

To all of the above and many more who know who they are, I extend my deep feelings of gratitude.

Table of Contents

"Life must be understood backwards; but it must be lived forward."

–Sören Kierkegaard

Prologue
1943

I saw a heron at the edge of the river, so perfectly blended with the reeds I hadn't noticed it standing there right away. Without warning, it rose up and immediately unfurled its wide wings. Gathering speed quickly with powerful strokes, it skimmed the river and then flew over the meadows. I watched its gray silhouette against the winter sky till it was completely out of sight.

What would it be like, I wondered, to fly away to the unknown? I didn't wish it for myself, even though we were in a war. I was anchored here. Holland was where I belonged. Even on a blustery winter day.

That day was a long time ago, but I remember it well, because flying away to the unknown would come to define and shape my life.

Chapter 1

Crossing
the Atlantic

The road to the airport was laid with bricks that made the tires on my father's car sing. Gijs was at the wheel and my father, too emotional to drive, was in the passenger seat. Gijs and I were on our way to America. I dreaded it. Emigration was not a move I had ever imagined for myself.

When we bumped over a railroad crossing, I felt a sudden movement inside, as if my baby were making a somersault, knocking its feet against the walls that contained it. I tried not to show how this jerking unnerved me, but my mother was alert and her hand took hold of mine. I would recognize that hand—its shape, its lines, and its energy—anywhere in the world without seeing it. I knew the touch and the unspoken words. They had seen me through bombardments, near-fatal blood poisoning, and childhood fears.

I leaned back into the plush upholstery and looked out over the meadows with the outlines of villages on the horizon. The familiar voices in the car, the sight of people in woolen overcoats pushing hard on the pedals of their bikes against the ever-present wind, these sounds and sights I would have taken for granted any other day. A sense of loss and emptiness pervaded my mood. Would I remember, once we'd made it to the other side, the everyday details of the life I'd known as a child, like the taste of a shiny raw herring; or the smell of a fertilized pasture on a damp winter morning; or the boisterous sounds of the farmers' market down the street; or the flat landscape under inky clouds that restlessly moved from horizon to horizon, letting the sun through only in patches?

Gijs had taken his board exam the day before. He was now an M.D., licensed to practice medicine in Holland. However, we were on our way to the United States. Under the provisions of the Eisenhower Special Immigration Quota, we were required to set foot on American soil by March 1, 1957, which would be the day after tomorrow.

The movers had come, and in the span of five hours all the wedding gifts we'd received the previous spring had disappeared into tissue paper. The few antiques we'd carefully selected to remember Holland by—an oak chest and a corner cabinet with a drawbridge painted on its front panel—were wrapped in our blankets. The towels and heavy linen sheets, embroidered with our intertwined last-name initials, found their way into cardboard boxes, and men in gray dustcoats had carried all of it down two flights of stairs. We'd pulled the door shut on the rented apartment in Rotterdam and headed for my parents' home in Breda.

Gijs had sounded remarkably chipper throughout it all for someone who'd stumbled up the stairs only hours earlier after a night of celebrating the good results of his exam with his father and some friends. A happy drunk doesn't get you hung over, he'd said, brushing aside my concerns. He was out of bed before dawn. But then, he was always upbeat, the kind of man who thoroughly believes in his own good luck. Even suffering through Japanese prison camp in the Dutch East Indies during the war

Entering the town hall for the civil ceremony

hadn't diminished his spirits. Life was an adventure, all of it, the good and the bad. Gijs didn't look back. The emigration was one more adventure. In his youth he'd moved across the oceans several times, following his father's navy career. He couldn't count on one hand the schools he'd attended.

When he proposed to me, he had a plan. We would get married right away and go to America within weeks. He had won a Fulbright scholarship and would earn a salary as an intern in a hospital outside of Boston. Presto! I was aghast, but I loved this big, cheerful, honest man and I said, "Yes." But the next morning I realized I'd only just met him. I didn't know his parents or anything about him. Who was this Gijs Bozuwa? I called it off. But Gijs was persistent and went to my parents to ask for my hand. I was sent to my room and an hour later—it seemed to take forever—I was called downstairs and they all looked very proud of themselves. Gijs would go ahead to the States and I would follow later so we could evaluate this land of opportunity together. My parents had offered to pay for my trip. They trusted their future son-in-law to make a considered decision for our future, and most amazing for the times, they allowed him to take their only daughter to a far-away place without insisting on a wedding first. When we came back from America, we had a big wedding. Emigration was certainly a possibility, but it generally took five years or more to get the papers. A lot could happen in five years.

Our last night in Holland we'd spent in the bed of my youth, where I'd heard the American bombers and German V Ones fly over, humming in a steady drone on their deadly missions. I'd said farewell to the good people who'd cared for me: my father's assistants in his pharmacy, the cleaning woman, and the neighbors who'd shared our basement during the last week of the war. They were tearful and mystified. America was very far away, incomprehensible in its newness. Good things came from there, to be sure, like corned beef when we were starved, cigarettes, and second-hand clothes that looked bright and funny while ours were drab and threadbare. America was generous, but they had a hard time imagining what they saw portrayed as daily life in the Hollywood movies, and they certainly couldn't place *me* in it.

When we stepped in the car, we had only three suitcases and some hand luggage for the gypsy-style living we were in for until our crated belongings could be shipped to a permanent address. The smallest suitcase held the baby clothes my mother had washed, bleached, and starched.

The first trip to America I had made alone on the *ss Nieuw Amsterdam*, and it had been unforgettable to float by the Statue of Liberty and see the Manhattan skyline come into view on a hazy summer morning. Today's trip would land us at Idlewild Airport, outside New York, in the dead of winter.

From the serenity of my father's car we stepped into urban confusion at Schiphol Airport. Inside, a sophisticated voice made crisp announcements over the loudspeakers, announcing departures to all ends of the earth in flawless English, French, German, and Dutch. Gijs's parents, his sister with her husband, and my two older brothers were waiting for us at the check-in counter.

"Did you bring your obstetrical kit?" Janneke asked her brother. Everyone laughed nervously. We all knew it was illegal to fly when more than six months pregnant. I was entering my eighth month of pregnancy. Gijs had fudged the papers. He'd had no choice, squeezed as we were between the earliest possible date he could do his board exam and the last possible day we could enter America under the special Eisenhower quota. We'd been in a race against time. I read concern on the faces around us, but I knew Gijs would see me through. There were no bounds to my trust.

"I did," Gijs said with finality.

"*Attentie als 't U blieft,*" the sophisticated, cool voice over the loudspeaker said. "Passengers for flight 207 to New York are requested to..."

I excused myself and went to the restroom. As I washed my hands, my mother came through the door.

"When your baby is baptized I will come over for it," she said. I was stunned.

"Will Pappie let you go?" I asked.

"He will have to," she said. Her eyes twinkled like stars.

We joined the line that was crawling toward the exit. Gijs put a protective arm around my shoulder. The gate was only a foot away now. Once through that gate there was no turning back. This was it. With Gijs I would not live in a provincial red brick doctor's house somewhere behind a dike. With Gijs there would be adventure, and the price to be paid was separation from the familiar. I saved my last farewell for the minute I could disappear from view. I tried to turn my mind into a void as the stout, warm body of my mother pressed into mine. I had thought all thoughts on the way to the airport, and long before, and I had seen the depth of my mother's love through the stirrings of the new life inside of me. She had encouraged me to emigrate, to follow Gijs. Where had she found the strength? When I looked into her lively eyes, I saw borderless love, the kind of love that knows how to let go.

"I'll take good care of her, Mammie," Gijs said. "Don't worry."

"I'm not worried, Gijs," she said, and gave him a big hug.

The big propellers hung like heavy fruit from the silver wings. They would have to twirl around for eighteen hours with only two breaks, one in Ireland, and the other in Nova Scotia. Underneath the wings I watched Holland's landscape turn into a map, printed on faded green pastures, delineated by black skeletons of bare February trees and icy cold rivers, until its contrasts blended into a mass without texture, the undefined color of memory.

Somewhere, halfway over the Atlantic Ocean, I felt a fierce tension, as if the elastic band that had tied me to home, to everything I had known so far, couldn't be stretched any further. I needed to let go of it or it would lash me. I felt like the robin whose nest has fallen to the ground and needs a new location to build another nest.

Millions of people had made this trip before me. Not in an airplane, not with a doctor at their side, not with the prospect of a certain job. Those millions had taken the uncertain step of emigration out of economic necessity or from fear of persecution. None of those conditions applied to Gijs and me. We were sitting in this plane because there were too many doctors in Holland and because Gijs wanted to make it on his own. In the end we had made the decision together, Gijs the initiator, I the follower. The prospect had felt like a limb was sawn off my tree of life, the branch that spoke Dutch and celebrated the Queen's birthday, the part of me that had been fiercely patriotic during the war.

The new life inside of me began to correct that outlook. Instead of a damaged tree I tried my best to envision a sapling that could adapt to American soil.

This vision was my prayer.

The wrenching farewells were history.

Before us was a blank page.

Chapter 2
A Difficult Message

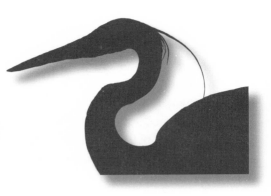

The hardest thing I'd had to do was telling my mother we might emigrate. It was October and we were in a restaurant called Americain. It wasn't typically French, in spite of the spelling, and neither did it remind me of America in any way. But it's where we were, in Utrecht, while Gijs and my father visited their alma mater.

I'd been married for four months. Mammie wondered why I hadn't taken a job as a Montessori teacher instead of a part-time secretarial one. After all, that's what I had studied to be. But I told her that I couldn't commit myself to a whole year and that was a requirement.

"Why not?" she'd asked with a quizzical look on her face. My mother could really zero in on things. I pulled my spoon through the hot oxtail soup, back and forth like the pendulum of a grandfather clock, wondering how I could evade her question.

"I don't know where we will be." My stomach knotted because I knew she would draw the right conclusion.

"Is Gijs still thinking about America?" she asked.

The waiter cleared the soup plates and lit the Sterno cans under a warming tray. A steaming platter with blackened sweetbreads, surrounded by a ring of mashed potatoes, materialized. The maitre d' lifted them expertly onto our plates while the waiter offered a variety of vegetables. Mammie pointed at this and that and, with authority, raised her hand when she'd been served enough.

"You know, Mammie, in America they bring in your meal on individual plates. I couldn't believe my eyes when we first went to a restaurant. A huge plate with a steak that would have been enough for our entire family. French fries and a vegetable called broccoli heaped next to it. No chance to say, 'This is way too much.' You just had to accept it."

"America fascinated you both, didn't it?"

Now was the time. I couldn't just sit here and keep her in the dark. She would worm it out of me anyway. But I only said, "Yes, it did."

"Would you like to go back?"

I told her Gijs had left his name at the American Consulate. It was an option. We didn't have to follow up on it.

"He has ambition," Mammie said.

My mother

She was on Gijs's side and it infuriated me. This wasn't like moving from Friesland to Brabant, as she'd done when she got married. I knew she would tell me that it had taken a whole day to travel from Sneek to Breda, not that different from flying from Amsterdam to New York these days.

"We'll be flying through time zones! Mammie, are you suggesting that the distance in miles is the only thing that would make me feel far away? I will have to become a citizen of another country. I will have to live with another language, other customs, another way of life." All my worries and turmoil poured out in anger at not being understood

But my mother understood me very well. She put her fork down and her indomitable spirit rose to the fore. It was what I feared and loved most about my mother. She pointed out that Gijs had been totally fair with me; that he had offered to forego his Fulbright scholarship because he didn't think it was reasonable to go abroad for a year when we had just got engaged. Besides, many women followed their husbands. Before the war they went to the Dutch East Indies. Gijs's mother had been one of them. They hadn't been asked if they liked to or not. They went because they promised to obey and follow their husbands when they got married.

I looked into her blue eyes that were as strong as they were soft. What she said was straight out of the Victorian book of conventions and convictions. Her sense of duty would always prevail.

From the corner of my eye I noticed the waiter. He discretely looked at our plates, which had hardly been touched. I picked at the capers with my fork. Mammie was oblivious to his presence. She was single-minded in her purpose to steer me in the direction she felt I should follow.

"*Titeke*," she went on. She only used that name when she knew I was vulnerable. "Have confidence in yourself," she said, "and trust Gijs's judgment."

"I know, I know. I do trust him. But it's just so difficult to project my life in America. What you said about those women going to the colonies is true, of course. But they didn't have to change nationality. After X number of years they would return and fall right back into their Dutch routine."

"It will all work out. You'll create your own way of life. You will have each other." Mammie said this with conviction. *She* should emigrate, I thought. She would relish the challenge.

We fell silent for a moment and resumed eating. The restaurant had filled and every table was taken. The rise and fall of voices mixed with the polite clatter of knives and forks on plates. The waiters moved swiftly between the kitchen and the tables without making a sound, like actors in a silent movie.

"There's something else I want to tell you, Mammie." This was the hard part. "I am pregnant."

Mammie lowered her knife and fork back to her plate. Her eyes filled and she reached for my hand across the table. Her firm grasp squeezed my shy hand. I looked down at the wrinkles on her hand, at the way the middle finger curved, at the ring on the next finger that looked like a crown. The familiarity of it suddenly overwhelmed me. I will be separated from this, I thought. That's what this was all about: separation. I looked up into her face and all my own thoughts were written there: joy and excitement about a new life; the continuation of blood; the recognition that while I mature she will grow old; that life is about coming and going.

"*Ach Titeke*," she said softly. Then, recovering, she asked, "When?"

"The end of April."

I could see her thinking to herself "Where will she be?" So I said, "I don't know where I'll be."

Five feet away, the maitre d' and our waiter exchanged a questioning glance. Our plates weren't ready to be removed. In fact, we had hardly touched them. What seemed tempting when it was dished up half an

I comtemplate my future

hour ago, now looked ready to be scraped together and fed to the dogs. The thought of food didn't appeal to me any longer.

I noticed tears welling up in my mother's eyes. The coincidence of our emigration and my pregnancy had opened unwelcome vistas for her later years. I wanted to hug her and wipe away the tears, but the formal atmosphere of the restaurant restrained me. What could I say to chase her black thoughts away? When a daughter becomes a mother, a mother becomes a grandmother. I was robbing her of that delight. It was cruel.

My mother's folded hands, the fingers interlaced, rested on the edge of the table in a characteristic pose of contemplation. I lurched forward and said, "Gijs would never force me to emigrate. He's said that several times. I don't even want to go. So. We won't go!" But I underestimated my mother.

"Nonsense. Gijs is absolutely right. There is more opportunity for him. Europe has always been a hotbed for trouble and the Russians can't be trusted. It will be safer to bring your children up there. Europe is old and tired, America young and vigorous. Don't just think of yourself, but also of your children and grandchildren. A man with foresight and ambition wants to go to America."

She made this speech while tears rolled down her face. My husband wanted me to go. My own mother wanted me to go. Obviously, I should go. It was my turn for tears. My heart was stirred by the magnitude of her strength and charity. How I envied her the courage, the abandon even, to face her own future.

The waiter was now clearly distressed by our lack of appetite. He came over to the table and looked at our tear-stained faces and asked if anything was wrong.

"Well...no," Mammie said slowly, "But could I have the check?"

"Wouldn't you like some dessert? Some coffee, Madam?" He looked troubled.

"No thank you. You can clear these dishes."

As we wove our path between the crowded tables, I felt self-conscious, my face twice the size from when we'd entered. At the staircase landing the maitre d' looked at us with curious eyes. The impressive menus were tucked under his arm and the gold-embossed letters of "Americain" stared me in the face. My mother nodded vaguely and breezed past him.

It was a relief to inhale the moist night air. Mammie hooked her arm into mine as we walked down the street and pressed it into her generous bosom. After the poignancy of our conversation, her physical touch was reassuring. We passed the shop windows in silence, absentmindedly registering the merchandise displayed under the floodlights until a "Back to School" sign drew my attention, triggering a nostalgic feeling about autumn, conjuring up musty smells of scattered leaves and sprouting mushrooms, blending the end of things with the excitement of things to come, of things to learn, of reaching broader horizons.

Chapter 3

Immigrants

We took off from Schiphol Airport at eleven a.m. on February's last day, and it was still morning when we landed at Idlewild Airport on the first of March. In Holland it would be four p.m. now and I pictured my mother having tea and wondering how our flight had gone.

Arriving by plane on a gray day in March had none of the wonders of entering New York harbor on an ocean liner and none of the awe of floating by the Statue of Liberty on a hazy summer morning. Hoisting my pregnant body out of the airplane's seat where I'd been anchored for eighteen hours, I had no thought other than to get a breath of fresh air.

In a daze, we followed the disembarking instructions for immigrants that led to a settlement of barracks at the far end of the airfield, our Ellis Island. It was reassuring to know we had tickets for flying on to Boston where we would be met by Pim and Jeannet Visser, a Dutch couple Gijs had befriended during his internship at Quincy City Hospital.

We stood in line. That's what immigrating was all about, it seemed. Back in the fall, we had stood in line to prove we were eligible for a visa and then we had stood in line to get medical tests. The American government took no chances on importing tuberculosis or venereal diseases into its country. I'd signed a piece of paper to the effect that I promised not to engage in sex for money and I'd solemnly sworn that I would not kill the President of the United States. When I had a chest X-ray taken in a drab, cold building in Rotterdam, I'd shared the experience with at least a hundred other applicants, many of them farmers who'd lost their livelihood in the terrible floods, one man-made through bombardments at the end of the war and one by nature's raging in the early fifties. And then there were others like Gijs, who'd repatriated from what used to be the Dutch East Indies. A middle-aged woman had seemed to be the one I always came after in line. She wore the native costume of the province of Zeeland and when her headdress, stiff and lacy and as wide as her shoulders, threatened to rake me, I'd ducked and she'd laughed heartily. Her house had been lost in the floods, she told me, their land left with salt from the seawater. Her husband was a farmer. What is a farmer to do, she'd asked.

Now, in America, we stood in line again to have all those papers checked by immigration officials in crisp uniforms who held the all-important stamping instruments. Finally, we were set free to find the plane to Boston. Gijs was busy making sure our luggage was put on the right plane and I trudged behind, willing to do anything I was told, as long as it would get me to a place with a bed.

"We made it!" Gijs said, squeezing my hand as we strapped ourselves into the seats of a small prop plane. The steady hum of the propellers beside my window drowsed me into a semi-conscious state. It had only been seven months since Gijs had told me he'd stopped off at the American Consulate on his way back from Rotterdam's Harbor Hospital, where he'd done his internship in surgery. On the last day of August, he'd stepped off his bike to watch an ocean liner dock at the other side of the Maas River. Just as he started to remount his bike, he told me, he noticed an American flag flying in the breeze from an impressive house in a row that lined the harbor. It was the American Consulate. On impulse he went inside, even though his watch said it was almost five o'clock. Since it was a Friday afternoon the woman behind the desk was packing her handbag, preparing to leave for the weekend.

Gijs asked what it would take to emigrate to the United States.

"Five years," she answered.

"That's a long time."

"Unless you are a victim of the floods or a P.O.W., of course."

"I am a P.O.W.," Gijs had answered. "I was in a Japanese internment camp on Java for over three years."

The woman looked at the clock. The long hand stood at eleven. She threw down her handbag and created a flurry of activity.

"Here," she said. "Put your name on this list, sign this form here and we can fill the details out next week. The special Eisenhower quota for victims of the flood and WW II runs out at five o'clock today."

Gijs was stunned. Only two minutes separated him from his dream to practice medicine in America. He quickly grabbed the pen the clerk held out to him and put down his name.

He probably didn't expect me to jump for joy as he told me that. In fact, my heart sank. But I could have known this might happen. Going to America had been in the cards all along. Gijs's sister had sung a German hymn at our wedding. *"Wo du hingehst da will ich ach hingehen, Dein Volk ist mein volk."* (Where you go, I will go. Your people are my people.) Shivers had run along my spine as her beautiful soprano and the accompanying organ tones washed over me from behind as I faced the minister who'd just asked me to love and obey my husband. It was crystal clear that both our families foresaw our future, while I was fighting the prospect of having to leave my country.

But Gijs asked me to give it some thought.

I bought a book by a Dutch sociology professor, who'd written a penetrating study about America. One of his observations shook me: the children of immigrants become alienated from their parents because they will be proficient in the English language much quicker than their parents. Their parents' foreign accent or total inability to express themselves in the language of their new country becomes an embarrassment to the children. This, in the professor's view, undermined the family structure in America.

Good God! What a prospect, I thought.

"Did you think that language was a barrier when you treated those stonecutter families from Italy in Quincy?" I asked Gijs.

"I remember one scene when an older man died," Gijs said. "It was a sudden death. The wife talked in Italian while her children just stood around not knowing what to do. I couldn't tell if they understood their mother, but they didn't respond to her in Italian. She looked pathetically isolated to me. So, yes, there was a barrier."

I felt choked up.

"What Professor Brouwer describes," Gijs said, "are the immigrants of the past; the people from Poland, Italy, Russia, Greece. You're ahead if you've learned to speak English before you go over."

"Our children will speak a different kind of English than you learned in Australia or the King's English I learned in England."

"Then you have to learn the way Americans speak. Think of it, most songs we sing these days come from the States!"

I laughed. "And your favorite is Doris Day."

"You seem to have raising children foremost on your mind," Gijs said with an inquisitive look on his face.

"I have good reasons to."

"Oh, I'll be darned," Gijs said, and jumped up from his chair to envelop me in his arms. His embrace exuded his immense joy. We held on to each other in a moment of pure bliss, pushing away invading thoughts of how a pregnancy would complicate our immediate future.

The stewardess came around with her food cart and woke me up from my reveries. Gijs had fallen asleep beside me. I motioned not to wake him up. He was just as exhausted as I was. I carried the baby. He carried the responsibility. I tried to peek around the propellers to get a look at what was below me. In the twilight, I saw lights pop up here and there in a mostly wooded landscape. Maybe we were flying over Connecticut? We could have been on our way to Oregon, but we had decided on New England.

Once I had listened to my mother's advice and given in to Gijs's dream of emigrating, we had spread the map of the United States of America on the carpet in the living room. There were forty-eight states and Washington, D.C. to choose from. I was bewildered. Should we throw a dart? We eliminated the Pacific coast, first thing, as it would put us twice as far from Holland. Then we wondered what the difference between Maryland and, say, Wisconsin would be. Our first acquaintance with America had been with the Atlantic coast. After some deliberation we agreed to narrow our search to that side of the U.S. The next choice

Studying maps with Janneke and Dick

was between the North and the South.

On my first trip to the States I had taken a job as governess for a family in one of the Boston suburbs. When they had to move to South Carolina, I was asked to bring the children down after the parents got settled in their new house, so I flew them to Myrtle Beach. I was there for only two weeks. The beach was beautiful, the countryside different and interesting. But when I was reprimanded for socializing with the black maid in the kitchen after the day's work was done, I knew I could never live in the South. My upbringing hadn't prepared me for the racial conflict that became obvious even during the short time I was there. As a child, I had happily spent hours in the kitchen with our maid. Mr. Wellman, whom I really liked, sympathized with me when I protested, but, he said, this was the way of the South and that was where we live now.

The most compelling determinant was which state would license a foreign doctor to practice solo medicine while awaiting American citizenship. Gijs's plan was to do a residency in general practice for a year and then hang out his shingle somewhere. Only two states qualified for that arrangement, it turned out. Oregon and New Hampshire. Oregon was too far away. The search had narrowed itself.

We landed in Boston around five p.m. Pim was there to greet us and take us to his home in Norwell, a suburb to the south. Jeannet had prepared a meal and a room. We could stay with them until we'd found a place to live in Hanover, New Hampshire, where Gijs would do a residency.

The radio clock next to our bed stood at eight p.m. when we turned in. We'd been up for thirty-three hours. I wondered when they would receive the telegrams we'd sent to both sets of parents, but my mind was too dull to figure out the time difference with Holland. I simply set my watch for the same hour as the radio clock. From now on we would live on Eastern Standard Time.

Chapter 4

First Trip
to Hanover

Route 4 stretched out before us like a black satin ribbon, glistening in the rain. Pim had generously lent us his black Dodge for the trip to New Hampshire.

Our way had wound through cities and towns, the distances between them becoming greater as we progressed from the south shore of Boston in a northwesterly direction. Pim had warned us that March was mud season in New England. It made for a desolate landscape of dead grass and tangles of untended brush under tall trees. The dirty snow banks reminded me of the crumbling walls of war ruins, and I was painfully aware that in Holland the crocuses would be peeking through the green grass at this time. There would be at least a village on the horizon and cows in the fields, but we hadn't seen a house for miles and there wasn't one in sight. Did people live here? How did they make a living? From the woods? We stopped wondering out loud. It just seemed too painful to admit that we felt acute homesickness.

How could I have been so happy and relieved when we finally received a telegram from the Mary Hitchcock Hospital in Hanover that stated "General Practice residency accepted. Expect you April 1," that I dropped a tray with crystal glasses? The Mary Hitchcock had been the only hospital in the state of New Hampshire that offered a residency in general practice. Gijs had put all his eggs in one basket by applying only there, but we heard nothing for months. Pim Visser finally cleared the mystery, when he heard about it. He mentioned it to a friend who happened to be the niece of Mr. Hopkins, a retired president of Dartmouth College. It turned out that the hospital didn't accept foreign residents because of the language barrier. The friend personally vouched for Gijs's ability to speak English fluently.

It was getting dark when we saw the first road sign with "Hanover" on it, and pitch dark by the time we pulled up to the inn where Gijs had made a reservation for two nights. A bellboy in a red jacket with brass buttons emerged to take our bags. I thought he was surprisingly well turned out for this neck of the woods, but I didn't question it. If only I could put up my swollen feet and rest the two bodies, the baby's and my own, after the day's confinement in the car. I needed to tune out those somber, frightening woods.

The next morning, Gijs jumped out of bed early and opened the heavy floor-length curtains aside to let in the light.

"Titia, look! You won't believe your eyes!"

I scrambled out of bed. Gijs could be so maddeningly enthusiastic if he wanted to put a positive spin on things. He couldn't have missed the effect the dark woods and crusty snow banks had had on me the day before. They still clouded my mind and I felt like I'd slept under a heavy blanket.

Outside the window was a huge rectangular field, partly covered with snow, enclosed by stately white buildings on one side and a red brick Georgian style building with a bell tower on top. The rising sun stroked the slate rooftops with its orange rays. It looked like a movie set, too perfect for reality, even at the dreary end of winter.

"It's absolutely beautiful," I said. "What do you suppose it is?"

"I'm not sure. I'll go and find out." Gijs pulled his suit on over his pajamas and left.

"That, sir," the bellboy in the red jacket had answered Gijs in utter amazement, "is Dartmouth College."

We should have known, but in Holland we had universities instead of colleges, and they constituted of a series of buildings that blended in with the rest of the city. The idea of a campus was not a Continental concept, just as the idea of an inn was very different. In Holland it would be the simplest place for lodgings one could find, but the Hanover Inn, it turned out, was anything but simple. We would have called it the Hanover Hotel. So, that was lesson number one in finding our way around. Gijs mentioned over breakfast that he was glad he'd found out this was the Dartmouth campus before he met Dr. Syvertsen.

"Yes, it would have cast you as rather stupid!" I agreed.

At ten o'clock sharp, a short, stocky gentleman with an engaging smile appeared. He looked at us as we stood waiting in the lobby. His gaze traveled from Gijs's wide-rimmed Eden hat and navy-blue full-length overcoat to my tailored cape with a white fur collar. They rested for a split second on my big belly. He took his hands out of his battered raincoat pockets and shook ours as an amused smile played over his face. After a short introduction, he ushered us into his car and drove us around Hanover to find a place to rent.

We were impressed by his kindness and mystified that a man of his authority would take the time to find housing for a resident. The homes he drove us by were grand. One even had a swimming pool in the yard. Another sat perched on a hilltop with a sweeping view of the Connecticut River. Dr. Syvertsen said most of these houses belonged to professors who were on one year's sabbatical. Gijs asked what the rent of these grand homes would be. The figures varied, but all ran into the hundreds.

"May I ask, sir, what my salary will be?"

"As a resident you will earn one hundred and eighty-five dollars per month."

"Well, it looks like we won't be able to afford these homes. Is there something less expensive on the rental market?"

Dr. Syvertsen turned to Gijs in surprise. He had misjudged our status.

"Holland put a limit on the amount of money that can be taken out of the country," Gijs explained. We were allowed to take 10.000 Dutch guilders. That equals about three thousand dollars. It will have to do for everything."

Sitting in the backseat as the silent observer, I could understand the dean's confusion. He had judged us by our appearance. I guessed that an American medical student wouldn't dress this way for an interview. Gijs looked older than the average medical student and his receding hairline reinforced that impression. Older or not, this was the way we dressed in Holland. We did what we'd been brought up to do, but in the eyes of the dean we'd turned instantly from mysterious foreigners into well-dressed paupers.

Once he understood, Dr. Syvertsen opened up another side of Hanover. At the edge of the campus a series of barracks had been built on the high river banking, next to the Tuck School of Business.

"This is G.I. housing," Dr. Syvertsen said. "We call it Wigwam Circle. Fifty dollars a month. Electricity included."

One of the apartments on the ground floor was empty. The dean was embarrassed by the condition it had been left in. We must have looked out of place in it, for he was exceedingly apologetic and promised to have a college crew paint the walls before we moved in. I told him not to worry, that it seemed roomy to me, that in Holland there was such a housing shortage after the war that we were grateful to have more than a few rooms in someone else's home.

"I never dreamed we would get an apartment with two bedrooms," I told him. He looked at my fur-lined cape and matching hat and shook his head in disbelief.

So that was lesson number two, I thought: people would have a hard time placing us.

The baby hung heavy on my stretched stomach muscles. Bleak walls with dirty fingerprints and greasy spatters behind the stove glared at me, but I stared back with dreams of bright curtains and the furniture that would remind us of Holland. The front room would be for the baby because it received the most sunlight. Gijs and I would take the back room with a view of the river down below and the mountains of Vermont rising up on the other side. A stand of pine trees next to the barrack lined a flat area. There must be a lawn under that mound of snow that could be a shady spot for the baby in the summer time. My mind took in the dimensions of the rooms and began to arrange the cradle, the bassinet we could borrow from our friends in Norwell, and all our belongings that could be shipped now that we had an address to pass on.

For a while we could drop anchor.

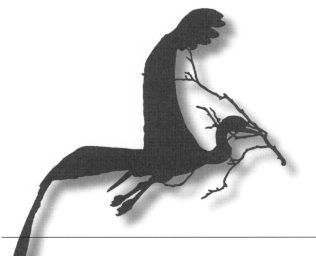

Chapter 5

It's a Girl!

A plump and middle-aged nurse met me at the maternity ward. She'd seen it all. What was new to me was old hat to her. She handed me a lump of cotton with strings attached.

"Here, take of your clothes and put this on," she said, as if I were a recruit.

"On the scale." Her stubby fingers moved the weight along the inscribed numbers until she found the perfect balance of the arrow.

The bed in the labor room was hard as granite and the plastic coverings of the mattress rustled with every movement I made. From the opposite wall a large clock looked down on me. Its black hands moved forward with frightening regularity, reminding me that I could neither stop nor forward time. I had to go through time.

"Let's see your belly, honey." A cold stethoscope landed on my tight-skinned drum after she turned up my johnnies, that equalizer of all hospital patients. The baby's heartbeat was recorded on a sheet of paper. The time between contractions and the baby's vital signs were noted.

"Not much going on. You could go home now. There won't be a baby for a while," she said to Gijs when he appeared at the door.

"Did you call the staff doctor?" Gijs asked.

"No use bothering him in the middle of the night," she said. Obviously, she was dealing with an over-anxious father.

"I'll call the intern," she added, and rolled a metal rig holding IV bottles next to my bed. The battle was on. The battle to avoid the use of the stuff they would put into those bottles. Friends of Jeannet Visser had told me they'd watched other women climb the walls, lowing like unmilked cows, when they were given a certain medicine. Gijs had confirmed these stories. I couldn't imagine such a scene in Holland. My friends delivered their babies at home.

"Why do doctors give that awful stuff?" I'd wanted to know.

"Because it's available to them. Don't forget, it's hard to watch someone in pain."

"Do you agree with it?"

"No, I don't. Giving birth is meant to be a natural process. But there are times when it is appropriate to use. The exception has become the rule here."

How arrogant, I thought. The doctors make it look like delivering a baby was *their* job. The woman's was to carry the baby around for nine months, eat right, don't smoke or drink, and knit little socks.

"I don't want that stuff," I had told Gijs.

My mother had firmly planted the notion of the sanctity of life in the fertile ground of my teenage mind. A woman's body was the sacred hall to receive the gift of life and her labor pains were the sacrifice to be willingly put on the altar. Enough of these preachings had stuck so that I viewed the use of drugs to lessen the pain as sacrilege. The image of a Chinese peasant woman squatting in the fields, the way Pearl Buck described it in her book The Good Earth, lingered romantically in my mind.

"I hope she won't hook me up to that rig," I said to Gijs when the nurse left the room for a moment.

"Don't worry about it. They haven't put 'the cocktail' in it yet. It makes good medical sense to put it there. You probably won't need it."

Gijs gave himself an out. Doctors are good at that. He had listened to my high-flying ideas, as well as my fears, during the pregnancy. I don't think squatting in a field was his expectation of the delivery. He'd been around long enough to know how Mother Nature can go awry, but he spared me the details. What he called "the cocktail" was a combination of barbaturics and scopolamine. Besides relieving pain, it caused disorientation and retrograde amnesia. As a result the woman would not remember a thing. To spare him the sight of seeing his wife with a brightly flushed face, doing things she normally would not do, her husband wasn't allowed anywhere near her.

The nurse had allowed that Gijs could stay for the time being since there were no other mothers in the labor room. The baby was quiet, the contractions mild. We amused ourselves with thinking up names, although we'd already decided that if it were a boy, he would be the fourth

Gerard Bozuwa. If it was a girl, we would like to name her after her two grandmothers, Johanna Marie.

"Do you think Americans can say Johanna?" I asked.

"Probably not. Or not the way we think it should be."

"Maybe it's better to stick with a name they can pronounce."

"Like what?"

We had been through this before. Every Dutch name we liked had sounded terrible when we rolled it around the way we thought an American would. A typical American name then? Ann? But Gijs would say, "God no, I can hear it now. Boyfriends at the door calling "Is Annie home? No, that's awful." And that's where the discussion usually ended.

"Why don't we anglicize Johanna Marie," I suggested between contractions. "How about Joan Mary?"

"Joan Mary." Gijs tried it out, repeated it several times. "It has a nice ring to it. Yes, I like that. Joan Mary. If it's a girl, that's what we should name her."

A sleepy man in a rumpled green suit sauntered into the room, the imprints of a pillow still on his cheeks. His eyes focused sharply from behind his glasses when he recognized Gijs. An hour had passed since the nurse had called him.

"How's it going?"

The nurse handed him the chart. With his back to her, he turned to Gijs, and as they exchanged some medical terms I watched the nurse's eyes widening with a new understanding. She was dealing with a father who was not only a doctor himself, but who, as a resident, ranked over the intern she'd called in. The sergeant major was acutely aware of the hospital's pecking order.

"I'll be back in a minute," Gijs said, and left the room while the intern examined me.

"Things are stable," the intern told him when he came back. "The head is engaged. Still very high. Two fingers dilatation. It will be hours. You could catch some sleep."

In response, Gijs asked the intern to show him the delivery room.

I looked at the clock. I'd been on this bed for over an hour. Gijs put his hand in mine when pain surged through the lower part of my body, and let me squeeze it for as long as the contraction lasted.

"Think of Nynke," Gijs said. "Remember?"

I was back on a narrow mattress down on the attic floor of a Dutch house where Nynke, a physical therapist, prepared expecting mothers for the deliveries of their babies in natural childbirth.

"Now, take a deep breath and let it out slowly. Relax. Totally relax. Don't think about anything else. Close your eyes. Relax." Three minutes later, Nynke hit the metal radiator with a stick. Full force. We all jumped. Nynke laughed. "Let's do it again."

After a few months we ignored the hard bangs. Relaxing was the secret weapon to keep the drugs away. Nynke told us over and over that if we tensed up during a contraction, we would go against what nature wanted to achieve: the relaxation of the cervix.

"Will you send a telegram to Holland" I asked Gijs.

"Of course."

He saw me through each powerful surge and monitored the progress. The nurse periodically checked in and pushed the IV rig closer to my side.

"No need to suffer, honey. Don't be shy." I didn't answer, just shook my head. I was concentrating on creating a passage for my child.

"You may want to call the intern," Gijs said to her. "There's rapid progress here." The nurse looked dubious.

By the time the intern reappeared it was past five thirty in the morning, and Gijs had run away to put on a surgical suit. *He* was giving the orders now. The contractions were coming fast and powerfully. He had seen the head crowning. He ruptured the membranes. I heard a gushing sound. Nature was pushing my muscles beyond their normal limits and I felt overpowered, swept up by forces past my control. Gijs ordered the nurse to get a stretcher and to hurry up about it, all the while coaching me in Dutch.

"*Goedzo*, Tiets. Keep it up. It looks like I'll help you deliver it after all." He chuckled. Gijs had asked for permission to deliver me himself, but had been politely refused. Not a good idea to treat your own wife, the obstetrician had said.

I was lifted off the bed, heaved onto a stretcher and wheeled at a trot to the delivery room by the dumbfounded intern and the bewildered nurse in tow. When I saw Gijs come into the delivery room in a green scrub suit and a small round cap on his sparsely populated head, I said to him in Dutch, "Gijs, it's coming!" He grabbed a pair of rubber gloves.

"Hold it Tiets, don't push." But Joan was ready to come. She was sailing her own ship.

Joan and me

"Don't push, Tiets," Gijs said in Dutch. I couldn't hold her back. She ripped through the prepared passage with a gusting force and met her father's hands. I heard a scream, a compelling sound like I'd never heard before.

"Het is een meisje!" Gijs shouted. We forgot where we were. We spoke our own language. The intern and the nurse could see for themselves that it was a girl. Gijs clamped the cord and placed the baby on the linens with her tiny feet facing me. The little bundle screamed, using her entire body.

"Joan Mary," I said, and held her head. It was incomprehensible that this tiny, soaking wet creature, not bigger than the doll I used to play with, had come out of my own body. I felt elated, split in half, and drained. Beads of perspiration on Gijs's forehead caught the bright overhead light. His eyes traveled from Joan to me, tracing a triangle within the larger spheres of the new society we'd entered.

"You did well, honey, " the nurse gushed. "Isn't she beautiful?"

Joan was covered with a slimy goop, her head shaped like a grapefruit that had sat at the bottom of a heavy bag for too long. It didn't matter. She was alive, she breathed, and she had ten fingers and ten toes.

"Yes, I said. "She's beautiful.

My muscles went limp and I sank back, drenched in fatigue. The bustle of metal instruments clattering on enameled trays, the baby's screams, the glaring light above me, the rubber soles of shoes squeaking over the linoleum floor, shadows of people in green suits moving about blended like counterpoints in a modern symphony.

The obstetrician, who'd been called too late, walked in and sized up the situation. He ignored the issues that would certainly be hashed over at the next staff meeting.

"You have a beautiful baby, Tisha," he said. My feet on the other end of the table framed his handsome face. "We'll have to sew you up. Do you mind if we give you some Novocaine?"

I hadn't even felt the tearing, so what difference would a needle make?

Joan caused a stir in the hospital. The story of how she arrived played well in the cafeteria during coffee breaks. It held intrigue. Her father was a foreigner. The approach to natural childbirth was a sensation. Hearing about the intern calling the staff doctor too late got a big chuckle. That Dutch doctor had probably manipulated the intern so he could do the delivery himself.

We listened and smiled.

We also learned lesson number three: Americans spring into unstoppable action when they see a need. The tribe at Wigwam Circle had circled around us like a family, seeing that we had none. When the big crate from Holland had been delivered and Gijs was still at the hospital, the men had rolled up their shirtsleeves and carried in the boxes and the furniture. The women helped me unpack what were mostly our wedding gifts. Just as their cutlery and china looked strange to me, they gawked at the different patterns of mine. We had compared and while I explained what various items were used for, we bonded and now they came to the hospital with flowers and pink baby clothes.

The mailman, who'd noticed the letters that came for us from abroad, gave Joan a silver dollar. The woman next to me on the ward had her young husband buy a silver spoon, engraved with the letter J.

The local newspaper, The Valley News, sent a photographer over to take a picture of Joan in my arms and put it on the front page on Mother's Day. Doctor Syvertsen brought a lily on Easter morning.

We were far away from home, but our little family wasn't an island onto itself any longer.

Chapter 6

Joan's Baptism

The reverberations of the pipe organ that pulled Hanover's faithful into hymn singing overpowered Joan's screams. The water on her forehead had startled her. The angry bright red face seemed out of place in its delicate lace cap. In her heirloom dress she looked like a fireball wrapped in white tissue paper. Her grandmother gently rocked her during the prayer that followed. She was quiet for a moment while she took a deep breath for renewed howling, and then she drowned out the Lord's Prayer.

My mother was prepared to shush her namesake for the duration of the service, but I felt uneasy with the stares of the congregation on my back. At my urging, the four of us made for the tall door that would put us back on the sunny street. It was a beautiful church, stately and Puritan in design, but I was a stranger, or I felt like a stranger, only distantly linked to the people inside. We might not have thought of baptizing Joan if it hadn't been for my mother's idea to come over for it. Gijs couldn't remember if he was baptized or not, and I had been baptized when I was a teenager. But Mammie lived up to her promise and had arrived in Boston, all smiles and proud to be one of the first people to traverse the Atlantic Ocean by jet.

Gijs held the car door open for his mother-in-law, who looked elegant and European in her black satin-trimmed suit and matching hat with a feather. I put Joan in her plastic car bed on the back seat of our pea-green Ford, and we drove aimlessly down to the Connecticut River, over the bridge into Vermont until Gijs found a meadow with a breathtaking view and a wide-branched maple tree. He parked the car underneath it.

The vibrations of the pipe organ and the rise and fall of the minister's voice receded. When she felt my warm breast against her face, Joan stopped crying, at peace again, fed and cradled in the nook of my arm. Mammie rolled down the car window and took a deep breath of the air that still carried the moisture of a lifting fog and the mushroom-like smell of things dying and decaying.

"I've never seen anything like this," she said with deep satisfaction as she clasped her hands together like a young child who's made a discovery.

Rolling hills and verdant meadows, dotted with white farm buildings and with a deep blue sky above, were laid out before us like a brightly colored quilt on this brilliant late-September day, so unlike the faded horse blanket that was Holland in the autumn months.

"Mammie, why didn't you have us baptized when Herman, Hans and I were babies?" I asked.

"I was baptized myself when I was sixteen. It was my own choice and I thought I should give my children that same choice."

Mammie had been brought up outside of the church because her father didn't agree with the way the Dutch Reformed Church was organized. All the same, he played the organ in the church every Sunday on the island where she was born and where he was the doctor. But the family never worshiped at the church. Instead, her father read to his family from the Bible at home after dinner. Every day.

"Then later," Mammie said, "when we lived on the mainland, I went to church by myself because I was curious. Of course, it was a way to prove my independence."

When she turned sixteen, she announced she wanted to be confirmed. Her father said if that's what she wanted to do, and if she'd thought about it long and hard, then that's what she should do.

With Joan asleep in my arms, I wondered why we do the things we do. The minister of the Hanover Congregational Church hadn't asked me anything beyond establishing that Joan's mother had been baptized and confirmed in the *Remonstrantse Kerk* in Holland, that her parents were married in that church and were desirous of having their child christened. We hadn't talked about choices.

"The minister asked the congregation if they would help bring this child up as a Christian, but I wondered if they would ever see Joan again," Gijs said.

"I liked the minister," my mother said. "Maybe you should go back there another Sunday. You would get to know more people."

When we'd walked into the church to take our seats, I had felt very much the foreigner. The pews were dotted with bright bunches of flowers seated on top of small hats, which in turn sat on blue-washed hairdos. Compared to the solemnity of a Dutch protestant church, it looked like a summer garden. Maybe that was good, maybe even better, but I asked myself if I could ever feel at home here and embrace these people as my Christian family. The feeling went deeper than the superficial observation of the funny flowered hats. Although I reasoned that people were people, and Christians were Christians, wherever you find them, I didn't feel it. America was a country made up of immigrants—first, second, third, fourth generations of immigrants—who accepted new immigrants not as foreigners, but as Americans-to-be. To feel like an American right off, though, was impossible. Too much of what I had been brought up with had to be erased before I could truly feel as an American did. It had to do with intangibles like tradition, customs, landscape, climate and taste. Maybe that was why we had to live in this country for five years before we were allowed to obtain American citizenship. On Joan's day of baptism, I knew we were a long way off. The importance of the ceremony had been the connection to God and the three generations. Gijs, my mother and I were standing there before God. I had not felt the connection to the congregation that I probably should have.

I put Joan back in her little plastic bed with elaborate care, so the maneuver wouldn't wake her.

"I feel closer to God sitting on this hill with this view than I do in a church," Gijs said.

"Even when we didn't go to church on the island," my mother said, "my father gave me a strong faith by example. It had to do with being in tune with the infinite."

Outside, a few yellow leaves whirled down on a puff of wind. The cloudless blue sky looked untouchable. What was beyond it? The Russians had surprised the world by sending a spacecraft into the atmosphere, but would the Sputnik answer age-old questions or pose more? Did it matter? If you were in tune with the infinite, you would have trust that however the universe was put together, it had a purpose. You could be at home anywhere in the world. At peace. Even if a war raged around you, you could feel God's endless love. In the end, the most lasting impression of the war years for my brother and me had been the way our mother had handled them. Although she probably could not rationally explain it, we noticed her innate trust. She never said, "Why is this happening to me?" Instead, she put her shoulders under Hitler's yoke, carried the burden, and countered oppression with high spirits. She always seemed to be in tune with the infinite.

"My family didn't go to church either," Gijs said. "My parents didn't read us from the Bible, but they had some strong ideas about what was right and wrong. I didn't always like their ethical discipline, but that's what they gave me instead."

"You can be sure that those strong values were rooted in the Bible," Mammie said.

Conscience, discipline, faith, custom. Were they related, or was each a combination of the others? Gijs had been given a strong conscience. It took precedence over all other considerations. Mammie had been given a sustaining faith by a freethinking father. Through the love of my mother I had been given an intuition to trust the purposes of the universe.

"Of course," Mammie said, "what the church offers beside dogma is community. American churches, I have read, excel at this."

"So, here we sit, on top of a hill, the four of us, alone in a car" Gijs laughed.

"We're going to lunch with the community of Wigwam Circle instead!" I said. "They may not be the faithful of Hanover, or maybe they are, but they serve a good meal and meanwhile they practice the so-called *good*."

"Well, in the end, upholding *the good* is the only thing that wins in life," Mammie said.

Gijs started up the car and turned onto the dirt road on our way to Hanover, to the farm on Reservoir Road that belonged to Dorothy Strong, the mother of our neighbor in the apartment above us. She had set out tables and chairs in her garden for all who wanted to come and celebrate the life of Joan Mary Bozuwa.

Chapter 7

My Mother's Visit

To prepare for my mother's visit we'd bought a bed at a flea market. Made of steel tubing, it was heavy, a bit narrow and the mattress only in so-so condition, but the price was right. The only available location for it was in Joan's room, against the wall that separated it from the stairwell to the apartments on the first floor. Late-for-class students thundered down the wooden stairs in the early morning like a herd of elephants. My mother was gracious about almost falling out of the narrow bed when she turned, and as for the noise, she had been well prepared by living on the marketplace in Breda for over thirty years, she said.

The house I grew up in was big and impractical in its layout. We had two maids and, before the war, a woman who looked after my two brothers and me. Mammie was used to having help in the house. All *I* had was a washing machine. Gijs tended it early in the mornings. He hung the washed diapers on lines he'd strung between the pine trees next to our apartment before he went to the hospital. One day, the young fathers of Wigwam Circle corralled him. He was setting a bad example, they said, and they were quite serious about it.

"Sorry, guys," Gijs told them. "I brought my wife over to a strange country, and the least I can do is the laundry!" That was the end of it.

My mother had high standards when it came to housekeeping, and she expected the same of me. I fell far short, even though I had attended a fancy school in Amsterdam to learn about these things. I had been handed my diploma on the condition that I would not do the internship that was part of the training. Keeping house was not my thing.

One sunny morning, after the newness of her visit had worn off,

Mammie suggested a thorough cleaning of our apartment. My mother's idea of cleaning meant moving all the furniture. I remembered those Monday mornings in Breda when the heavy chairs of the living room were piled into the hall. The maid, under the watchful eye of my mother, would don a kerchief over her hair and attack the floors and the walls with soap and water, and for the rest of the day the house smelled of furniture wax. Lacking a hallway in our apartment meant we would have to put the furniture outside.

"The neighbors will think we're moving again," I said, trying to get out of it.

My mother didn't wait for me to fall in line. She rolled up her sleeves and started to move the chairs through the front door onto the street. I'd never seen my mother move furniture before. She meant business. But whose house was this? She was stealing my initiative! Although a little voice inside whispered I wouldn't have cleaned the house to begin with, I concentrated on how I could duck this unpleasant task. Why did these tensions always surface when Gijs wasn't around to defend me? She wouldn't have uttered a word about housecleaning if he were home. Well, I had other things to do, like feeding and changing the baby.

Mammie's pace of moving furniture was picking up. When I fastened the second safety pin onto Joan's diaper, I heard the front door slammed shut. I was curious enough to look out the window. There she was, walking down the street toward town, her stout body propelled by anger. I only saw the back of her head, but I could draw the expression on her face from memory: the eyes flashing bolts of lightning, the lines around her mouth set like a rapidly falling barometer.

It had the same effect on me as when I was little. My stomach curled with a painful cramp. I placed Joan in her bed and ran outside. Mammie had turned the corner and was out of sight. I couldn't very well leave all the furniture sitting in the street. There was only one solution and that was to do what she'd wanted me to do in the first place. CLEAN.

I grabbed the broom – we didn't own a vacuum cleaner yet – and started to sweep furiously. Then I remembered that our maid used to first pick up the rugs and drag them upstairs to our roof garden. If she was strong enough to carry them up those steep stairs, I was rugged enough to pick up these puny oriental rugs and drape them over the rope Gijs had strung between the pine trees to hang Joan's diapers. I faked a big smile when Chris VanCuran, our upstairs neighbor, walked by on his way home from class. I prayed he wouldn't have time to stop and talk. He was a gifted teaser.

I went in to get a red bandana and checked Joan who was awake and studying the design of woven reeds that formed the sides of her cradle. I promised her that when she got to be my age, I wouldn't stick my nose into her business. I would respect her individuality.

I beat the rugs as if my life depended on it. With each blow, my inner landscape alternated between a wicked tornado sweeping everything in its way over a flat prairie, and a pelting hail over a black street, badly denting cars with the icy mothballs that fell out of my inner sky. I created a cloud of dust, a tornado in its own right. I stepped back to get a breath of fresh air. It was actually a nice day. An Indian summer kind of a day. The crisp, bracing air filled my dusted lungs. Maybe Mammie was right. It was a perfect day to air the house, beat the rugs, and wash the floors before winter would muddy them up again.

Mammie rounded the corner of the grand tree-lined campus avenue that led to our humble corner of town as I was brushing the seats of the chairs with a stiff brush that I'd found in a basket with cleaning tools. The movers had packed it by mistake. It had belonged to the maid who came with our apartment in Rotterdam. Mammie might be impressed I even had such a practical housekeeping tool.

I pretended not to see her. Her stride had lost its vigor. She was ambling along, I noticed from the corner of my eye. What would she say? What would I say? My heart started racing.

Neither one of us said anything when she stood before me. Her eyes twinkled as she held out a brown bag with cookies. Before I could peek inside, she embraced me and smiled. I smiled back. Then she went inside to make tea. Fifteen minutes later we sat down in our living room chairs on the street, munching the cookies she'd brought from town. Neighbors came by and asked, "Is this the way you clean house in Holland?"

"Yes," my mother said, and smiled graciously "This is the way we clean in Holland," with emphasis on each word.

I went inside to get Joan and put her in Mammie's arms. After all, that's what she'd flown in on a jet for. To become a grandmother.

Gijs had asked for a week's vacation.
"Let's go to the Niagara Falls," Mammie suggested.
"Niagara Falls?" Gijs asked. His mother-in-law never ceased to amaze

him. "Do you know they are a good four-hundred fifty miles away from here?"

"So, what of it?" Mammie said. "Joan seems to be happiest in the car. She'll sleep through it, if that's what you're concerned about."

In our "pea-green," equipped with maps of New England and New York State, two overnight bags, a picnic basket, and the red plastic baby bed on the backseat, we set out through Vermont. Mammie beamed as we drove though picturesque towns and valleys, and she was still beaming when we cruised over the endless highways that led westward, where the landscape was as flat as Holland's.

"Ah, this is exactly how I imagined America. In Holland we have no notion of the scale of this landscape. And look at these roads! Straight as an arrow. The wonder of this century. "

Listening from the backseat, I marveled at how two people can look at the same landscape and have such different reactions to it. Mammie looked at it to satisfy her curiosity about the world, checking her book knowledge against reality. I looked at the landscape whizzing by the window with emotion. And what the flat, endless stretches evoked in me was unsettling. I found the dreary landscape without Holland's quaintness terribly inhospitable. Where was the next farm, the next sign of human life?

After two days we reached the Niagara Falls at dusk, without hotel reservations. Our Wigwam Circle friends had said we could chance it, and chancing it appealed to both my mother and my husband. We'd landed at the local fairgrounds, it looked like, as we passed an endless strip of hotdog stands and neon lights. A stork appeared on every commercial building we passed. When I inquired about it at the least seedy looking motel, I was met with the same incredulous look the bellboy at the Hanover Inn had given Gijs when he asked what "those buildings" were.

"Well, this is the number one place for honeymooners, ma'am," the clerk behind the desk said.

"Oh, great," Gijs chuckled, "I'm here with my mother-in-law." Mammie was waiting in the car with Joan.

"Don't forget your wife," I piped in.

"Oh, yes, and with my wife. Do you have room for us?" Gijs asked.

"We have a bridal suite," the clerk said looking at a chart on his desk.

"You don't mean for us to share the bridal suite with my mother-in-law, do you?"

"Well, I have another bridal suite for your mother-in-law."

"Do you only have bridal suites?"

"Well sir, that's the bulk of my business." I winced at the use of his words. Business was not a concept I associated with a wedding night.

We ushered Mammie into her bridal suite with her overnight bag. A lamp with a colored bulb was aimed at the wall behind the king sized bed, dousing everything in the room with a gaudy pink hue. It looked like a nesting place for storks. They were everywhere. Painted on the lampshades. Carved out of wood on the dresser. Woven into the bath towels. Printed onto the soap wrappers. And to top it all off, the bedspread was covered with pink satin bows.

"I'll ask the stork to bring the baby in from the car," Gijs said.

"Our timing is a little off, don't you think?" I said.

Mammie took in the unusual surroundings and her eyes sparkled with amusement. I could tell that the words to describe this scene to my father were forming in her mind. When Gijs walked in with the red plastic basket holding Joan, who was startled into crying, Mammie burst into laughter, almost choking, just looking at Gijs standing there with a crying baby. She couldn't make herself stop, and I started laughing too, falling onto the bed with tears streaming down my face. Joan increased her volume. The gaudy room overflowed with howls.

"Rather a suggestive room, isn't it?" Gijs said carefully to his mother-in-law.

"Yes. Rather!" she said, composing herself.

Chapter 8
Scouting for a Place to Settle

"**B**ring the baby," the lady from Woodstock, Vermont, said over the phone when Gijs responded to an inquiry from a search committee for a general practitioner. We did. Living on one hundred and eighty-five dollars a month didn't leave spare money for a babysitter. My mother had unexpectedly gone back to Holland because my father needed to go in for immediate prostate surgery. After she left, we realized we had two big tasks before us. Gijs had to prepare for the necessary exams to get his license and we needed to find a place to practice and live. We had inspected a good deal of New Hampshire's countryside with my mother, driving through one village after another. The first thing we saw driving into almost any town was the cemetery. Although the flaming red maple trees holding watch over the weathered headstones were pretty, being greeted by the dead at the outskirts of town created an ice-dam around our hearts.

"Do you want to be buried here, Tiets?" Gijs would ask. The answer was written on my face. No. But my mother laughed at us. That was no way to look at the future, she said.

"Why would you have to be buried here?" she said. "Don't project your life that far ahead. See it in phases of five years. If you still like where you are, sign up for the next five. If you don't, make a change!"

Woodstock turned out to be a picturesque town, one of the prettiest we'd driven through so far. White clapboarded homes circled a well-maintained green and breathed an air of stability. The types of stores in the main street clued us in on the type of people who populated this town. The fancy restaurants and a high-end antique shop didn't look like they catered to the indigent.

We climbed a steep hill over a rutted dirt road in a cloud of dust that settled on the ferns under an arch of old maple trees. At the end of the road sat a spacious Old Colonial house with meadows spread around her like a green apron. We were greeted at the door and ushered into one of the tastefully appointed bedrooms, where, it was suggested, we could leave Joan in her car bed.

Joan couldn't care less that she was in a beautiful home. She howled at full capacity. We could hear her at the other end of the house where we were served cocktails. It didn't let up during dinner or while we sipped coffee in the pine paneled den afterward. Our hosts were gracious about the disturbance, as they were about everything else. I slipped out as often as the formality of the evening allowed to sing Dutch lullabies to her, cradle her in my arms or offer her my breast. None of my tactics changed her mindset. This was a strange place and she didn't like it one bit.

On my trips back and forth to quiet Joan, I absorbed the décor of the house. Our hosts had described it as "the farm." It looked more like an estate to me. Antique furniture pieces stood out against carefully chosen wallpaper that didn't look like it had come from the local hardware store. The kitchen was filled with gadgets advertised in LIFE magazine: a blender, a dishwasher, an electric percolator, and a magnet for storing different lengths of knives. The tools used by the people who'd made a living farming the land had been painted black and hung around the huge fireplace as ornaments. The house was like a museum except for the den with its TV set and bulky Lazy Boy chairs.

Back at the table I tried to tune into the conversation, led by our host. He'd just retired from a life on Wall Street. They had long owned this property. The restoration had only just been completed. It had been good fun to do.

"Why did you choose to live here?" Gijs asked.

"We bought the farm on our honeymoon and spent many summers with our kids here," our host said as he stood at the head of the table carving a leg of lamb. "I wanted to get out of the city's rat race; the roads have improved, cars are more comfortable. It's not the undertaking it used to be to visit the city,"

"Besides, you can order everything through the mail," his wife said. "S.S. Pierce even makes deliveries here!"

She read from the look on my face that I had no idea who or what S.S. Pierce was, because she said, "You know, the grocery company from

Boston. They're excellent. You phone in your order. It's as simple as that!"

She was seated at the other end of the table from where her husband placed generous portions of lamb on a Wedgwood plate. Gijs passed it through to his wife, who filled it with a variety of vegetables.

"These are from our garden," she said. "We've had to put a fence around the vegetable garden, because the deer like the corn as much as we do."

Through the large picture window, aimed at a view of the mountains, I noticed a fenced-in area. I was mystified. Where I came from nobody but the Queen would have to worry about deer coming into the garden. Few people owned property that didn't have a neighbor in sight or a city close by. These people lived out in nowhere and owned all the land around them.

Our host skillfully steered the conversation to the purpose of the visit.

"Where were you trained, doctor?" he asked of Gijs.

"In Utrecht, sir," and Gijs ran quickly through his curriculum vitae. The man was satisfied.

"What we need in this town is a man just like you. There are more and more people moving into this area to retire. It's a wonderful life. Lovely countryside, pure air, lots to do, but you have to be inventive. It's a real challenge to live in the country. I raise our own vegetables and do the haying myself. Very satisfying." He leaned back from the table to offer Gijs a cigarette.

"But medical care is a problem," he went on. "The doctor in town is a turkey. We need someone better than that."

"I don't know the man," Gijs said diplomatically.

"Well, of course, we can go to Hanover, to the Mary Hitchcock Clinic. But that's almost an hour away. It's a comfort to know there are good specialists nearby. But when you have a cold you don't want to travel that far and see a specialist. Not for a cold, you know."

"Do you use the clinic for your medical needs, sir?" Gijs asked.

"No, no. I have my own cardiologist on Park Avenue. Fine man. Gone to him for years." Our host inhaled deeply from his Marlboro.

When we got ready to leave, he said, "Let us know what your plans are, Dr. Bozuwa. Call me anytime, but not after Thanksgiving. We spend the winter in Florida."

"What do you think, Gijs?" I asked as we drove back down the dirt road.

"I think they would buy medical care through the mail, if they could." Gijs chuckled, "Like their groceries."

"Seriously, would you like to practice here?"

"No!"

We were back in Woodstock village. Whatever its history, it was now a rich man's playground. The new doctor would be captive to the minor medical needs of its wealthy migrants since, as our host indicated, they provided him with a well-equipped office to practice in. The doctor in this village would be a kept man and he wouldn't treat much more than colds.

Joan was at peace again after crying from beginning to end. All through the formal dinner I had fought with myself if I should just bring her to the table and take her in my lap, but the house rules were palpable and they didn't include a crying baby tugging at a corner of the heavy linen tablecloth, so I had complied. I wasn't proud of it.

"Maybe Joan was sending us a message," Gijs said. "It's funny, this town has the looks we like, but I don't think we would be happy here."

There was always the lure of specializing. As he rotated through the various hospital departments, Gijs toyed with the idea of becoming an internist or a dermatologist. Either choice would require three more years of residency. He was encouraged by the department heads who themselves had chosen Hanover to live because of the combination of a relaxed lifestyle with the stimulating environment of the college. Gijs was tempted. On the surface it seemed ideal. Hanover was a lovely town, filled with intelligent, sophisticated people. Some college graduates couldn't tear themselves away from its uniqueness and would do anything to stay, even if it meant running a grocery store.

But what of the ideal of being a solo practitioner in a place where he would be sorely needed? The dream he had chased during those long, hard years of medical school?

All the weekends Gijs was not on call we spent visiting various towns that needed a doctor. We went to New London, Jaffrey, Plaistow, Littleton and Franklin and several other dots on the map. I would remember them by the peculiarities of the people we met. A doctor whose desk was littered with financial magazines personified one town. His field of study seemed to be the stock market. Another town we nicknamed "The Dark Closet."

After we'd be wined and dined by a general practitioner who said the town badly needed another GP, Gijs was shown the local hospital while I stayed in the car with Joan. When he returned, I could tell from the expression on his face we were probably not going to live in that town.

"You won't believe what happened to me, Tiets," he said when we were driving away. "As I walked through the corridor, a hand reached out of a closet and pulled me by my sleeve. A male voice whispered, 'Don't be fooled by the old man. We don't need another doctor here. The staff is against him and he badly needs an ally. Don't fall for it!' That said, he pushed me back into the hall."

"Do you know who it was?" I asked.

"No idea. It was pitch dark in that closet."

Every place we went had a barely visible crack in its New England façade. Underneath its pretty main street ran a river of tensions, usually between the natives and the new people of the sort we'd met in Woodstock, or real estate developers who brought change and big ideas the local population wasn't ready for. Medical care, or the lack thereof, was usually one of the issues, as well as a specialist versus a GP.

"Where is that place you're needed?" I asked on the way back from one of our expeditions.

Gijs sighed. "Beats me."

The process was eating at him. In a letter to his parents, I read an unsettling paragraph. "The remote village in the mountains is beginning to lose some of its charm when you look behind the scenes. Maybe we should begin to look at either a college town or a suburb close to Boston or New York City."

Was this the same man who'd wanted to drive a white jeep through Africa to bring medical care to the outposts? A sort of Albert Schweitzer without the religion? Hanover was like a seductive woman: pretty, well proportioned, sophisticated and alluring. She had unsettled his thinking as well as mine. It would be an easier life, on the surface of it, to be part of a group practice. It would have more prestige to be a specialist. Being part of the Clinic was no pipe dream. He'd been encouraged along those lines. Hanover, lying in her manicured valley amidst the undulating hills, wearing her dignified college buildings like heirloom jewelry, appealed to the side in us that had seen a bit of the world from an advantaged perspective. When Gijs was ten years old, it was a matter of fact that the whole world saluted his father. When he followed his father up a gangplank to board a ship, a sharp whistle was blown and the entire crew jumped to attention on deck, because his father was the commander. Gijs had delighted in the extravagant first class luxury of the ocean liners that brought his family back and forth to the Dutch East Indies before the war.

Yet, the most decisive exposure in his life had been to the war. When I met Gijs at a Dutch beach resort where my family had rented a cottage and where Gijs was camping with a friend, he presented himself as a wild and irresponsible student who wrecked borrowed cars and regularly flunked his exams. But my female intuition sensed that a mature man was hiding beneath his boisterous and amusing stories, and not only because he was six years older than I. My intuition was backed up by facts, I discovered much later. Gijs had gone into the war with dreams of becoming a navy officer like his father. But by volunteering to empty the bedpans of dysentery patients in the camp's sickbay, he'd gradually become interested in medicine. It hadn't been scientific interest and it wasn't the prospect of big money that had gotten him involved in medicine.

The war years had left their mark on both of us. Gathering material wealth, we had seen, was a relative goal at best. One bomb could wipe it out. Twelve silver spoons were all Gijs's family had left to their name after the war was over. His mother had held onto them as she was being dragged from one internment camp to another. In the face of war, there was no safe place, no security. The only safe place was in the hammock of our own moral threads. We weren't streetwise. We had become "warwise" as we'd watched people we'd taken for granted in our everyday lives turn into heroes, because they resisted the enemy or saved others at their own peril. Then we watched the very people who had been brought to their knees only a few years earlier erase the ruins and rebuild our badly beaten country. Life went on. It always would. We had witnessed a powerful will to survive.

This we knew down deep. At times, it didn't surface enough for us to have faith in our own undertaking.

The fall lost its colorful luster and one day the wind blew the leaves into a thick brown carpet. The naked trees looked as desolate as they'd seemed to me in March. The wind had a frosty bite to it and the floor in our Wigwam was getting too cold for Joan to crawl over. To get us out of the house Gijs took Joan and me for a ride along the Connecticut River.

It looked like a gray sock as it reflected the leaden sky above it. The entire landscape with yellowed fields and black tree trunks deeply alienated me and I lost heart. Back at the house, we each wrote a letter to our parents and announced that we were going back to Holland. We just didn't see living here for a myriad of reasons. Gijs went out in the dark of night to bring them to the post office.

        After a sleepless night, we looked at each other the next morning and said, "What have we done?" We raced to get dressed, woke up Joan, got her dressed as well, and took the car to town so we could be at the post office at opening time. The clerk retrieved the letters for us and I locked them away. I did not dare open them for fear I might fall into the same trap of giving in to homesickness. Finally, after twenty years, I did. I read our thoughts of that gloomy day in 1957 and laughed.

Chapter 9

A Surprise Visit

One bright December day, a black Jaguar pulled up in front of our Wigwam Circle apartment. Out stepped our announced visitors. He a handsome, dark-haired man in a well-fitted gray flannel suit, in his late twenties I guessed. She a stunning, tall blonde, her hair done up in a simple bun. Paul Hugenholtz – that was how he'd introduced himself over the phone – opened the backseat door of the Jaguar. A chow jumped out with an air of great self-assurance. I'd last seen this rare Chinese breed with the bold face and blue tongue in Holland. The threesome looked exotic against the backdrop of the GI housing we lived in and younger than I had expected. Gijs had announced that a cardiologist from Boston would drop by, and automatically I had placed him in his forties. They were Dutch and they'd heard about us from a friend of my father. We hadn't received any visitors yet, outside of my mother, and I had quickly polished up the living room the way she would have wanted me to, then ran some errands and picked up Gijs at the hospital. As they approached I thought with satisfaction that we'd made it back in the nick of time.

"Come in," Gijs said, extending his right hand. "How do you do?"

"Very well, thank you, Dr. Bozuwa."

"Gijs is my name."

"This is my wife," the man said, touching the woman who was almost a foot taller than he..

"I am Loes," the woman said with an amused smile. Her manner was at once shy and sophisticated. She looked very proper and very Dutch in her charcoal gray dress with a delicate white trim. Joan stopped pushing blocks around in her playpen and fixed her eyes on the tall woman and smiled. Loes went over to her, placed her finger on Joan's nose and made a clicking sound with her tongue. Joan was immediately engaged.

"Do sit down," I said, and offered them tea.

"How long have you lived here?" Paul asked.

"Oh, just half a year. I am doing a residency in general practice."

At that, Paul and Loes burst out in laughter.

"To tell you the truth," Paul said, "we got here a little early and we thought we were at the wrong address, because Dr. Loeb told us you were an established cardiologist. We thought it a little funny you should live in GI housing. Just to be sure, we opened the door. We saw some Dutch antiques and typically Dutch things. We didn't know what to make of it, so we drove around to check if this was the right address."

"And nobody was home, because Titia came to pick me up at the hospital!"

The conversation turned to our immediate past histories. Paul had been in the States longer than Gijs. He'd served in the Air Force and was currently doing a residency in the Boston City Hospital. They lived in Cambridge. Loes was a social worker. It turned out I had lived in the same student house in Amsterdam as her sister. Small world, wasn't it, and how did we like to live in the States and especially here in Hanover? Paul had his eyes on the Hitchcock Clinic and hoped Gijs could be a valuable connection. He loved Hanover's location, close to skiing and sailing, two of his favorite sports.

The men got involved in the pros and cons of the Hitchcock Clinic, and the opportunities for doctors of Dutch origin in general. Paul had thought about doing general practice, but now he leaned toward a future

Loes and Paul Hugenholtz

in specialization. Probably cardiology. I could see fires burn in Paul's dark brown eyes. Fires of ambition. He would create a future that would put him on top. Of what, I didn't know, but of something that had power and potential.

Loes seated herself close to Joan and played with her.

"Do you have children?" I asked.

"No, not yet," she answered, and quickly changed the subject. "Do you know where you will live after Gijs finishes his residency?"

"No. I find it very confusing, this decision making process." I gave her our various options.

"Would you want to live in Hanover?" she asked pointedly.

I thought about it. Hanover was a beautiful town in every respect. That wasn't the problem.

"I don't know," I said carefully. Would this woman understand? I knew nothing about her. Well, that wasn't entirely true. She was Dutch and, because I had lived with her sister under the same roof, I knew she was a baroness. It explained her easy social grace and natural authority. But Dutch blood and blue blood were negligible clues to character.

"What don't you like about it?" she asked with disarming directness.

"I don't know if I would fit into this tight circle. There's a lot of brain power and wealth here."

"Wealth?"

"Yes, many of the doctors chose the clinic because they liked Hanover and its lifestyle, and they have the means to fund that lifestyle. But that's really only part of it." And I told her how I felt uncomfortable with the older women I had met. They were far more competitive than I knew my mother's generation to be. It seemed they wanted to outdo each other in one field or another. You either took up gardening and raised the biggest tomatoes anywhere, or Japanese flower arranging and bragged about a prize at a juried show. You had to be the best at something, be it reading books in French, painting, music, whatever. I couldn't remember my mother being engaged in that kind of rivalry. Her friends and she had been totally absorbed by trying to survive the war. When her life returned to normal after the war, I was a student, living away from home. Mammie would write to me about a history of art class she took. That was all. It scared me to have to excel at something.

"What about the residents' wives?" Loes asked.

"I don't feel particularly at home with them either." Loes invited honest answers. At social gatherings with the residents' wives I had felt out of place. Even though my English was good enough to understand what was being said, I seemed to speak a different language. Their expressed interests centered on babysitters, clothes, what they would buy once they had money. They complained about the housing they had to live in. They spoke of colleges I'd never heard of, about TV shows I'd never seen.

"I tried to connect to them, but that only worked if I used *their* topics, hooked into *their* interests," I told Loes. The real me had been hiding out, as though I had no past, as if all the experiences in my life had been flushed away. I don't think they'd noticed. Maybe I'd even looked like the life of the party for all the talking I did.

"Where would you like to go?" Loes asked.

"I don't know. Somewhere Gijs is needed as a GP. I really think he'll regret it if he goes against that."

I got up to pour more tea, but Gijs waved the teapot away and got out the bottle of Dutch *jenever* that Mammie had brought.

"Why do you think he would regret it?" Loes asked. She wasn't going to leave the topic unfinished. Her head was tilted towards me, her widely set blue eyes fixed on mine. The social worker emerged.

"Well, it's flattering to be asked to specialize and maybe stay here, but I'm afraid Gijs will get bored concentrating on one thing. He'll feel boxed in."

"You think he'll be happier as a GP?" I wondered where she stood on the subject of specialization.

"Yes. I think he is a born caregiver. More than a scientist. He'll make a great GP."

Loes sighed. "I wish Paul would be a GP."

We would stay in touch, we said to each other when they got ready to leave.

We did.

Chapter 10

First Move

───────────────────────────────

I n that first year of our marriage it became abundantly clear to me that Gijs was a man of action. Having his baby crawl over the cold, drafty floor of a building without a cellar underneath went against his common sense. The oil burner in the living room was inadequate and dangerous. Why wait till Joan got sick or burned by the stove? An ad in the *Valley News* by a retired couple looking for someone to occupy their house while they spent the winter months in Florida caught his eye.

Before the snow started to fly in the bitterly cold winter of 1957/1958, we had moved into a modest house on Route 5 in Norwich, Vermont. Our belongings were parked in the garage and, with the couple's permission, could stay there for a while.

Cut off from my friends at Wigwam Circle, with Gijs away at the hospital most of the time and without a car, I didn't have many options for getting through the day besides keeping the immaculate house in the shape we'd found it in. The layout—with the staircase ending in the living room, the kitchen and eating area all one, the shiny gadgetry, the bland color scheme, even the very size of the Bates' bedspreads—reminded me that I was far, far away from home. The skippers of the river barges I used to watch from our apartment on the Zalmhaven, a small harbor in Rotterdam, had the right idea. They were like snails that carried their house on their backs. No need to feel like a stranger in another country. With their cheerful red geraniums in the cabin's window and the familiar ticking of the coo-kook's clock on the wall, they took Holland with them as they plied through the waters of the Maas and Rhine rivers on their way to Germany to deliver a load of grain or coal.

When I held a mirror to my soul, I saw it was desperately trying to find solace in my mother's view of being in tune with the infinite. Mammie had been right, that night when I told her we were emigrating, that I'd often been homesick as a little girl. I had to admit to myself that even as a big girl I was homesick. Not so much for the people as for the familiarity of Holland's landscape, its food, its ways, its customs. This wasn't like being on a fascinating sightseeing trip. Living in America was for life, and it scared me to death. Was I just a snail that had lost its shell; that yearned for the familiar ticking of the Friesian clock, now neatly wrapped up in a box in the garage? I felt suspended in a new and strange reality, where Joan's cooing or crying and the sound of Gijs driving into the yard at night made up my own familiar. It was my secure triangle within the infinite and I wasn't ready to step out of it and embrace the new world. That would take work.

Wherever we would ultimately land, Gijs needed to pass the national boards exam before he could apply for a license to practice medicine. He would be examined on every possible subject he'd ever studied at the University in Utrecht. The snowbound winter served him well to prepare for it and jog his memory on the basics he'd learned back in 1946, like organic chemistry and physics. The exam's date was set for several days in March. Never having taken a multiple-choice exam before—in Holland he'd only taken oral exams—Gijs left the house for Concord early in the morning of the first day of the exam with trepidation. But he passed. It was a major accomplishment, by anyone's standards.

The next hurdle was fulfilling the obstetrics portion of his general practice residency. The Mary Hitchcock Hospital had made arrangements for their obstetrical interns and residents with the Providence Lying In Hospital where more than 8,000 babies were delivered each year. Hanover had far fewer. Besides, the wives of professors and doctors preferred not to be delivered by interns and residents.

We had to move again. Our amazingly generous friends, Pim and Jeannet Visser, offered that we could stay with them in Norwell for the three months Gijs needed to do obstetrics. Even though it would be a bit of a drive for him from Norwell, Massachusetts, to Providence, Rhode Island, it was a marvelous solution. He would be on 36-hour shifts, then a day off, and so on.

We wondered how they would manage adding a family of three to their household. Would there be room for all of us? They had a pleasant medium–sized house and three children between the ages of nine and five. When we arrived, Pim and Jeannet directed us to their own bedroom, where they had placed a crib for Joan. Their own family they divided over the remaining bedrooms. When we objected, they said it was just common sense. The only other available place was the unfinished attic, which they deemed unsafe for an exploring one-year old, so they moved there themselves. We were flabbergasted.

When Gijs had left Holland to do his internship in Quincy City Hospital in 1955, he'd been given the name and address of the Vissers by Robert Steendijk, a Dutch doctor who'd also done his internship there. He told Gijs how they had given him and another Dutch intern a chance to catch up on sleep, to speak Dutch, to adapt to the American way of life. They were born teachers, he said, and had challenged them with hands-on lessons and practical jokes. While I was still in Holland, Gijs was on a ladder in no time, taking off old wallpaper room by room. He'd never done anything like it in his life, but Jeannet, who'd become a pro at it since they'd recently bought this old farm, coached him.

It wasn't without its hilarious moments. Pim, five years older than Gijs, made a sport out of testing the boisterous interning doctor. Feeling somewhat lost and lonely, Gijs would do anything to be able to spend time in Norwell. Looking around in Pim's workshop, he noticed an ax on the wall and remarked that he'd always wanted to use one and was there a tree that needed cutting? Pim pointed to a 7-inch wide beech in the yard.

"That will take no more than fifteen minutes!" Gijs said.

"If you can take that tree down in fifteen minutes, I will give you one dollar for each minute," Pim said. He set the kitchen timer at fifteen minutes. Forty-five minutes later Gijs finally had the tree down, but it fell into the crown of another tree. It would take more than an ax to get it down. A chainsaw was a tool he wasn't familiar with, so he tried to pull it down with a rope. That didn't work. He needed to use the chainsaw. Pim showed him how and positioned himself in a lawn chair to watch. It was a lovely day in May.

Although Jeannet warned both that it might be an expensive bet if Gijs damaged his hands – after all, a doctor needs his hands – neither listened to the sound advice. Gijs hacked away at the stubborn tree, but it just hung there. What was needed was horsepower to pull the tree over. Gijs alone couldn't budge it. Pim and Gijs together could not budge it.

They needed a car. Jeannet's old jalopy was brought around and they tied the heavy rope to the bumper. Revving the motor on full throttle didn't have the desired result. Jeannet's car was now without a bumper. A wrecker was called to pull the tree in the right direction and relieve the car from its dug-in place on the lawn. It was a hard thing to live down. Instead of fifteen minutes, the project had taken up the better part of the Sunday, with unexpected expenses to boot.

Pim and Jeannet had emigrated from Holland right after the war where they'd both been involved in the Underground. Pim had been in solitary confinement in one of the worst prisons, the infamous one in Scheveningen, because he had spread illegal news bulletins. Jeannet's father was one of the top leaders of the Underground movement, while her older sisters and their boyfriends were in constant danger of being caught with illegal radios and doing undercover spy work. When the war was over, Pim immediately left for America and found a position in Boston's wool business. Jeannet followed later.

The Vissers embraced the American way of life, everything about it, from the neighbors' hospitality to its seemingly limitless possibilities. They'd come without a penny, they told us, and, "Look, here we are, in our own home, with a job and two cars in the driveway." The American immigrant's dream-come-true. They made the will-do, can-do attitude they encountered in America their own. After three months of helping to get their old farmhouse in shape, I couldn't wait to follow their example. My mother would always call the carpenter or the painter if something needed repair. It wouldn't have entered her mind to buy a gallon of paint to do the job herself. My mother on a ladder with a paintbrush in her hand was simply unimaginable. I was in awe of the skills Jeannet had acquired, and of her energy to hang wallpaper while she kept house and supervised three young children. Another facet of their life that I took note of was how they shouldered the work equally. It didn't matter what needed to be done—the dishes, painting, weeding, putting linoleum down, shopping for food—the one at hand would do it. It seemed a perfect arrangement to me, a true inspiration. Pim and Jeannet were into this adventure together, all the way.

I had never set foot in a hardware store, and I doubted my mother ever had. In Holland hardware stores were for carpenters, electricians, and painters. Not for housewives like Jeannet, who covered their hair with a bandana and thought nothing of steaming the wallpaper off the walls and bringing the resulting trash to the dump. Here the storekeepers weren't snickering when Jeannet asked for a paint roller. A sympathetic industry had sprouted up around the do-it-yourselfers. America exuded energy.

One day, Gijs received a call from a doctor on Cape Cod. His name was Langdon Burwell, and he'd set up a group practice in Falmouth and was looking for a fourth doctor. We were invited for an overnight visit and encouraged to take our barely one-year old with us. Remembering the formality of the visit in Woodstock, Vermont, I wasn't looking forward to it, but I shouldn't have worried. Langdon Burwell was an utterly charming, energetic, sophisticated man in his early forties who was used to visitors of all ages. He lived with his family in a large house on the beach in Woodshole, where many relatives and friends flocked. Barbie, his wife, had developed an effective system of entertaining guests. A make-it-yourself breakfast set up in the kitchen made you feel you weren't holding them up in the morning. Her other rule of thumb was to leave the guests to entertain themselves. "We'll see you at supper," was the motto. It was wonderfully relaxing.

These people had seen a lot of the world. Everywhere I looked I saw framed maps, paintings and memorabilia of the places they'd visited. Walls were lined with bookcases that held well-read books. Through the picture windows we watched the ocean roll toward their beach below in foamy waves, and throughout the night we heard the hoarse and repetitious sound of the harbor's foghorn. During breakfast we noticed that yesterday's breathtaking view had disappeared in a veil of mystery.

Joan felt at home almost immediately, surrounded as she was by the four guileless and friendly teenagers who doted on her. She took her very first steps to loud acclaim on the second day of our visit. A good omen, I thought.

It turned out that Dr. David Bradley in Hanover had recommended Gijs. We had baby-sat his children for a week when we still lived at Wigwam Circle. Gijs was excited about the setup of Lang's practice. He'd never considered being part of a group practice, but Lang's infectious idealism to bring the best medical care possible to an area that was, at that time, still rural, appealed to him. The closest hospital was in Hyannis. Lang said he would change that. He was determined to build one in Falmouth itself. With energy and vision he designed a modern state-of-the-art facility, and with its blueprints in hand he went to the wealthiest summer people to beat big bucks out of their pockets. At the time we visited, Lang had enough pledges to start the project.

We all felt very comfortable with one another and reaching the decision to join the group wasn't hard to make. But there was one catch. The medical licensing board of the Commonwealth of Massachusetts made it very hard for a foreigner to obtain a license. Gijs was well aware of that stumbling block, but Lang was not the kind of man to take no for an answer. Neither was he going to sit around to wait out the tedious application process. He went right to the top, there and then, by calling the chairman of the board. He and Gijs left the next morning for Boston in good humor and full of hope.

They came back empty-handed. Lang was incredulous that the reason the board didn't want to give a license to Gijs was because Gijs could not produce his high school grades. Of course, Gijs had missed most of high school because he was in prison camp. Lang was fuming at the myopic policy of a board that wanted to keep out as many foreigners as it could out of competitive considerations. Boston had become the Mecca of modern medicine. The whole world flocked to it for training and prestige. The medical profession in Massachusetts had become a closed shop. Lang had not been able to poke a hole in it and he was very disappointed, as were we.

Yet, in spite of the outcome, we had made friends for life.

Chapter 11

Discovering Wakefield

Dr. Sawyer was the one who brought us to Wakefield. For years he had hunted for a young man who could take over the practice he'd reluctantly started when, in fact, he'd come to this area to retire. He had returned to his native New Hampshire in his late fifties from Fall River in Massachusetts, where he'd practiced as an obstetrician. He'd bought a grand house on Cooks Pond in Brookfield, the next town over. The time was just before WW II. He realized he'd walked into a hornet's nest when Dr. Louise Paul, a native of Wakefield, asked him to sign a paper that would allow her to join the navy. The American government, at war with Japan and Germany, had ruled that practicing physicians could only enlist if they found coverage for their patients. Dr. Sawyer had served in WW I and felt he should do something for his country again. He obliged. However, Dr. Paul, who was in her late thirties, met an old sweetheart, Frank Heck, in an officer's mess in San Diego. He'd become a widower and had also enlisted in the navy. They married and after the war went to live in Minnesota.

It was not what Dr. Sawyer had expected when he signed on the dotted line. As he got on in years, it became too much to be on call seven days a week, and he frantically looked for a replacement, or at least for an assistant to help in the busy summer months, when the population of 1800 tripled with summer residents in the cottages around the region's many lakes. He called Dr. Syvertsen at the Dartmouth Medical School, who told him about a Dutch doctor who was about to complete his general practice residency. Gijs was invited for a visit.

Gijs declined Dr. Sawyer's kind invitation to stay overnight in his impressive house and instead asked permission to park our car on their lawn bordering the lake. Mrs. Sawyer looked dubious when Gijs assured her we just loved to camp. He'd immediately fallen in love with the lake called Cooks Pond (now renamed Kingswood Lake). A white cabana sat at the Sawyers' stretch of the shore, partially covered with ivy and surrounded by flowerbeds. It sparkled like a piece of glass in the lawn. There were no bedrooms inside, but it was an ideal place to park next to. Gijs wanted to get the feel of the area he might one day call home through his own frame of mind, without the distraction of polite conversation. Woodstock was fresh in his memory. So, even without the proper equipment like a tent, we preferred spending the night in the car to being put up in the formal house. After a pleasant dinner with the Sawyers we drove down to the lake leaving behind a bewildered hostess, who probably chalked up our strange desire to camp in a car—with a one year old—to coming from abroad. Of course, she was right. She knew about black flies. We didn't.

We were closer to the night than the day when we maneuvered our car down the path to the lake. Through the shrubs and tall pine trees the lake looked like a liquid backdrop to a ballet. In the twilight, the view was divided in sweeping areas of dark and silver highlights. The gently rolling mountains that bordered the lake on the west side presented themselves in positive and negative images as the water doubled their contours in reflection. I wasn't aware of any air movement until tiny silver ripples rolled playfully over the lake's surface like marbles being shot over a polished sheet of glass in a never-ending stream. Dr. Sawyer had told us at dinner that the lake was spring fed. Close to the shore, granite boulders rose up out of the sandy bottom and were so sharply delineated that they gave me the sense of looking at them through a magnifying glass.

"This is magic," I whispered to Gijs. Joan sat on his arm, totally fascinated by the silver rippling and the gentle sloshing of water against the dock.

We tried to make ourselves comfortable in the car, curled up under borrowed blankets in the front seat and Joan sprawled out over the backseat because she had outgrown her red plastic car bed. The warm late May air soon became stifling, so we opened the windows to catch a breeze. With the fresh air came the black flies, maddening creatures we couldn't hear or see, but whose vicious bites we felt. They invaded our small space in swarms, hid in cavities like nostrils and ears and, worst of all, left big welts on Joan's fair skin. Our first night in the Wakefield/Brookfield area was spent wildly swatting at flies that were microscopic in size, cursing under our breath, opening windows, closing them again, and scratching various parts of our bodies, which were trying to adjust to curled-up positions not conducive to sleep. Unfamiliar rustlings of the wind through pine trees and the hauntingly mocking cries of an unidentified bird on the lake warped my dreams into scary scenes with otherworldly creatures, and I was relieved when the day announced itself by spreading light into the sky. Slowly, the snakes and monsters that had inhabited my dreams changed from the nocturnal shapes outside the window into recognizable objects I could name. The dark whirlpool became a lake, the grizzly bears transformed into flowering shrubs, the snake into a border edging.

Gijs winked at me when Joan stirred in the backseat. In sign language we decided to get our sleep mobile on the road. The horizontal rays of the newborn sun highlighted the roofline of the Sawyers' house, throwing a mysterious shadow over the flagstone terrace. Gijs drove at a snail's pace by the house like a thief who's just made off with the heirloom silver. Once on Route 109, he picked up speed, and a delicious breeze swept through the car, sucking out the tiny black flies.

It seemed like an eternity before we saw another house. Yet on the map we saw that Brookfield and Wakefield practically ran into each other. Eventually, we passed a cluster of homes, a gas station and a church that looked like a barn with a cross on top. Dr. Sawyer had told Gijs on his first trip here that Wakefield was made up of several villages. The original settlement was on a hill, called Wakefield Corner. Sanbornville lay at its foot in the valley. Union was a few miles to the south, East Wakefield toward the Maine border, and then there was North Wakefield.

We had entered Sanbornville, which went by the name of "French Town" because French Canadians, who'd moved down from Quebec to cut trees from the woods and ice from the lake, largely inhabited it. They'd lingered even after refrigerators replaced iceboxes and the need to ship chunks of ice by train to Boston was taken away by progress. A huge barn where the ice blocks used to be stored in sawdust hung precariously in its wooden hinges, barely holding together at the side of Lovell Lake. And because land barons had raped the forests around the turn of the century, little was left to cut for the next generation of woodcutters.

The houses looked like the clothes I remembered from the war: worn to a thread without any supplies to repair them. The long body of the narrowly fronted general store ran parallel to the railroad tracks. In more prosperous times, a jolly artist had painted a man on it, seated in a rocking chair and smoking his pipe, his feet up on a pot belly stove. It was one of two gathering places. The other, called "Sarah's Spa," sat next to a tall brick building with the words Town Hall inscribed on a large piece of granite above the door. "Sarah's Spa" fronted the center of town, marked by a triangular raised bed of grass. Before we reached the lake we passed by the barbershop, a fishing and hunting store, a shoe repair shop and a small grocery store next to Mixer's Real Estate. On the corner sat the funeral home and around the bend Bob Duchano's garage, surrounded by a parking lot with secondhand cars.

"That's it," Gijs said. "You've just seen the town of Wakefield."

"Wow!" I said. "How long does he want you to be his assistant?" I couldn't imagine what I would do in a barren place like this.

Gijs turned around in Duchano's parking lot and let the tired body of our "pea green" crawl by the rows of spiffed-up metal and chrome. I was incredulous that the biggest part of commercial real estate by far was the car dealer's, while otherwise the town had little more to offer its inhabitants than the bare essentials. In my hometown of eighty thousand people, I didn't even know where the car dealers were. Owning a car in Holland had been a luxury few people could afford. As I was soon to find out, a person could not live without one in these parts.

"Let's go up this hill," Gijs suggested.

At the top of the hill, the same mountain range that hovered over Cooks Pond dominated the view over rolling pastures. A spectacular big barn stood on one side of the road and a white church with gothic windows and a slender steeple on the other. Intrigued we continued on, first dipping into a valley, then climbing an even steeper hill that leveled off to form a long ridge lined by old colonial homes in meadows that seemed to roll away, bringing into view distant mountains on both sides. It was obviously the part of Wakefield that had been settled first.

Joan woke and hoisted herself up so she could look over my shoulder. I reached for her to put her in the safety of my lap. The three of us looked through the front window on the front seat as we advanced slowly, careful not to wake this pretty maiden so early in the morning. There was no sign of life, but my spirits were lifted by the stately homes, which looked unspoiled behind their white picket fences, breathing an air of history and as deeply rooted as the elms that created an arch in front of them.

After seeing so many villages, candidates for Gijs's practice, this part of Wakefield was like a strong white chrysanthemum amidst decaying petunias.

We turned around and took it all in again: the three-story Elmwood Inn, another church, the library, the original Town Hall, the general store with a gas pump in front, the granite watering trough, a hay scale on the spot where the road forked off toward Maine. This part of Wakefield reminded me of Woodstock, but without the pretense.

Gijs took the job of being Dr. Sawyer's assistant for the three summer months.

Chapter 12
Living in Brookfield

O n the first of July 1958, we drove to Norwich, Vermont, in a U-Haul truck and loaded our belongings that had been stored in the garage of the house we'd rented during the cold winter months. Dr. Sawyer had found a house we could rent for the summer. What was once a working farm stood on a knoll in the encroaching woods and offered many empty rooms. With the little furniture we owned, we concentrated on making the kitchen livable. The owner, Mr. Baker, had recently been widowed and had moved in with his caretaker.

Gijs threw himself into the rural practice he'd dreamed of. Early in the morning, he took off for Wolfeboro to make rounds at Huggins Hospital. In the family of towns in the Lakes Region, Wolfeboro was the wealthiest with a prime location on Lake Winnipesauke, the largest of the lakes in the region. It had attracted many interesting and wealthy people, among them illustrious doctors who came to spend the summers and who made themselves available on the consulting staff of Huggins Hospital. This set Huggins apart from other hospitals Gijs had visited.

The house's kitchen area was large but depressing, taken for granted by an aging couple, who had ignored the grease stains and the veil of gray. With Mr. Baker's permission, I availed myself of light blue paint, a stepladder, and a roller to roll away the spatters of their bacon breakfasts. Joan was asleep upstairs, taking her morning nap, while I was on the ladder watching the patterned wallpaper give way to my latex paint. When Joan made her wake-up noises, I lifted her out of bed and installed her on the floor of the empty dining room next to the kitchen and barricaded the lower half of the open door. She was happy loading and unloading cardboard boxes, leftovers from our move, lifting objects with her busy little fingers and trying to fit them into spaces she was convinced she could fit them into.

My ladder was positioned so I could watch her. My glance fell on a note pad a pharmaceutical company had sent in the mail to push their latest blood pressure pill. Two pills were inserted behind plastic at the top of the pad. Two??? One was missing. I jumped off the ladder. One piece of plastic had been worked open. Pill gone. I reached my finger into Joan's mouth, but found nothing. I combed the floor on my hands and knees. No pill. My heart filled with panic. *She has swallowed the pill. What are these ingredients? They're listed. God, what do these names mean? She will die if I don't do something. No car! It's a twenty-minute drive. I have to get to Gijs. Never mind my paint-splattered clothes. Act, for God's sake! Hit the road! They have to pump her stomach out. Oh God, she's going to die.*

The closest neighbor was one mile away, and I knew nobody in town but the Sawyers. I picked up Joan, dashed out the door, and started walking blindly down the very long lane that led to Governor Wentworth Road. Joan sat on my arm and smiled. She didn't show any sign of physical distress.

God, how incredible to be walking here, with the birds singing in the trees, earthy smells rising from the warm woods, the brilliant sky above me and knowing that soon Joan will go into coma, be out of touch with me forever, and then die. Gone! Never to see that dear little face again, those lively blue eyes, that sweet little mouth already full of wit and intelligence. How long will it be to Wolfeboro?

I heard a car behind me. It slowed down.

"Hi, it's a hot day to be walking. Wanna ride?" The driver had rolled down the window. He looked like a young farmer.

"My baby! She's swallowed a pill. I've got to get her to the hospital. I have no car."

"Get in, lady," the man said. The woman in the seat next to him jumped out of the car and opened the back door for me. I wormed myself onto the seat in between bags of groceries. The floor was strewn with candy wrappers and plastic pistols. They must have kids. Boys, probably.

"Excuse the mess. Aren't you the new doctor's wife?" the woman asked.

"Yes, I am." How did she guess? My accent?

"A doctor's wife letting her baby eat pills?" the man said.

"Now, Bob, don't give her a hard time," the woman said, almost under her breath.

"We live around the corner from you. We are Bob and Bea Smith," the woman said.

Bob was putting his foot to the gas pedal and we made it to Wolfeboro in record time. He knew the shortcuts. I ran straight into the emergency room, bypassing the ER nurse, and rushed by the examining rooms till I found the one with Gijs in it. Instinct had told me that of all the places he could be at that moment in that big building, he would be in the ER.

"Gijs!" I shouted, oblivious of rules that forbade patients to barge in on busy doctors.

He lifted his handsome face from being bent over a patient. He excused himself, stepped into the wide hallway, and took in the scene of his daughter in diapers and his wife in a sweat-soaked painting outfit. Joan reached for him and he took her from my arm.

"What happened?"

I produced the pharmaceutical pad and pointed at the empty space at the top.

"Did she eat it?"

"I don't know. I found this on the floor next to her. She didn't have a pill in her mouth, but I couldn't find it anywhere." I was close to tears. "Hurry up! Do something, Gijs!"

Gijs took me in his arms, then released me and smiled.

"It's a fake pill, made to look like a real one."

"You mean, there is no poison in it?"

"More likely sugar."

I felt taken. Those drug companies should know better. What a stupid way to advertise. The nurses and other doctors gathered around us and had a good laugh. I figured the best part of the adventure was that I had discovered I had neighbors. Bob and Bea Smith. They even knew me by name. They'd helped me unasked.

After the shock wore off, I went back to my paint job. While putting the finishing touches on the born-again kitchen, I heard a knock on the front door. With Joan on my arm, I answered the door to face a man who took off his Stetson hat and held it against his old-fashioned business suit.

"Good afternoon," he said, throwing back his head in a gesture of great self-confidence and a convincing smile. "I am Bert Holman, and I would like to speak to the doctor."

I told him the doctor wasn't home, would it do to talk to me? He said it would and I invited him in.

"I come with a proposition," he said "We very much need a doctor in this town. Dr. Sawyer is getting on in years, and Dr. Bozuwa is well liked by the people here."

I nodded.

"We would like to keep him here. We would arrange for him to have an office. We would buy the equipment and instruments. You know, he wouldn't have to put up any money."

Joan was getting restless in my arms so I let her down to play. It gave me time to think.

"You mean the townspeople would own the office and everything in it?" I asked.

"That's right!" Mr. Holman said, obviously pleased he'd been chosen to deliver this golden opportunity. He relaxed in his seat and leaned back.

"That's incredibly generous." I said "But I'm not sure he would take you up on your offer."

Mr. Holman sat up straight again. "Does he have other plans?"

"No, there are no definite plans at this point, but I think he will want to earn his own equipment and office."

How could I explain that Gijs was a proud man, who wouldn't want to be kept by anyone?

"But it's offered to him. Why would he refuse?" Mr. Holman was incredulous. Here he was, bringing an office on a silver platter and this young woman in her paint-splattered clothes wasn't jumping at the idea.

"I don't know how to explain it to you, Mr. Holman, and maybe I shouldn't speak for him, but if I tell you that he refused my father's offer to buy a practice in Holland for him – in Holland you have to buy a practice, you see – then you can maybe understand it's just not his way."

"But a father-in-law is different from a community in need, Mrs. Bozuwa," Mr. Holman said, like a teacher talking to a pupil.

"I think, Mr. Holman, that one of my husband's concerns is how it would work out to charge patients for, let's say, an ECG if the machine he takes it with had been paid for by the patients themselves. That might not sit so well after a while."

"Well, now," Mr. Holman was quick to reply, "that's no problem. The people would understand a doctor has to make a living."

"I don't know, Mr. Holman." I stroked Joan's fine blond hair since she had come to stand at my knee, staring at the stranger. "It's a very generous offer. But maybe you'd better check with my husband."

Mr. Holman took his leave. His gray Stetson hat went back on his balding head and he shook my hand as politely as he had coming in, with the same set smile on his lined face. I later learned he was the local bill collector.

As I watched him get in his car and drive off, I hoped he wasn't angry with me, and more importantly, that Gijs wouldn't be. No doubt Gijs would have handled the encounter with more diplomacy. He had a way of steering people away from their intentions or even angry suppositions without them being aware of it in the slightest.

Joan

I tossed a ball to Joan on the lawn and thought how curious it was that in socialistic Holland one had to buy a practice while in capitalistic America they came to offer one for free. I had understood the American spirit as meaning that you made your own way. No free lunch, but opportunities for everyone. When I talked with Gijs on the phone, he agreed: it wouldn't work.

He didn't come home that night, tied up at the hospital with a delivery. It had been a hot and windless day. Joan was listless, her shirt clinging to her little body; nothing interested her, nothing pleased her.

The trees, the flowers, the fields, everything had lost its luster in the gray light. The air trembled with heat and the earth waited for release. It came with a vengeance that made old myths about angry gods riding the sky in rumbling chariots, throwing spears and flaming swords through the air, comprehensible.

Joan huddled next to me on the couch and crawled into my lap with the first distant rumblings, which sounded like the artillery fire that had preceded the liberation of my home city. For days we had heard explosions getting closer and closer. We hungered as much for the end of the war then as I looked forward to the release from the oppressive air and humidity now. My mother always displayed her greatest calm when the bombs started falling around us. She acted with icy self-restraint. I always tried to stand next to her because her whole body exuded confidence. Now I would have to give that confidence to Joan.

For a split second the world lit up. A loud crash followed. Rain clattered on the roof. I couldn't see even the closest trees, but I heard the wind twirl their crowns. Joan clenched her fist around my ring finger and whimpered. Did this house have a lightning rod? Another bolt of lightning, a deafening thunderclap, a quick snapping and a slow downing of branches, heavy with wet leaves. The earth shook. *God, this is close by!*

I jerked out of my seat with Joan still in my arms and ran to the window. A big tree lay sprawled over the lawn and the dirt road. I was a prisoner! I picked up the phone, but there was no dial tone. The lights had gone out without me noticing it. Why did this have to happen the night Gijs wasn't home? But if he'd been home, the pregnant woman couldn't have reached him on a dead phone and even if she could have, he couldn't have gotten out the road. I looked again. The tree had come down on the exact spot where Gijs usually parked our car. Our "pea green" would have turned into a steel sandwich. Worse, if Gijs had been in it? No, don't even think it.

Instinctively, I moved toward the wall my mother would have chosen, in the middle of the house. One explosion after another. The only thing lacking was the smell of gunpowder to bring me back completely to the last days of the war, when we hid in the cellar for almost a week. I pressed Joan against me while I searched my soul for traces of my mother's calm. I couldn't remember any storm in Holland that had come close to the violence this one unleashed.

A light crept over the wall and stopped. My heart pounded, but

I walked over to the window and watched a man step out of his car, a raincoat draped over his head. He approached the house. I didn't know him, but that was not surprising because I knew nobody in this town. Except for Bob and Bea Smith. I opened the door before he reached it. He stepped inside, a puddle of water forming around his shoes.

"Are you all right here?" he asked.

"Yes, I think so. The phone is dead and the lights are out, but other than that, we're all right." Was that all he wanted to know? Who was this man? As if he read my mind, he said, "We're your neighbors. I am Earl Brown. My wife and I thought we'd check to see if there was a hit. This storm came right close. I see you lost a tree. I'll get a man here to get the worst out of the way."

"Thank you very much, but you really don't have to do that."

"Oh, no sweat, I'm a contractor." He was a bear of a man, big and hulky. I liked his no-nonsense approach and the twinkling, intelligent brown eyes. He turned around, not waiting for a thank you, and quickly ran back to his car. He backed it all the way to the road.

I felt Joan's heaviness on my arm and set her down. Earl Brown had acted as a lightning rod for our panic and driven our fright into the ground. It was still raining hard, it was still blowing, and the thunder rumbled on, but Joan went over to her toy box and started to take things out. By the time I reached Gijs, the biggest limbs of the fallen tree had been removed.

Now I knew that I had two sets of neighbors, people who acted when the chips were down.

We kept looking for a place in New Hampshire to practice until we asked ourselves, "Why not here?" It was an established fact that Gijs was needed, that people took to him. The area hospital with an outstandingly gifted surgeon, Dr. Ralph Adams, and a good staff was a big attraction. It made him feel safe.

The clincher was a call that came into Dr. Sawyer's office from a wealthy woman, a summer resident, whose servant had taken ill. Dr. Sawyer dispatched his assistant. It was a Friday evening. Gijs followed the directions that led to the top of Cotton Mountain at the end of a dirt road. There he saw an extensively remodeled cape on a level stretch in the cool shadow of old maple trees. It was situated to take advantage of the view of the White Mountains.

Gijs told me all about it afterward with his considerable talent for feeding his listeners the details they needed. When he saw that the wide driveway was filled with spiffy cars, he decided to park his trusty "pea green" out of view. With his black doctor's bag in hand he rang the bell. A servant in a white jacket answered and, seeing the black bag, led Gijs to the servants' quarters without a word. In the background he heard the rise and fall of voices emboldened by the loosening effect of alcohol, sounding like the tuning up of an orchestra before the conductor steps onto the podium.

It was the servant's wife Sophie who was ill in bed. Both were Polish and spoke poor English. Gijs examined her and concluded she'd suffered a slight stroke. He asked to see their employer. A woman about sixty years old, he guessed, in a rustling silk dress, met him in the hallway and took him to the study. She gestured for him to sit down with the ease and the authority of the society hostess she was.

"Sophie suffered a mild stroke," Gijs informed her. "I gave her some medicine and I'll wait to see if it takes effect. Bed rest will be of the greatest benefit to her."

"I have the house filled with guests over the weekend," Mrs. Burwell said. "We have to get her to the hospital."

"I beg to differ in opinion, Mrs. Burwell," Gijs said firmly.

She looked surprised to hear opposition to her plan and she made it clear that she wasn't going to let this young man get away with it.

"I'll have Emil take her to the hospital," she said.

"No. It will be harmful to her condition to transport her and put her in a hospital where she'll be met by a language barrier. That will be anxiety provoking, far better to keep her here. I'll stay with her for a while and I'll be back tomorrow morning."

Gijs must have said this with great aplomb, and I think that Mrs. Aubrey Burwell quickly evaluated this tall, balding man with his strong blue eyes and made up her mind to give him a chance. When Gijs came back the next morning, Sophie's condition had markedly improved. To Gijs it was just common sense, but Mrs. Burwell was awed. She trusted him in all things, medical and otherwise, from then on. Sophie remained living proof of his good judgment for many years.

With his medical authority established, Mrs. Burwell invited him into the living room, which was dominated by a beautiful grand piano. She seated herself in front of it. There wasn't a trace of the previous party.

Gijs was shown a Chippendale chair close by. His hostess was not the most beautiful woman he'd ever met, but she definitely bemused him. She was vibrant and eccentric. Music was her passion, she told him, and she was practicing to perform a concert in Cambridge soon. He couldn't help but notice the flamboyance of her dress and the cloud of perfume that surrounded her. Before she put her hands to the piano, she took off four spectacular rings and placed them in a china dish. Her fingers moved rapidly over the ivory keys, reaching for them with confidence, her bracelets jingling with her elegant upward gestures. She could really play!

It was his turn to be impressed. But what impressed him most was her willingness to accept advice from a general practitioner. It was a very different attitude than the Woodstock couple had shown. There would be an interesting blend of patients here, he thought. Mrs. Burwell gave the last push Gijs needed to make up his mind to start a medical practice in the Wakefield area.

Chapter 13

Cocktail Party

Whathen Mrs. Sawyer learned of our decision to stay in Wakefield, she thought we should meet other young couples. Soon an invitation arrived in the mail. It read: "Rear Admiral and Mrs. Lloyd Thomas request the pleasure of your company." We would attend a cocktail party in Melvin Village, a picturesque town on the north shore of Lake Winnipesauke.

Joan sat on our bed looking at me while I frantically took out dresses from the closet. There wasn't much choice. My collection could be divided into maternity dresses and the dresses from before I got married, and those were a tight fit. I took the hatbox down from the top shelf and pulled out the hat I'd worn as part of my "going away costume." My mother had insisted that I wear a hat. She thought I needed at least two hats when I got married.

"Are you ready?" Gijs called from the bottom of the stairs.

"I'm coming," I answered, and threw a last glance at myself in the mirror. Something was lacking. I looked in the closet and noticed the summer parasol Gijs had bought for me on our honeymoon in Italy. A white silk tassel hung from the curved wooden handle, and its cloth had light blue, soft pink and white sections. All three colors were visible in the swirl it formed around the stick. I put the crook of the parasol over my wrist and went downstairs.

"Well, look at you!" Gijs said.

We left Joan in care of a babysitter and drove halfway around Lake Winnipesauke to the Bald Peak Colony Club. A uniformed security guard stepped out of his sentry box and checked our names against a guest list. The driveway wound gracefully through a well-kept stand of trees. Tall

ferns turned into gilded fans as the late afternoon sun peered in shafts
through the branches. We came out on a wide expanse of lawn, freshly
cut, and in places given a crew cut. People, mostly men clad in colored
slacks, walked over the fairways followed by young caddies with golf bags
slung over their shoulders. My father played golf, but not in such brightly
colored slacks or on such rolling countryside. In Holland nothing rolled.
Everything was flat, with few exceptions, and whatever rolled was usually
manmade.

We drove along the fairways edged by white houses that were
designed to look grand with the help of pillars and terraces. They faced a
spectacular view of the lake and the Belknap Mountains. We were among
several guests as we walked up to the house. Nobody wore a hat, I quickly
noticed. Furthermore, only one elderly lady wore gloves like me, and
absolutely nobody carried a parasol. The zest I'd felt at home when I came
down the stairs with Joan all excited on my heels, drained out of me fast.
"Who is this pretentious young woman?" I could feel them think. Their
thoughts—the ones I imagined they had about me—fastened on my back
like deerflies.

Admiral and Mrs. Thomas stood in the hall greeting their guests,
obviously accustomed to their role of hosts as they chose the words with a
kind of controlled informality that would make their guests feel welcome.
The admiral looked smashing in a dark blue blazer with an embroidered
emblem of the Bald Peak Colony Club on the breast pocket, probably
reminiscent of the insignia he must have worn on his navy uniform when
he was on active duty. His blue eyes, set in a masculine, weathered face,
had a kind look. His wife Harriet was a plain woman who dressed well.
She had an executive air about her, and I could imagine her as president
of the Garden Club, the local Red Cross, that sort of thing.

Gijs clicked his heels when he shook hands with the admiral, a
gesture triggered by years of watching his military father.

"Dr. Bozuwa, how are you? Dr. Sawyer told me about you. He's very
happy you will stay in the area," Admiral Thomas said.

"Make yourself at home," Mrs. Thomas said to me. "We have many
young people here for you to meet."

We stepped into a spacious living room. Everything in America
seemed to be of a larger scale than in Holland: the cars, the forests, the
hills, the ice cream cones, the steaks, just about everything we came into
contact with was king sized. Gijs steered me to a corner where a bar was

set up. A man in a vest with brass buttons asked me what I would like to drink. I was confused by the array of bottles, plates with lemon and lime slices, bright maraschino cherries and buckets of ice. The choices were numerous and had strange names like martini, daiquiri, Manhattan, planter's punch, bloody Mary. At home the choice was between sherry, red vermouth for the ladies and Dutch *jenever* for the men. All without ice. Gijs saw my confusion and suggested a gin and tonic. "It's a warm night."

Dr. and Mrs. Sawyer came over to introduce us to a group of couples, who were about Gijs's age, who was thirty-two. These were the people Mrs. Sawyer wanted us to meet. It worked.

"Hi, I am Henry Maxfield," I heard someone say to Gijs. An amused curiosity played in his light blue eyes when Gijs introduced me to him. A handsome man, with blond wavy hair, probably in his late thirties, I guessed. The type of man I remembered from right after the war. My friends and I drooled over men like that, our liberators, with their self-confident air, looking very dashing in their leather jackets that were a sensation after the dour gray uniforms of the German soldiers. I wasn't surprised to hear him talk about the war. He seemed to be eager to tell his story.

"I was shot down over Germany on a bombing mission and made a P.O.W," he said to Gijs, who didn't volunteer his own war experiences.

"I am in real estate," he went on. "Came to live here a few years ago. I'm a writer. I've just finished my first book. It will come out this winter."

"What's its title?" I asked.

"Legacy of a spy," Henry said. "I sold the movie rights to it."

Henry loved to talk. He made the book come alive. If the scenes in the book were as well written as he described them, it would be a best seller. He'd worked in the C.I.A. for some years after the war, he told us, but didn't like the life. He'd quit and wanted to devote himself to writing. Of course, one had to make a living, so he became a real estate agent.

"Why did you pick Wolfeboro?" Gijs asked.

"You wait! This area will be booming."

The roads were improving, he said, people wanted to get to the lakes and there were miles and miles of undeveloped shore frontage waiting for them.

Young couples were gathering around the dining room table, which was laden with large trays with deviled eggs, rolled-up ham slices, filled mushroom caps and cherry tomatoes. Henry steered me over to his wife Betty, and soon I found myself within a circle of women who looked like young mothers.

"Hi, I am Di Hopewell, how do you do?" one of them introduced herself to me. She was Canadian, she said, born and brought up in Montreal.

"Are you on vacation?" I asked.

"No, I'm not. We moved up here this summer to live. My husband bought the North Country Smokehouse in Wolfeboro. We moved up here from Tarrytown, New York. Before that we lived in Brazil. Bob worked at the Canadian Aluminum Company as a geologist."

"He's made some interesting switches," I said to the woman, who looked like she would be more at home in a New York suburb than in a mining town in Brazil or a rural area in New Hampshire. She spoke proper English and moved with social grace. Good manners were part of her persona, they were important to her, I could tell. Using them made her feel comfortable.

"Do you have children?" I asked.

"We have a daughter," Diana Hopewell said.

Gijs came over and led me to the other side of the room where Dr. Sawyer introduced us to his contemporaries. Graying hair surrounded us and I pegged the average age at around mid sixty. The automatic, introductory question, "Where do you come from?" served up a map of the Eastern border of the U.S. No one in the circle answered with, "I was born here." The men had retired from work in the big cities, from corporate jobs – I heard General Electric, General Motors, New England Telephone and other names that were household words even I recognized – and they had moved to the country. They relished their sense of adventure to let go of city conveniences and the orderly lives they'd led. Everyone, it seemed, was into remodeling an old farmhouse. The men swapped stories about salmon fishing and clearing land, the women about antique hunting and decorating their homes. Their conversations were sprinkled with anecdotes about the locals who did jobs for them.

The way in which these people circulated without getting stuck in a corner with one person, absentmindedly twirling ice cubes in their cocktail glasses, and tossing out topics like Ping-Pong balls as a lull threatened in the conversation, gave them an air of self-evident propriety that reminded me of our visit to Woodstock. They'd been around.

Standing back from the party hum – I had repeated our story over and over – I took in the scene. In the course of the evening, the room clearly became divided into relatively young people on one side and relatively old people on the other. Age was only one factor in what set the groups apart. The older men had retired from jobs the younger men spurned. It didn't have to do with level of education. They had all, as far as I could tell, enjoyed a college education. Harvard, Yale, Dartmouth were names I'd overheard. Bob had worked as a geologist, Joe as a chemical engineer before they'd landed in this area. When asked where they came from – and it seemed the right question to ask – they mentioned Boston and New York. For some reason they'd traded the city for a rural area, a city house for a farmhouse, a conventional job in line with their education for small town enterprises. Bob had bought a smoke house; Joe had started a hardware store, Charlie an oil delivery business, Doug a furniture store, Henry a real estate office. Their fathers, they said, had pursued more traditional careers in business or had fallen into them through inheritance.

On the way home, Gijs and I compared notes. None of the communities we'd ever lived in had a comparable structure, we agreed. Gijs had spent his growing-up years in towns that were ports with naval bases. You were always aware of rank, he said. My own growing-up years had played out in a city divided in levels of standing. My father's standing was not defined by the amount of money he might have in the bank, but by the type of work he did. Professional men like civil servants, doctors, high school teachers and engineers, had a higher standing than shopkeepers; and the nobility, even if they were shoestring aristocrats, ranked above all else. This was such an accepted way of rating people that we were hardly aware of the prejudices we held. What had amazed us at the admiral's cocktail party was the ease with which people like Bob and Joe had stepped over lines that were seldom crossed in the societies Gijs and I had grown up in. They didn't seem hampered by societal codes in choosing careers that were unconventional for the education they'd received.

"Did you notice how many old people there were?" I asked.

"Yes, we're part of a tiny minority here."

"What do you mean?"

"Well, it's simple. The population in this area divides into locals and imports. There are summer imports and year-around imports. In the year-round group are retired executives and the like, and then young, educated enterprisers. But very few of those."

"Why do you think they moved up here? Can they make a go of it?"

"Most spent their summers here, going to camp or their parents' summer home. Nostalgia, you might say. I talked to several and they said those were the best times of their life. They'll have to work hard to make a living here, especially during the summer months. That's when you make money here."

It took almost an hour to drive back home. A hostess in these parts had to cast far and wide. People seemed to think nothing of driving an hour or more to have a drink with someone.

Gijs slowed the car. Lake Wentworth had turned into a black and white picture. The vibrant daytime colors had been pocketed by the falling night. The mountains on the horizon, the same Belknap Mountains we had seen from Bald Peak, looked like a camel's humps. Gijs stopped the car, and we sat down on a log by the side of the road. The lake lapped the beach close to our feet.

"Let's enjoy it," Gijs said, and added, "Joan will be all right," anticipating my objection.

"It's amazing how much I took for granted in Holland," I said.

"What do you mean?"

"I don't know exactly, but it all seemed so natural when I grew up. Everybody knew my father. I never gave much thought to how he'd gotten to where he was. My parents had interesting friends. They did more or less the same things my father did."

"You mean to say: it's different here."

"Yes, I suppose so. Like, I wonder how Diana Hopewell feels. You know, the woman from Montreal."

"Yes, I remember her."

"She said she'd lived in Brazil and now they came from a New York suburb. That's quite a change!"

"Bob's family owns a house on Lake Winnipesauke. He's spent a good deal of his life here already. His brother moved up here too, he told me."

"I understand how *he* wanted to get up here. But his wife? How did she feel about it? Does she expect to become part of the local population or will she chum with the retired women? That's what puzzles me."

In my heart I knew the answer. Grin and bear it. That's how these wives had come up here when their husbands decided to leave the city or their suburban lives. I belonged to the same category of grin and bear it, but I knew what reconciled me. I fully understood the reasons why Gijs had emigrated and I loved his idealism and his sense of adventure. The women I'd met tonight must have similar understandings to reconcile the radical changes in their lives, and their husbands probably also came with some ideal in mind. Or, I hoped they did, for their own sakes.

We got back in the car. I sighed as I settled into the passenger seat. How could we fit into this heterogeneous community, made up of old farmers and their struggling families, some wealthy retirees, and a handful of young, educated people with lives I didn't fully understand? In Europe, I had lived in cities where people with different backgrounds only crossed paths in their daily work situations. In our new environment a large geographic area constituted, in essence, a small community. The fundamental difference with Europe was the tradition of equality that had shaped the social interaction here for almost two hundred years. These people actively governed their towns together, their schools and their church life. It seemed to work. Lines were crossed that I'd never seen crossed in Holland. It was intriguing, but I wondered how long it would take me to measure relationships with a different ruler. How could I acquire that new ruler, and was I really ready to toss my own in the dustbin?

Chapter 14
A House
of Our Own!

"I hate it, I hate it, I hate it," I said out loud, even though nobody but Joan was around to hear me say it as we stood in the backyard of the white clapboard farm house we'd just signed the mortgage on. Gijs had gone off to tend to some administrative details. Fire insurance or something like that.

I stared at the rooflines of the old colonial that went from high to low on the attached shed on the back, to even lower on some outcroppings that hung like pimples from the main frame. The various roofs were red, like on most Dutch houses, and as such they were the only aspect that reminded me of home.

"I hate it," I repeated passionately.

Joan sat on my arm and played with my necklace. I hugged her close and she looked up. Blue eyes looking into blue eyes. Mine were veiled with tears. She didn't sense my mood and smiled. A disarming, trusting smile that unsettled me even more.

"Don't worry, Joan, we'll make it work."

But how? Anxiety weighed on me like the heavy static air before a violent thunderstorm. You know it's coming and you shiver to think where it will hit. What I didn't realize at that moment was that the storm had already passed. The emigration, the separation, giving birth and taking the exams with a lot riding on them, all crowded into a little over one year, were behind us. I didn't stop to think of that. The house looked alien to me. It embodied all my private agonies. I hated it.

Oddly enough, after worrying where we would find a town to live in, it was the certainty that scared me. We had committed ourselves. The monthly $94.63 mortgage payment was only part of it. The finality of my signature on the lengthy document began to sink in. Gone were the days of choosing this or that. This was it. This house. This town. This country. We had nailed ourselves to a decision. What had it been like for my mother to follow my father to Breda in 1927? Mammie had been like a New Englander moving to New Orleans. She never did feel completely in tune with the more ebullient, light-hearted nature of Holland's Southerners. The summerhouse she convinced my father to build became her shield. There she raised beautiful gardens and played the piano for hours.

The signing of the mortgage had been somewhat of a ceremony. At exactly two o'clock on the first Saturday of September 1958, a small group of men in dark suits met at Mixer's Real Estate office. I was the only woman present. The owner of the house, Mr. Carlton Spencer, presided. He hadn't ever lived in the house we were about to buy, but his wife had inherited the big house diagonally across the street and he'd bought the Roberts place (our house) as well. Mr. Spencer was a dashing man of about fifty, a Boston lawyer who came up for summer weekends with his family.

The other men were locals. Civic-minded people who guaranteed Gijs an income of $100 per week in the first year to match his present salary as an assistant to Dr. Sawyer in case he wouldn't collect this amount from the patients. Also present was Dr. Sawyer, who handed over $3,500 in an interest free loan, so we could pay the $1,000 real estate fee, as well as for medical instruments and the installation of a heating system in the house. Mr. Spencer took on the mortgage himself. It was obvious that he didn't approve of the real estate dealer who charged the normal fee, while everyone else was bending over backwards to get a doctor in town.

Mr. Carlton Spencer read his own words from the legal documents that lay spread out over the desk, ready to be signed if there were no objections. Done reading, he scanned the faces around the room. His dark brown eyes flashed between charmingly engaging and icy cold, hinting at a fierce temper underneath his affable appearance. I didn't know if this man was loved or not, but I sensed those present had at some time or other decided it was best to stay on the right side of him. Even the usually boisterous real estate agent was subdued in Mr. Spencer's presence. There were no objections to what had just been read.

The mortgage deed redefined the borders of our property. The fifteen or so acres on the Spencer side of the street that used to be pasture for Mr. Roberts' cattle were now Mr. Spencer's. We didn't care about the loss of land. The five acres directly around our house constituted more land than all the members of our families combined could call their own back in Holland. What would we have done with all those fields? It was rumored that Mr. Spencer had bought "the Roberts place" because someone harbored wicked plans to build a drive-in theater on the Roberts' pastures right behind the house his wife had inherited. He had decided to take control.

Mr. Spencer's professional manner turned the signing of the various documents into a solemn occasion, as well it should be, for it was truly remarkable how the town's citizens had gotten together to enable a penniless immigrant to set up a medical practice in their town. The three thousand dollars we'd been able to take from Holland were long gone and we were living hand to mouth. All we had to our names were some Dutch antiques, our 1950 Ford and a two thousand dollar debt to Dartmouth College. We didn't even bother to go to the bank. Mr. Spencer had drawn up a document stipulating that no down payment was required and that no payments needed to be made in the first six months. He charged an interest rate half a percentage point below the going rate. What a deal!

One by one, we placed our signature at the "X" on the various documents. Signed and sealed. The tension broke and Gijs was slapped on his back. Not to worry! He would make it! Then the other men all slapped one another on the back. They'd done a fine thing for the town.

We were on the street again where Mr. Spencer's black Cadillac and Dr. Sawyer's two-tone beige/brown one flanked our pea green Ford. Across the street, Mr. Kenneth's black Cadillac was parked in front of his modest funeral home. This was the America I had studied in pictures back in Holland. Main Street U.S.A. with Cadillacs parked on both sides. But it was deceiving. Driving through Wakefield's main street showed a town hit by crisis. The farmers in the area had recently lost their sheep and hens to the South, where it was cheaper to raise them. The railroad, an important player in the town's economy because it was a junction, was flat broke. Wakefield was hurting and it showed in the peeling paint on the houses.

Joan held onto my hand as we walked to the shed over the sharp stubbles of the freshly mowed hayfield. We stepped into a dim space that seemed like an underground hole after the outside brightness. Some leftover firewood lay heaped in one corner, hardly distinct from the rough framing that had turned deep amber through the many years of

Our new home

just being. In the cool darkness I made out five doors. Five escapes! Like a woodchuck's living quarters! How would I stay ahead of Joan in this place? Mr. Spencer had warned me about a well under the wooden floor that should be closed off, and I could feel the planks with loosening nails dance under my feet. I opened each of the doors to see where they led: the driveway, the barn, the fields, and the house. We could do away with at least two. Joan ran inside the house like a penguin in a hurry, moving from side to side with her arms spread wide for balance, as fast as her fat little legs would propel her. She stamped her feet and roared with laughter at the echo she created in the unfurnished rooms.

The wallpapers used throughout the house reminded me of the house in Woodstock. I ran my fingers over the thick layers of paint in the elaborate designs. As soon as I could get my hands on a paintbrush I would cover them. Mrs. Spencer had done all the decorating, we'd been told. Hopefully, she wouldn't visit us. When I'd asked Mr. Spencer if we could make a few changes to the house, he'd laughed and said, "My dear, it is *your* house now." But it didn't feel that way. We hadn't paid a cent for it. It was all a promise. What if we couldn't make it? It didn't seem to bother Mr. Spencer.

When I was very little, my mother had created a family war when she had the gall to rip off the real leather wall coverings, delicately imprinted with gold designs, in the house that had belonged to her parents-in-law.

She had replaced it with stark white wallpaper. I grew up in a house with white walls. My mother thought they did more justice to her paintings and in that, as in many other things, she was ahead of her time. The current wallpaper in this colonial house would swallow up our own modest wall hangings. A vivid painting of purple and pink tulip fields under a dark Dutch sky would clash unbearably against a chartreuse-colored wallpaper with endless rows of horses and carriages riding through a hilly, nineteenth century English landscape. This paper suited the taste of a woman in her fifties, born and raised in New England, but not a young twenty-six-year old woman from Holland.

Joan bounced around like a little rubber ball through the empty spaces. I reached for her hands and together we danced circles through the rooms, as if we were moving through revolving doors, from one side of the house to the other. Gijs walked in and beamed when he saw us. His dream come true: a town that really needed him and a house of our own.

I never told him how I'd felt just before he walked in on us.

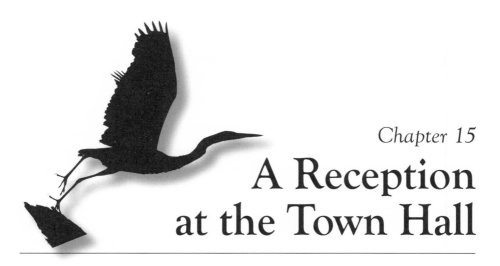

Chapter 15

A Reception
at the Town Hall

The contemplative peace of the summer was blown to bits by the autumn that followed. We became a sort of public property the minute we declared we would stay in Wakefield. The generous American spirit poured over us as benignly as water over thirsty flowers. Albert Drew, one of Dr. Sawyer's patients, insisted on moving our scant belongings from Brookfield to our new home in Wakefield. Dressed in baggy green twill pants that hung on red suspenders, he arrived with his wife Maud at our rented house and loaded the boxes we handed him. Joan sat like a little princess in Maud's lap and rode over to her new home on the front seat of the old pickup truck, an American marvel.

We had barely unloaded when a mason appeared, offering to put a damper in the living room fireplace. Another stranger, Mr. Albert Wiggin, cranked the big, clunky bell on the front door and delivered a dainty ladder-backed chair, compliments of him and his wife. The Episcopal minister, Father Gasson, and his wife Esther gave us their own harvest table with four thumb-back chairs. Mr. Lewis, down the street, asked if we could use a wing chair. The Lions Club bought a scale for the office. The sprinkling can of generosity never seemed to dry up. The big house filled up with somebody's spare bed, a vanity, and a bureau, representing a hodgepodge of styles.

On the day Gijs's practice officially opened, on the first of October 1958, Loes Hugenholtz and I stood with our noses against the windowpanes of an unfinished attic room above the office to see the long-awaited patients arrive. Loes had come over from Cambridge to help. Donned in dungarees and an old shirt of her husband Paul, with a red bandana over her blond hair, she attacked Mrs. Spencer's expensive wallpaper with a roller and off-white latex paint as if this was going to be her own husband's office. She wouldn't have minded if it had been, she confessed, but Loes knew she was headed for Boston's suburbs, the wife of a successful super-specialist who would work at a hospital. As we painted side by side for a whole week, Loes shared some of her life's varied experiences, which included working on a ranch in America's West, rounding up cattle on horseback. With Paul, who had served in the Air Force, she'd lived on various bases. The last one was in Arizona, she said. That's where they'd found the Jaguar they had arrived in when we'd first met in Hanover and which had impressed me so much. It had stood unwanted and forlorn in a used-car lot and they'd bought it for a song.

"Look, Tiets, that's a classic," Loes said, and pointed at a black model A Ford that pulled up at the curb. An older man with a red hunting cap over his longish white hair slowly swung out one leg, then the other. It looked like a painful maneuver.

"Oh, that's amazing," Loes said. "Do you see his white gloves? I saw a pair like that at the general store this morning! They're cotton work gloves. A farmer with virgin white gloves, that's a sight to behold. I bet he bought them especially to come and see the new doctor. Oh Titia, aren't you excited?"

I was. I was moved by the man's appearance. He was exactly what Gijs hoped his patients would be like. To me he was the American version of the farmers I remembered from my summers in the country. Where this man had a red cap, a blue jean jacket and leather boots, my *Boer* Jansen would have worn black corduroy pants, a suit jacket, a shirt without a collar, a gray wool cap and wooden shoes. But it was all the same. Under this man's loud red cap was probably the same tough mindset. Both were men who made their living from the land, who had to overcome or accept the elements day in and day out.

"Well, that's it." Loes said. "The first patient is in. We're rolling." She was all smiles. "Dr. Bozuwa. Country doctor. That farmer fits the image to a T."

The town fathers organized a reception for us that Saturday afternoon. Paul and Loes took care of Joan. We put on our most formal clothes and took the "pea green" downtown. The three selectmen were waiting to welcome us on the granite steps of the Town Hall. Unlike in Holland, where even the smallest village would have a mayor appointed by the Queen, these men were locals who ran the town for very little compensation. Johnnie Nason was a plumber, Bill Twombley a farmer as well as the state's road agent and Ed Drown the town's road agent. I could feel the marks of their daily toils in their handshakes. They ushered us up the wide staircase into a large assembly hall and invited us to stand in front of a stage, flanked by the American and New Hampshire flags. A wheelchair carrying a man in uniform was pushed in and stopped next to Gijs. He was the local police chief whose legs had been amputated only weeks before.

A wide circle of faces surrounded us, and the curious glances went through me like needle pricks. Instead of twenty-six, I felt fifteen. This was my first public appearance. Maybe, if they'd so readily accepted Gijs, they would take to me as well, but I realized keenly that we were not just strangers to them, but foreigners. I consoled myself with the thought that Gijs and I were like millions before us, and that Americans had a strong tradition of being hosts.

The selectmen spoke warm words of welcome. Father Gasson had been given the job of handing Gijs a box. This, he said, was a token of appreciation for the fact that Dr. Bozuwa had decided to stay in Wakefield. The people were happy for Dr. Sawyer that he could finally retire. To help Dr. Bozuwa buy the right equipment for his practice, the town's people had collected some money.

Gijs bowed and took possession of the box. He hesitated. Was he supposed to open it? A silence of suspense hung in the hall. He looked over at me and we smiled at each other. We didn't know what else to do. Then Gijs rattled the box and made a funny face.

"It feels heavy and it sounds heavy," he said as coins rattled inside the box. "We better see what's in it at home!" Laughter.

He handed the box to me. More Laughter. Then he rose to the occasion and made a rousing speech with hopes for the future and gratitude for the reception the town had given him. He deftly drew the attention away from himself by taking the wheelchair by the handles and asking for a round of applause for the Chief of Police.

When we returned home, Paul and Loes sat at the dining room table, which was nothing more than a door resting on makeshift legs. Gijs turned the box upside down on it. Silver dollars flew everywhere. Joan delighted in catching them. Her little fingers worked hard to get hold of the coins. The adults sorted out the rest of the trophy. We counted twice because we couldn't believe the final tally of seven hundred and forty-nine dollars. Although most of it was paper money, the amount of silver pieces amazed us. Maybe they'd been taken out of socks stashed away under beds. We were moved to tears. The people of Wakefield and Brookfield had made a big statement and we had a lot of goodwill to live up to.

Paul and Loes returned to their city lives. Paul said he had his doubts about how wise it was to start a practice in an economically depressed town in the poorest county of one of the poorest states in the union. Only Alaska's statistics were worse, he said.

Chapter 16

A Horse
in the Barn

The Roberts Place, as the locals called it, had five fireplaces around a center chimney but lacked central heating. The electric wiring was haphazard. To turn the wing of the house into a medical office required major adaptations. The Spencers recommended Vic Bezanson to do the work for us. Vic taught us everything we needed to know about a house made of wood, about the difference between hardwood and softwood, two-by-fours and two-by-sixes. He built cabinets, took down walls and brought the 1780 farmhouse into the twentieth century.

Gijs hired an eighteen-year-old girl to babysit Joan so I could help in the office. Cynthia was a very young bride. She lived in a small Cape on a dirt road, an hour's walk from the center of town, and had no money for a car. When Gijs found out she owned a horse but no wheels, he swapped our "pea green" for the horse and bought a second-hand bright red station wagon for ourselves.

Like most little girls, I had loved horses for as long as I could remember. I was three years old when *Boer* Jansen let me ride his workhorse bareback, nine when he let me drive her to market with a load of milk cans. After the war, a retired cavalry officer barked his commands from the center of a dusty arena to teach me the finer points of riding. My mother's tailor outfitted me with an elegant black riding jacket when I was made a member of the student riding club in Amsterdam. My mounts were well behaved, expertly trained and always presented groomed and ready to be ridden.

Dreaming about having a horse wasn't the same as owning one. The stark reality of a horse standing in our barn sank in when it whinnied to be fed or pawed the wooden planks to be let out in the pasture. Heaped on top of my new roles as secretary and receptionist was one of fixing old barbed wire fences, throwing hay down from the loft, filling buckets of water and mucking out stalls. Cynthia told us that Louise (what a name for a horse!) had come from the racetrack.

On a day that nobody came to the office because Gijs was delivering a baby, I found the trunk with my riding breeches, which reeked of mothballs. I pulled on my riding boots and tacked up the horse—a job I'd never done before.

We made it safely out of the driveway. For a while we looked like a picture from an English country magazine, walking sedately through the colonial village, horse and rider nicely turned out, as if ready for the foxhunt. People passing by in cars craned their necks. A rider in a black riding coat, elegantly flared over the hips, beige breeches and shiny black riding boots seemed to be a novelty in this part of the world.

I asked the horse for a trot by applying slight pressure with my booted calves against her rump. She obliged.

Hmmm. There's speed in this animal! Better take her back a little. Pull on the reins! She goes faster! Shifts into a different gear…what is this? My body felt twisted. Hold onto the reins! Oh God, she goes faster! What did that Dutch cavalry officer say? Does this horse know how to slow down?

We went lickety-slip over the road as if it were a racetrack. The sound of irons scraping the tar rang in my ears. The black pavement blurred, eaten up by the gigantic strides that made me feel as if my bowels were being rearranged.

Joan! I have to get back to Joan! God, my baby!

We careened around a corner to the top of a hill with a spectacular view of Moose Mountain. Drivers, seeing the new doctor's wife hang onto the reins for dear life, veered to the left and the right of us. Then, for some reason, my horse came to an abrupt halt. I was almost vaulted out of the saddle. My head banged against the mare's neck and, for a moment, I felt nothing but manes in my face. The world spun around, then came to a stop. Horse and rider were still together, but I could only think of one thing: get off this beast.

With my feet on the ground, I decided that I would not mount again. This horse would only double her speed to get back to the stable. Louise knew she'd gotten the better of me. In my black riding jacket with the elegant flare, in my beige breeches and shiny black boots, I walked with the horse, sweet as a lamb, behind me. When a school bus came by, I looked into forty incredulous and amused faces. They'll wonder what happened, I thought miserably, but at least they didn't see me getting bucked off. Cars stopped. People asked if I was all right, if they could help. I would never live this down.

When I came home and confessed to Cynthia what happened, she seemed amused and gloating.

"Yep, Louise's a pacer," she said smugly.

"What's a pacer?"

"She got trained to lift her feet on the same side of her body and put them down together in the trot. They only train harness horses that way. And when you pull on the bit of a racehorse he goes faster. It's a trick to get her out of pacing mode into regular trotting."

I wondered why she hadn't taught me that mysterious trick before I went out on the road and risked my life. Was this a practical joke, an example of the Yankee humor I'd heard about? Maybe the answer was as simple as a teenage girl, who'd gotten married and needed to get rid of her horse. Her parents might have pressed her into it. They probably said they weren't going to take care of her pet. Where she lived now she certainly couldn't keep it. She needed our car for transportation, and we needed her to help out in the house while I did the bookkeeping and assisted Gijs. It had all seemed very logical. Now it infuriated me, but I was realistic enough to know that getting mad at Cynthia would certainly make me lose face.

When Gijs came home after he delivered the baby, he asked what was wrong.

"Nothing's wrong," I said, and kept on setting the table for lunch. My body felt rigid. I tried to avoid Gijs's puzzled looks. I didn't know how to admit defeat, and I knew Gijs would be disappointed that his clever scheme hadn't worked out. What a mess. Why hadn't I put my foot down before the horse walked into the barn? Cynthia's wicked little smile stuck in my side like a knife. I was furious at her, I was mad at the horse and, worst of all, I hated myself for being so pigeon-hearted.

Gijs went into the office after a silent lunch and I dragged myself through routine activities. A fire raged inside me. I felt trapped. In the barn stood a horse I was supposed to love but couldn't ride. In a few hours the whole town would know it. How could I get rid of a horse that wasn't fit to ride? With all we had to do and worry about to make this house, this practice, this immigration adventure work, I would spend my time agonizing over this impossible creature in the barn. When this dilemma was firmly established in my mind, I finally told Gijs how my first ride had gone.

"Don't worry, Tiets, we'll fix that horse," he said, and threw his arms around me in a protective gesture. I fumed. I was in a box. What did *he* know about horses?

"There's nothing to fix," I declared. "You can't turn a pacer into a pleasure horse. It isn't her fault. She was trained to pace and go as fast as she can. And that's what she did."

I waited for him to say, "But Cynthia rode her." Instead, he pulled me close and told me not to worry. I stood stiff as a broom in his embrace. Gijs didn't know what he was talking about.

Gijs kept his own counsel on how he was going to fix this unexpected "barn problem." One crisp Sunday morning, he got out of bed and announced he was going to ride the horse that stood in the barn doing nothing. I went limp at the thought.

"Did you ever ride a horse?"

"Sure. I used to ride some mountain ponies in Indonesia when I was a kid."

"Well, let me tell you, Gijs Bozuwa," I almost shouted as I jumped out of bed. "This is no packing pony for a slow track into the mountains. This is a race horse!"

"We'll see," Gijs said.

He pulled on a pair of dungarees and sneakers and went to the barn. I picked up Joan and followed him out. With a bridle in his hand, he walked up to Louise, who contentedly munched on plentiful hay.

"Well, let's see who's boss around here," Gijs said, and with his baritone voice mesmerized Louise, who stood like a statue to let this amateur tack her up.

Joan watched from my arm. "Wisa," she said, pointing her finger at the horse. I hugged her close as I watched my husband fit his sneakered foot into the stirrup while trying to hold the horse still enough to mount. Louise winced under the weight that fell on her back and shot forward, straight ahead, through the open barn door into the driveway. I darted out of the way. The last we saw of "Wisa" and Gijs was when they rounded the corner, still together, heading the same way I had days earlier: down the hill toward the center of town.

There was nothing to do but wait. Wait for Gijs with or without his mount, or the ambulance or the hearse. Movies of his ride through town were fast-forwarding through my mind. I saw a bay horse snorting and bucking, Gijs flying through the air like a football and landing, head first, on the black pavement. How would I tell his parents?

"Your son's emigration adventure has ended in a fatal accident. No, not in a car. On a horse!"

The early November day had a brittle edge to it. A stiff breeze was playing with the piles of fallen leaves and tugging at the few still clinging to the trees that rose into a deep blue sky. I shivered and carried Joan inside. A cool, breezy day was just what a racehorse needed to get fired up and trot her heart out.

Me and my horse

Minutes crept by till they added up to more than an hour. Still no sign of a horse. I lay stretched out on the floor in the playroom, surrounded by the toys that Joan pulled down from the shelves. I didn't want to think about the ride Gijs was on. Yet there was no other thought in my mind. Nerve, I thought. That's what's keeping him in the saddle. The same nerve that he'd had to emigrate. The same grit he'd entered the Japanese prison camp with. Only wincing when he got beaten by a prison guard, who wanted to snatch his one and only blanket. He hadn't given in, held onto his blanket even though he was a bloody mess. He had a scar six-inches long from the laceration the whip had carved into his shoulder. He was probably holding onto our crazy racehorse with the same tenacity. Wouldn't it be ironic if he succumbed to a horse after surviving three years of prison camp?

My thoughts were going round and round, like a cat chasing her tail. Joan hammered two blocks together to get my attention. She abruptly stopped. In the sudden silence I heard the unmistakable sound of gravel grinding under irons in a slow but steady four-beat. Joan ran to the door. I jumped up, grabbed her and ran to the barn. An exhausted Louise and an exuberant Gijs rode in. Both were drenched in sweat. Clouds rose from Louise's heavy winter coat, like fog lifting from a warm lake on a frosty morning. Her head hung low, her sides heaved. It had been established who was boss, no matter how the ride had gone.

"How did it go?" I asked.

"Great! Absolutely great!"

"Where did you go?"

"All around Lovell Lake."

"What?" I was incredulous.

"You'll have a ball," Gijs said. "It's so beautiful. Unbelievable. Once Louise settled down and we got used to each other, I had time to look around. The trees around the lake were spectacular. You'll love it!"

He didn't doubt for a moment that I would grab my boots the next day and set out for a ride around the lake. But the next morning I found a thousand things to do that seemed more urgent than tacking up a horse. With Joan, I led Louise to the pasture. We cleaned the stall together. I picked up the droppings and Joan tossed some fresh hay in her bin, getting most of it inside her jacket. Once in a while Louise, grazing peacefully in the large meadow, caught my eye. She represented everything I'd once dreamed of. My mother wouldn't let us have animals like dogs and ponies. We were allowed a cat, a rabbit and a goat until the goat got too rambunctious, walked through the kitchen door, jumped on the counter and left her droppings there. I had dreamed of a horse of my own. I would groom it, care for it, ride it through the woods. I would take a map and a rucksack and go on long rides. Gijs knew about my horse dreams. He had watched me ride with his brother-in-law in a city riding stable. I had probably looked pretty confident, riding a well-trained horse; the very confidence I lacked now that I finally owned a horse. It was a bitter discovery.

Gijs couldn't walk straight for days and he didn't get back in the saddle. Not for lack of courage, but because the hunting season had opened and we were told not even to let the horse out in the pasture when the countryside was filled with hunters who had their fingers on the triggers for anything that moved, especially something with a brown furry coat. When the hunting season closed, the snow had already blanketed the landscape and the lure of skiing became greater than the urge to ride a racehorse over roads banked by piles of snow.

Louise spent the winter frolicking in the field and growing a dense winter coat. Cynthia left for another town. Every day, as I scooped up the products of Louise's internal hay-burning machine, I wondered where I would find the courage to mount her again. At times I thought I could triumph over her, but most of the time I thought it would be a disaster if I tried. Yet the daily tasks of cleaning the stable, inhaling the familiar odors of manure and horse sweat were a pleasure. I began to look forward to the impatient whinnies of Louise when I entered the barn, to the sound of teeth grinding in a steady rhythm. It was exhilarating to push the wide barn door open early in the morning and watch the sun throw low-slanting rays over the trees, drawing pictures of daddy longlegs on the virgin snow.

Louise was sold for fifty dollars, saddle, bridle and all, to a shrewd horse trader, who'd listened to the scuttlebutt in town and bided his time till the level of frustration in the Bozuwa household would ripen to a point where any offer would be a blessing. That time had come in the spring. Irving Tuttle, Sr. walked into our barn, leaning on a cane, stooped but sharp-witted, wearing a sardonic smile on his thin, wrinkled face. He threw arrows of poison at my last vestiges of pride concerning the part of my life that had to do with horses.

"Looks like a great horse to ride to me," he said. I didn't take the bait and let the arrows whistle by me, relieved to see Louise being loaded on the truck.

Maybe this horse had come into our lives to give Joan the very confidence I lacked. Joan, not quite two, had already accepted the overwhelming size of a horse, the loud whinny and the wet muzzle in her face.

Gijs never mentioned riding, especially me riding, again. Instead, he surprised me at Christmas with a big box that contained all the equipment needed to set up a darkroom. He'd taken it over from Pim Visser. Vic Bezanson immediately went to work transforming part of an attic passage into a dark area. It was makeshift and required placing two pieces of plywood over a stairwell each time I went to print, but it worked and I was beside myself with excitement. Photography had snagged me during my teens, and it had been a main attraction between a boyfriend and myself when I studied in Amsterdam. Jan, who worked at the Rijks Museum as an art historian, had taught me a lot about composition but nothing about camera controls and chemistry. I sorely lacked know-how, but with blissful innocence I bought the chemicals Pim said I would need.

During Joan's naps I snuck upstairs, put down the plywood over the stairwell and gave myself over to the magic of the darkroom. It was an easy enough procedure for making prints that beat the drugstore quality I was used to, yet difficult enough to challenge me. The rich blacks, the fine gradations of gray, the brilliant whites enchanted me and I was hooked.

In my childhood dreams about horses I had never questioned whether I would be a good rider. Of course I would be. I would be a star on a horse. I had a more realistic attitude toward photography. I bought a book to study how I could improve the making of expressive pictures. Painting over patterned wallpaper, pitching out manure, answering the phone, sending out bills was all good and well, but I couldn't help, at times, to think about what my life would have been like if we'd stayed in Holland. I suspected that my roommate in Amsterdam, who studied History of Art, led a more sophisticated life. In some ways I envied her. None of my friends had emigrated. Living the country life, running an office and a household was an adventure, but I prayed that the part of me that had grown up in European cities would not be rudely awakened from its slumber some day.

Chapter 17

Irving and Aubrey

The melting snow unveiled the landscape of the backyard after our first winter in Wakefield. People told us the largest barn in all of Carroll County had once stood there. Farmer Roberts had kept a hundred cows in it, but the Spencers had the barn pulled down because it was in poor repair. Now a mound of granite boulders was all that was left. Not a pretty sight. It had to go, I observed one morning at breakfast.

Gijs went immediately into action. Bob Doe, one of our neighbors, drove into the yard the next day on an egg-yellow bulldozer. The shiny steel blade of his machine overpowered the age-old granite slabs and boulders, scooped them up and banished them to the side of the field. What had taken oxen weeks to set in place was rearranged in a matter of hours. The entire field was leveled. When Bob Doe left, our backyard looked like corrugated cardboard.

Paul Hugenholtz surveyed the new look of our yard during one of their frequent weekend visits and convinced us to build a terrace. He didn't waste a minute and dispatched me to buy a crow bar, a wheelbarrow and a few long-handled shovels, and then put us all to work. We dug up part of the mound the bulldozer had left and heaped the sand up to create a platform that was prevented from sagging back into a slope by the rocks Paul hauled from the field in the brand new wheelbarrow. He used his recollection of building a terraced garden in Italy, where he had spent a good deal of his youth, to create tiled drains for melting snow and heavy rainfall. Paul had the determination of a terrier, the physical endurance of an Arabian horse and the authority of a general. By the middle of the hot Sunday afternoon most of his troops had dropped. Joan was in bed in sandy underwear. Gijs had retreated to the hospital to make rounds. Loes was fanning herself in a chair. I was the only soldier still standing, preparing dinner.

Paul hauled stones from the field till after dusk. The following weekend he came by to check on his handy work and planted a Macintosh apple tree next to his masterpiece. I was inspired. The pitiful condition of the backyard didn't need to be taken for granted. We could change it. This was a do-anything, do-it-yourself country, and I could feel myself becoming a part of it. As long as I could stay busy landscaping I wouldn't miss my life in Holland so much. I overlaid the sight of weeds and messy underbrush with sweeping designs of borders, filled with flowers and curving edges. There would be a lawn instead of a hayfield. My memory of Dutch gardens served as a guide. I had never gardened, only watched gardening, but the details could be found in a book, I figured, like learning the ropes of developing film.

"Turn the soil," the Better Homes & Gardens book Gijs brought me decreed. It didn't make mention of the granite rocks my spade met every time I jammed it into the ground. Besides rocks I dug up broken medicine bottles dating to earlier years of the century, rusted parts of tools and square nails. The spot I had innocently chosen for our flower border had been the farmer's dumping ground. Healthy long worms hastily slithered over the rich black soil to get away from my spade as I disturbed long-established clumps of witch grass. As I chased yard-long roots, the skin of my hands turned as brittle as outer onion scales.

Irving Tuttle, the son of the horse trader who'd bought Louise, sat on the examining table in the office and watched me through the window.

"That your wife, Doc?" he asked. "What's she tryin' to do?"

"Make a flower border,"

"With her bare hands?"

"You got a better idea?" Gijs asked.

"Yep," Irving said. "I'll get it and bring it over."

He drove back later in his pickup truck and unloaded a machine that looked like an oversized potato masher. Iron tentacles protruded from the front axle.

"Hi," Irving said, as I watched him come across the field. His body had the same lean and lanky build of his father, also slightly stooped, but it was the tough, muscular body of a much younger man. He stopped next to a pile of witch grass roots that looked as white as the precious asparagus our neighbor farmer in Holland used to dig up in an almost ceremonial manner.

Irving stood there silently for a while, observing me yank out the stubborn weeds. He wore his father's sardonic smile, dangerously mixed with masculine charm. Gijs had stepped out of his office to tell me that I could expect him, so I got up from the weeding position on my knees.

"Hello. Are you Mr. Tuttle?" I asked.

"Irving. You Tittia?"

I cringed at the way he ruined my first name and at the familiarity with which he breezily used it. In Holland, this would be an unthinkable transgression of code. But in these parts, people didn't wait to be introduced. Plumbers, painters, carpenters, everybody tried to pronounce my first name. Most didn't succeed. Yet, I had to admit, they did it with pleasant joviality. There was a certain appeal in the way it erased part of the distance between complete strangers.

"Yes, I am. My husband said you might come by." I intuitively hid behind the protection of a husband.

"You tryin' to kill yourself?" His beat-up boot kicked against the pile of roots. "Here, let me show ye something."

Irving walked over to his machine, pulled a cord and the thing started to sputter and belch smoke. He moved a handle and the iron tentacles clawed at the hayfield like an impatient horse pawing the ground. The matted weeds got chewed and mixed with the dark soil. Irving roughed up a large patch. The muscles of his bare, tanned arms – he only wore a once-white T-shirt over his dungarees – bulged like ship rope as he yanked the greedy machine from left to right.

Joan, who had been picking grass blades and feeding them to her rabbit through the mesh of his cage, looked up and came running over. She held my hand and watched the snorting machine from a safe distance.

Irving stopped and mopped his brow with a red handkerchief.

"How big you wanna make this?" he asked in his New Hampshire accent.

I took my spade and outlined the area I had in mind with the handle.

"You crazy?" he asked, aghast. "Forget that! You'll be lucky if you get the weeds out of this here patch. You know," he said, for encouragement, a wicked look in his light blue eyes, "you c'n never get rid of witch grass."

"We'll see," I said.

This man was annoying. Yet there was something about him, and after all, he was digging up our hayfield, or a good part of it.

"You'd be better off with a swimming pool," he said. He walked around, pacing the open area closest to the house. "Yeah, this'd make a grand place for a pool. Forget about the flowers. You'll never grow flowers in this field." There was a ring of triumph and finality in the way it came out.

"With all these lakes around here, " I said, "I do not see any need for a pool."

I adopted his tone of finality. He looked me over with renewed interest, but he didn't say anything. He loaded his red machine, which he called a rototiller. I thanked him and he drove off.

He returned after a week and found me on my knees in the garden. "You still at it?"

"As you can see," I said, and went on weeding. I hadn't been impressed with what the rototiller had accomplished. The long witch grass roots had been divided into a million bits and they sprouted in a day of just lying around. So, instead of fewer weeds I had the prospect of the thickest carpet ever.

"You'll find out," he said. "I still say a pool would be nice here. Think of it, you won't have to go to any lake. You can swim right here!"

"You sound like a salesman for pools," I said while I flung the weeds on a heap.

"I am."

"Then you'd better know that my husband and I have no interest in any pool."

I continued weeding. That should do it, I thought. This man probably thinks a lady who was gullible enough to buy an old trotting horse off the track would be fool enough to sacrifice her backyard for a plastic pool. But I underestimated the gift of gab a taciturn Yankee could crank up when he wanted to make a deal. Irving was the son of a horse trader and he could probably sell a donkey in his sleep.

He set himself down beside me in the dirt. I wondered if Gijs could see us from his office window. I wished he would come and rescue me. I felt unprotected in my own yard. People simply walked in! The farmers in Holland wouldn't dream of doing such a thing. I could count on one hand the times *Boer* Jansen came to the door of our country house, cap in hand. What would Mammie do in this situation? No matter. This was a different country and I was the guest.

So, I sat and listened to a long list of virtues that Irving ascribed to the pool he was determined to sell me. He finally got it. A Dutch woman can be as stubborn as a Yankee. He left after getting two no's, one for the pool and one for the rototiller.

Irving returned a few more times, teasing, pushing his wares with a look on his face that would vaguely unsettle me. He didn't realize I was secretly avenging his father's belittling remarks when he paid fifty dollars for the horse I couldn't master. The weeds might be tough and stubborn, but they couldn't make a spectacle out of me. I would make a spectacle out of the flowers I replaced them with. Inch by agonizing inch.

When Irving Jr. walked into our yard years later, I was the mother of teenage children and standing in my finished garden. His temples were graying, his muscles softer. He complimented me on the borders, said he never thought it could be done. The look in his light blue eyes, extending to the fine wrinkles around them, was still there, charming and luring. But older now, I also saw a hard edge to that charm. I had been spared more than an ugly pool in our backyard, I thought. It was the kind of charm that could raise havoc in the life of a married woman.

I fell asleep over the Better Homes & Gardens book every night. It offered a whole new vocabulary. I recognized the flowers from my mother's garden, but not the names. Where would I find these perennials? Only a limited variety was sold at a local farm. Petunias, geraniums, that sort of thing. People here were into raising vegetables, stuff you could eat. But Mrs. Lewis, up the street, had flower borders that reminded me of Holland. When I walked to the post office at the end of the street to pick up the daily bag of mail, I stopped and peeked over the white picket fence and soaked in the sight of her neatly edged borders. Mrs. Lewis had given careful thought to different heights, colors and the effects of foliage. She ordered her plants through the mail, she once told me. Through the mail? I hardly believed her, but she sent me home with a detailed catalogue, a reference book in itself, and I placed an order with the Wayside Gardens in South Carolina, which sounded as far away to me as Hungary from Holland. Ten days later, I picked up large boxes at the post office with plants and shrubs, their roots carefully wrapped in moist peat moss and instructions on how to first soak and then plant them.

Joan followed me around with her miniature trowel and helped me weed. During her afternoon nap, I raced outside to replant her mistakes. As patients filed in to consult the new Dutch doctor, I was pushing the wheelbarrow with topsoil over the sidewalk.

"Hello, Titia."

I turned around and recognized Mrs. Aubrey Burwell. I put down the wheelbarrow, wiped my hands on my khaki shorts, then thought the better of it and did not shake her hand.

"Mrs. Burwell, how nice to see you!" Oh Lord, I thought, what am I going to do with her?

"Are you making a garden, my dear?"

Was she nosy, mocking or genuine? Her eyes sparkled. Everything about her seemed to move: the muscles in her face, the heavy bracelets on her wrist that jingled with her gestures, even her lips moved with rapid, unspoken words. She absorbed me in her field of energy.

"I'm trying. There's so much to do, I don't know where to begin."

"Show me! I love gardens."

Was she really interested?

"Oh, how lovely!" she exclaimed when we entered the backyard. Mrs. Burwell herself had the most unusual geranium trees I'd ever seen: two spheres of carefully trained blossoms that sat above a thick stem, a yard tall. In earthenware pots they flanked her front door. Was she faking her praise? My garden was only a promise. Were American women given

Joan and her rabbit

to making undeserved compliments, or were they just more ebullient in their expression than I remembered my mother's contemporaries to be?

"You are so ambitious! Did you have someone dig up the border?"

"No, I did it mostly myself," I said. Mrs. Burwell looked at the stone wall that I had arranged as a backdrop for the flowers and shook her head. "Darling, that's hard work. I know this soil. It's backbreaking. Tisha, I am simply amazed." She looked at the flowers and knew them all by name.

I suddenly remembered I'd left Joan for a nap in her room a long time ago. She must be howling by now. I excused myself, but Mrs. Burwell said she would love to see Joan and followed me into the house. We walked into the kitchen via the new terrace. There on the floor—it was hard to miss—were rabbit droppings. Joan had insisted on bringing the rabbit inside, to feed him there and leave a dish of water. In spite of my sensible warnings that rabbits weren't dogs that could be house-trained, the rabbit had come to live inside during the day. Neat little balls and not so neat orange puddles dotted the cream-colored linoleum tiles. The rabbit looked at us from under the refrigerator where it liked to hide from Joan's crushing love. I quickly led my unexpected guest through the living room to the hall and opened the door to Joan's room. She sat in her crib with a triumphant smile on her face and her diaper in her hands. The brown content she'd smeared over the railings. Evidence of parental neglect abounded. Toys had been flung through the room; books with pages ripped out littered the carpet. It resembled a farmers' market at the end of a long summer day and it smelled worse.

Mrs. Burwell's good humor was undaunted by the scene and she withheld judgment. I picked up the neglected child, who stared from my arms at the strange woman in her silk dress. Joan's inquisitive blue eyes responded to Mrs. Burwell's amused brown ones. They were each other's match in liveliness and curiosity. What to do next?

"I think I'd better clean up this little disaster," I said, and put Joan down, who quickly ran off, bare-bottomed, to the kitchen to find her rabbit. She came back lugging him by his front paws.

"Yes, I can see you have your hands full," Mrs. Burwell said with a smile, looking at the dirty diaper I held in my hand. She laughed.

"I marvel at you young women today. When I had children Joan's age, I had servants. I admire the way your generation copes without help."

She left through the front door, walked to her shiny dark blue Cadillac and moments later tore through our tranquil street like a teenager who just got wheels.

My next encounter with Mrs. Burwell was ten days later. It was after dark on a mid-summer night at the Huggins Hospital Street Fair in Wolfeboro, a popular fundraising event. I paid five dollars to have my fortune told. An attendant drew back the canvas curtain of a small tent when it was my turn. As my eyes adjusted to the darkness, I made out a gypsy sitting behind a table with a kerosene lamp on it that threw eerie shadows all around. Gradually, I realized that it was Mrs. Burwell who sat there with a deck of cards in her hands. She usually favored large jewelry, but this night she'd outdone herself with earrings the size of bracelets. Her wrists were hidden below a mass of slave bands; a burgundy red shawl was tightly pulled over her hair and knotted at the nape of her neck. When she moved, her black skirt rustled—and she moved a lot. I was fixated by the outrageous pattern of large flowers on her glistening white blouse. She motioned me to sit down. A flicker of recognition lit in her eyes, but she treated me as a perfect stranger. As the session wore on, I wondered how she could come up with the things she said. After all, she really only knew my name, my husband and the country I came from.

My fortuneteller shuffled the cards several times and then laid them out. I recognized a king of hearts, a queen of diamonds and a black jack.

"Hmmm," she murmured. She looked up at me and gave me a look that penetrated my whole being.

"Hmmm," she said again. With an impulsive gesture she gathered up the cards, reshuffled the deck furiously, restacked them several times and laid them open-faced on the table again in what I presumed was a fixed pattern. I saw a diamond king, a queen of hearts and the same black jack. My fortuneteller looked shocked. She was weighing her options, I sensed.

"Well, my dear," she said, "the most important person in your life is your husband." She touched the diamond king. "People around you may think you are a people person, but in reality there's only one important person in your life." She touched the king again. "Although," she went on, "there is also a strong woman in your life. It is your mother." She touched the queen of hearts, and then looked at the cards with numbers on them. They seemed to tell her something.

"Your husband will make a lot of money." That was a safe bet, since she knew he was a doctor, and being a doctor was considered to be a lucrative occupation, although I wondered how rich any doctor, good or bad, could become in the poorest county in the poorest state.

"I see you lead a busy life." The light of the kerosene lamp flickered, and it lit up her eyes as she fixed them upon me. "You are putting so much physical energy in your daily life, it blocks your ability to conceive a child."

I gasped.

"And this child wants to be born," the gypsy woman said. I shifted uncomfortably in my straight-backed chair.

"Now, this black jack," she went on, "He's not good news. Let's see." Abruptly, she swept the cards up in one quick motion and reshuffled the whole deck. One by one she turned them over in another pattern. I was breathless and tried to match each turned-over card with the expression on her face. Dismay was what I saw when the black jack came up again. She picked the card up with resignation. She knew that, according to mysterious rules, she had to come to terms with the meaning of the black jack. She preambled her conclusion by asking if I had a sick brother, or an uncle maybe. I answered that I had two brothers and four uncles but that, as far as I knew, none were sick.

"Someone, some young male, whom you're connected to, will become sick or die, or be in some sort of danger." She sighed. "But your cards look good. You will have a happy life."

On that note I left the tent.

"Well, what was it like?" Gijs asked with a barely hidden contempt for fortunetellers.

"You will be rich and happy!" I answered, and for a long time I kept the rest to myself.

Chapter 18
A Child on the Way

I knew I was pregnant when the marigolds in our early autumn garden made me nauseous. Mother Nature had sided with Mrs. Burwell's subtle warning and broken the dam in the undercurrents of my soul. Joan was told she would have a brother or a sister.

"When can we get it?" she asked.

"In a while," I said vaguely.

Shortly after this exchange, Joan spotted a pile of towels in a quiet corner of Russell's Market. She crouched on the wooden floorboards and watched a cat nursing her young and ran over to Russell. He told her the kittens had just been born and were drinking milk from their mother. I don't know what else he explained while I did my grocery shopping, but she caused consternation in the store when she announced in her crystal clear voice that a baby would soon crawl out of her mommy's tummy. Filled with the excitement of a new understanding, she ran over to me and asked how many babies I thought would crawl out of me.

"One," I told her.

"Only one?" she wanted to know in front of a very interested audience.

"Yes, only one." I said, and quickly paid for my groceries before I would have to answer more questions.

I sensed early on that delivering this baby wouldn't be as simple as "crawling out." A mystical fear throbbed in my heart. I couldn't name what I was scared of, but I was on the lookout for trouble.

"Do you want me to deliver the baby, Tiets?" Gijs asked. "Feel free to say no."

"Of course I want you to deliver it. I thanked God you were there to deliver Joan."

He put me on the scales and a low salt diet and took blood samples, all the routine preparations and precautions. An uncomplicated tool to hear the baby's heartbeat that Gijs had brought on our flight when I was pregnant with Joan – just in case – looked like a cross between a vase and a trumpet. The wooden trumpet end was placed on my belly and he held the narrow base to his ear. The day Gijs heard the baby's heart beat for the first time, he let Joan put her ear on it. She crawled next to me on the bed and Gijs held her over my body. There was puzzlement on her face, then a flash of surprise. Her eyes turned inward as she concentrated on the strange sounds she heard, magnified by the wooden trumpet.

"Tick, tick, tick," she shouted. "I hear it, Pappie!"

From that day on, Joan would sneak into the examining room to steal the trumpet and put it on my stomach. Her awareness of another person coming into her life was growing. A cradle materialized and she put some of her own toys in it, and then took them back again, depending on her mood.

My mother also prepared for the baby. Pappie and she would come to New York by boat, she wrote, well in advance of the baby's birth so Joan could get to know her grandparents and feel comfortable with them. They would take care of her while I was in the hospital. I wondered who was more excited. It had been three years since I'd seen my father, and the thought that Mammie would take care of Joan was a relief from the guilt that continued to nag me for having taken the joy of grandchildren away by emigrating.

I thought I'd finally discovered what the black jack in Mrs. Burwell's deck of cards stood for when our fifteen-year-old neighbor, Peter Brown, walked into the house one Sunday afternoon in February. He and Gijs had taken off early in the morning in our brand new blue Volkswagen beetle and gone skiing in North Conway.

Peter told me Gijs had broken his leg, but not to worry.

"Where is he?" I shrieked. Before he could answer me, Peter reached out to catch me because I had turned as white as a sheet. He expected me to faint, but I didn't.

"In the car," he said. He looked rather meek.

"Did he drive?" I asked incredulously.

"I drove." Peter almost whispered this piece of information, fully

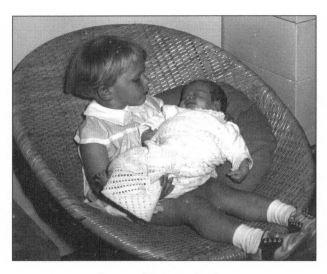

Joan and her new brother

aware he didn't possess a driver's license yet.

I rushed outside.

"Don't worry, Tiets, it's nothing," Gijs said, looking pale and faking a smile. It took a joint effort to get his big frame out of the little car.

To prove there was nothing to worry about, Gijs didn't break his stride. He made his hospital rounds, saw thirty patients in the afternoon and delivered a baby, all the while on crutches. A wise colleague reminded him of Dr. Otsler's famous saying that "The doctor who treats himself has a fool for a patient and an ass for a doctor," and hospitalized him for a few days when phlebitis threatened.

After the scare of Gijs's accident, I told myself the black jack problem had faded. Of course, the endangered male was no one else but Gijs, and Gijs was on the mend, so stop worrying. But sometime in March, that most miserable of months, when Mother Nature throws the State of New Hampshire into a season of thaw, mud and unpredictable snow storms, Gijs took me into the hospital to have blood drawn that would be sent to the Blood Grouping Laboratory in Boston for evaluation.

"Just routine," he said.

There was more to it than that, I sensed. I hadn't told him of my torments, that I knew I was carrying a boy, that some form of bad luck was going to befall a male in my immediate environment and that these fears derived from Mrs. Burwell's predictions. Gijs would—and I knew this for sure—dismiss out of hand any fears brought on by a fortuneteller. He had a deep suspicion of people who made predictions through mystical powers. The man I was married to relied on science as his guide in these matters. If a statement couldn't be proven, he wouldn't buy into it. Miracles were not what he believed in after three years in an internment camp. What he'd witnessed there had turned him into a realist and a humanist, an idealist even, but not a believer. He had responded to his predicament with the hands-on service he could give as an orderly because of the ethical standards he'd been brought up with.

During the first months of his imprisonment a young Catholic priest, who was his roommate, had impressed and influenced him, and for a while Gijs thought he wanted to be converted. The priest, however, told him it would be better to think about that after the war was over. It is easier to see God through barbed wire than through a stained glass window, the priest said.

In the days of our courtship, Gijs had not presented himself as a man of faith. What had attracted me was his intuitive understanding of people, his compassion for them and his reverence for Mother Nature. For me it was only a small step from there to religious faith, but for Gijs it meant a giant leap he wasn't willing to take.

I felt somewhat lonely in those months of secret anguish. The church across the street had a nice enough congregation and a nice enough minister, but I felt like a complete stranger in their midst, and my grasp of the English language wasn't sure enough to touch on such a private and vague matter. Loes Hugenholtz would have understood, but she was grappling with infertility herself at that time, and was in the hospital for corrective surgery.

The lab results showed high levels of antibodies that my blood was making against the intrusion of the fetus, which had a different Rh factor because of the incompatibility of Gijs's and my blood groups. If this situation continued, Gijs explained, the antibodies would destroy the fetus's blood. Labor could be induced a month earlier than the due date of May twenty-first. That way the anti-Rh titer couldn't rise to intolerable levels. In the worst case, a cesarean section would have to be performed. If the baby were carried full term it would either die intra-uterine or be "damaged."

A flag should have gone up in my mind when I was tested for blood grouping. I should have remembered how shaken Gijs had been after he delivered a baby that died soon afterward when he was interning at Quincy City Hospital. He had explained why it died and asked if I wanted to have our blood groups determined before we got married. We agreed we didn't. We would cross that bridge when we got there. Now we stood at that bridge. I had conveniently stuck my head in the sand. Gijs had taken on the burden for me. He had protected me by not unduly worrying me about the possibility. And I had kept from him the fear induced by Mrs. Burwell's black jack. It was time to fess up.

Gijs didn't immediately rip my story to shreds, as I had expected. Instead, he said, "Don't worry, Tiets."

"How can you say that when the baby in Quincy died? Remember?"

"Yes," he sighed. "I remember. But that was in 1954. We know so much more now. In our case we're ahead of the game. We won't let it get out of hand."

"How?"

"We'll know exactly what condition the baby's blood is in as soon as it is born, and a team of specialists will be ready to tackle any irregularities."

"In Wolfeboro?"

"No, not in Wolfeboro. It will be better to go back to Hanover for the delivery and the aftercare."

"Look, Tiets," he said gently. "Mrs. Burwell saying something awful is going to happen doesn't make it so. I won't say it isn't serious, but I will say that we're awfully lucky we live in a time when these problems are recognized and that there are ways to do something about it. The baby in Quincy didn't have a chance, because the Rh factor in its blood had not been determined. Our baby is at a great advantage. We know what's going on."

I took his word for it. If a cesarean section was necessary, then so be it.

The frequent blood tests showed that the antibodies in my blood were rising at an alarming rate. It was time for action. Gijs brought me back to the hospital where Joan was born and gave up his dream of delivering his second child himself. The first try at inducing labor failed, but on May seventh I packed my suitcase for the second time with Joan's help. She picked out clothes for the baby's homecoming. When I reminded her that the baby might be a girl, she looked at me with her wise eyes and said it was going to be a boy. We compromised. Joan put a white baby blanket in my suitcase.

It took two-and-a-half hours to get to the other side of the state where Hanover lay in the valley of the Connecticut River like a bright, ripened berry on a vine. How different the landscape looked from the day we arrived in March of 1957, when I was eight months pregnant with Joan and sunk low into the passenger seat of the borrowed Dodge, trying to hide my misgivings. Then we had driven through the dead landscape of a late winter month. Now we traveled through early spring. Courageous young grass blades worked their way through the matted yellow grass of last year, shooting for the sun. The budding trees were ready to let life flow, like my own breasts.

The old battle-ax who'd met me in the middle of the night for Joan's delivery was not part of the day shift. There was an advantage to arriving in broad daylight, announced and at the side of a licensed physician. Our credentials had improved over the past three years, as had our command of the English language. A young nurse took me in and put me at ease. She attached me to I.V. bottles with the magic potion that would tease our baby into the world. It dripped for twenty-two hours. Drip, drip. Tiny droplets joined my bloodstream without causing labor pains. This was leading to a cesarean section, I thought.

I was wrong. The little boy inside me finally awakened to his task of working his way into the world. Gijs wheeled me to the delivery room. I felt a strong determination behind the surges, and it seemed to take no time at all to deliver this baby. At five p.m., on Sunday, May eighth, I heard a loud cry and Gijs shouted, "We have a boy!" He placed the miracle in my arms, as he had done with Joan. Then Dutch had been on our lips, because we'd felt like we were on an island and didn't care whether anyone around us knew what we said to each other or not. Three years later, Gijs used English.

The baby had everything he needed to have. He breathed. He moved. He screamed. The worries and fears I had carried around for the months of gestation melted away. I let my head fall back on the pillow when the nurse took the baby away for his first scrub. The young resident doctor said he'd never witnessed a natural childbirth before. He was an instant convert, he told Gijs, and offered to give his blood for the transfusions that might be necessary to keep the baby alive.

But the black jack still wasn't done spreading its fear. Gijs warned that not until a few days had passed would they know the extent of danger caused by the antibodies. It put him in a bind. He had to drive to New Jersey, to meet my parents. It would take a few days to show them at least a little bit of New York City and then drive back with them. I urged him to go. I had visions of my parents, never light packers, on the docks in Hoboken with cabin trunks and suitcases.

The baby's skin grew more yellow by the hour, as yellow as a buttercup. I watched the doctors in their sterile green suits and masks through the window of the nursery as they guided shiny steel instruments into the umbilical cord, which had been left long so tubes could be inserted; one side for the inflow, the other for the outflow. Gijs had compared it to washing out an ink bottle. It takes a long time, he'd said, if you put an ink bottle under a streaming faucet for the water to come out only faintly blue. The blood the baby had been born with was being sucked out of his tiny body and replaced by the on-the-spot donation of the generous resident.

I felt helpless and fearful as I watched through the window, the primary fear of a mother for her child. No words exist in any language to allay that fear. Three days in a row, the baby lay on his back on the examining table and screamed through the process of having his blood "purified." Finally, the pediatricians were satisfied they'd saved their little patient whom we had named Gijsbert Paul, Gijsbert in the Bozuwa tradition and Paul after Paul Hugenhotz, because we felt compassion for Paul and Loes that they would not have a child of their own.

The nurse brought him to me to be fed. He was a peaceful sight as he calmly lay at my breast, sucking rhythmically, his little shrimp-like fingers curled into a firm grip. If it was true that our lives are a repetition of the period of conception through birth, I wondered what this meant for the life of this little Paul. Mrs. Burwell's extra-sensory perceptions had foreseen a darkness surrounding a young male in my life. I had interpreted this as a deathly danger for the child I carried. It had convinced me I was carrying a boy, and that premonition had been correct. There probably would be many black jacks throughout Paul's life. External dangers that would cross his path or that he might even flirt with. But with the intensity of giving birth, I had the clear notion that this child knew how to make his path smooth, never mind the dangers. He would be a survivor. He might make me worry myself sick about him, yet—and I knew this just as clearly—he would be honey to my soul.

When Mrs. Aubrey Burwell returned to her summer home, Gijs

Paul and me

told her he never wanted her to tell fortunes again. She had upset his wife, he told her, with the notion that the black jack could mean the death of our baby. He'd had his hands full reassuring me and guiding me through a difficult pregnancy. Gijs maintained that even if fortunetelling was done in jest, some of it would stick and could influence people into actions they might later regret. At the least, it could cause unnecessary anxiety. Mrs. Burwell listened. The Hospital Street Fair never saw her again as a gypsy.

I had different feelings about it, and in due time, I told her so. Yes, she had scared me, but she had alerted me. She had found a switch and turned it around so my body could receive the stream of a new life. It had sat waiting, blocked by my preoccupations with Joan, the house, the garden, the practice in our home and the new ways of life. Mrs. Burwell had hit the nail on the head, and I appreciated her unusual gifts of perception. Some people see what's hidden from ordinary eyesight. Aubrey Burwell was one of those people.

Yet, I faulted myself for not having had more faith. I had let a playing card bedevil me? Had I learned nothing from my mother? Where had my trust in God been?

I pondered these things for a long time.

Chapter 19
Visits from
Our Parents

W e hadn't known, when we said good-bye to Holland back
in 1957, that we would see our friends and families again
in the opaque future. Everyone who saw us off felt the
same way, except my mother who had decided on the spot to make the
trip no matter what it would take. She lucked out. Only months after
we left, the jet engine was put to use for commercial air transportation,
which meant ten hours were cut from crossing time.

Before the war, Gijs's parents had traveled between the Dutch East
Indies and Holland several times. *Vader* Bozuwa had sailed the oceans as
a young navy officer and set foot on every continent except Antartica,
though he'd never anchored in a North American harbor. My parents
had made many trips within Europe. Yet in spite of all this travel, I do not
think it would have entered the mind of any of our parents, once they
were retired, to take a vacation in America. America was thought of more
as a concept than as a destination, as improbable as that may seem today.
The idea of going on an eight-day sea journey to visit the New World
seemed rather far fetched. For our parents, who had seen the advent of
electricity, the bicycle, the automobile and the radio, the idea of climbing
into a jet-propelled flying machine was downright outlandish.

But blood speaks loudly. The initial shock of our emigration wore
off, and America morphed from a concept into a reality, one that came
ever closer through our letters. Close enough to make plans for a visit.

Each one had a different reaction to making this long trip to the much
talked-about young country. Those of my mother and Vader Bozuwa were
predictable. Vader relished the voyage on one of the Holland-America
Line's spectacular ships. *Moeder* Bozuwa got seasick, as she always had,

Our parents: (left to right) Pappie, Vader, Mammie, and Moeder

and my father didn't have very strong sea legs either. But all of them, on separate trips, were deeply moved when they entered the Hudson River and saw the Statue of Liberty rise up in the morning sun. They had lived through the part of history that saw citizens of Poland, Italy, Germany and Ireland flee Europe. And again, just before the Second World War, they saw the persecuted Jews leave for America. They could well imagine what emotions must have coursed through the minds of those immigrants when their ships sailed into the arms of the tall woman who symbolized justice and equal opportunity. Their eyes popped when they disembarked on Hoboken's docks and saw the skyline of Manhattan, more overwhelming than they had imagined from the two-dimensional black & white pictures in magazines. These skyscrapers were taller than any cathedral in Europe.

While I was in the hospital nursing Paul, Gijs showed my parents New York City, where he took them to a musical. Back in Hanover, he took them around the campus of Dartmouth College. Pappie was incredulous that such gorgeous college buildings had been set down in, as far as he was concerned, an uninhabited part of the country. When we took Paul on his first car trip to his home through a verdant New Hampshire landscape, my father remarked, "Vox clamantis in Deserto."

"What did you say?" I asked.

"That's the motto of Dartmouth College," he answered.

"My Latin is a bit rusty. What does it mean?"

"A voice crying in the wilderness."

Next to me in the backseat of our second-hand fire-engine-red station wagon, he looked thoroughly European in his tailored suit with a vest and an Italian silk tie. It wasn't hard to read his thoughts as he looked out the window and tried to make sense of the tangled woods; a startling contrast to the woods in Holland that were more park than wood. He commented on the farms that looked in poor repair.

"What's their best crop?" he asked.

"Rocks," I said.

He shook his head.

The road from Hanover to Wakefield led through small towns like Canaan, Bristol and Moultonboro, spread far apart by miles and miles of hills, woods and quiet countryside. It looked excruciatingly lonesome to my father, who'd spent his entire life in cities. I was already sufficiently steeped in New Hampshire's lore that I could tell him how the first settlers had subdued and battled this demanding landscape, and how the suffering to make a living off the land had made self-sufficiency their goal; how they had equated taming the land with bringing order to chaos, changing evil into good, and how this attitude had fit nicely with their Puritan breeding.

He shook his head again. Life was chaotic enough in itself; why go out and look for land made up of boulders and unforgiving granite? He simply could not imagine that anyone could enjoy that amount of physical hardship. The very thought made his soul shiver. Mammie didn't share his misgivings. She looked at the beauty of it. Born and raised on an island, she understood the land and the people who loved it.

But once he let his anchor down in Wakefield, Pappie perked up. The people who'd come into our life embraced my parents. The neighbor across the street, whom we had nicknamed "The Squire of Wakefield" because he looked the part with his Dunhill pipe and tweed cap, invited my parents for a day trip around Lake Winnipesaukee. Rollins Brown was of old Wakefield stock, a successful businessman who sold mutual funds to doctors and lawyers. My father, a keen investor, felt at home with this jovial man, and he couldn't get over the size of the Oldsmobile they traveled in, how it had floated over the macadam like a boat on water while my mother was entertained in the backseat by his wife Lillian.

The local car dealer Guy Neilly and his wife invited them for a slide show about a trip they'd made through America. The Burwells had them over for dinner, as did the Hopewells. America worked like a tonic on my mother, who, having lived through two world wars, thought of Europe as broken and dispirited. She embraced America's vibrancy and had no difficulty seeing us building a life here. I don't think my father felt really at home, though he was happy to see that friendly people surrounded his daughter and her family. A European to the core and steeped in the classics, he wasn't in tune with the youthful American culture that had taken the world by storm after WW II. But Mammie wrote me after their return that he'd regaled his friends at the coffee club with tall tales about America, its skyscrapers and the vastness of its landscape. He told them that a country doctor in America practices medicine in ways that would be unthinkable in Holland. At the top of the list of advantages that Gijs had over his colleagues in Holland, he said, was the fact that he was on staff at a hospital and could treat his patients to any extent, including setting broken bones. Accompanying Gijs on house calls had been an eye-opener for my father. He'd watched Gijs free a kid who was nailed to the dock on the side of Great East Lake. The boy had stepped in a protruding nail that went in at the sole and came out the top of his foot. He'd stood there, shivering in his bathing suit, waiting for the doctor to come. One visit in particular, my father would never forget. Gijs had received a call from someone in Brookfield who stated, "Father isn't well. Can you come over right away?"

Pappie stayed in the car while Gijs went in. Gijs had quite a story to tell on the way home. Asked where the patient was, the son said, "In the barn. I'll get him." Moments later, he wheeled the patient into the kitchen in a wheelbarrow. Not sick, but very dead.

The previous summer, Gijs's parents had come for a one-month visit. What immediately struck them was how much the sunset, the outlines of distant hills and the temperatures that could soar well into the nineties reminded them of the Dutch East Indies. Their life in the tropics, hand in hand with their war experiences, resurfaced. Vader huddled in a corner with Admiral Thomas at a cocktail party going over the strategic aspects of the infamous navy battle in the Java Sea. One evening we invited Father Gasson and his wife Esther for dinner. Before Father Gasson came to Wakefield, he had taught history for many years at a boarding school for boys, and it didn't take long before he queried

Vader about the war. It started out with historical generalities, but soon veered off to personal experiences, and the Episcopalian priest showed himself a skillful questioner. I got to hear the story about what happened to my father-in-law after he escaped the Japanese when they overran Java.

Vader, who commanded a naval airbase in the Indies and later the Allied Reconnaissance Division, had been ordered by the Dutch Vice-Admiral Helfrich to burn all the airfields before leaving for Australia with what was left of his fleet of airplanes. They flew from Bandoeng to the harbor Tjilatjap to take on fuel before crossing over to Australia, but Tjilatjap had just been bombed and gone up in smoke. The planes had to be abandoned and Vader made it out of Java on the last ship to leave: the *Poelau Bras*, a Dutch merchant ship. What happened to that ship has been described in two books, one by an American journalist, William H. McDougall, Jr. and the other by another survivor, Helen Colijn.

An estimated two hundred and forty people were aboard the freighter

Vader Bozuwa

when it set sail in the night of the 27th of February in 1942. It had a crew of ninety, which was more than a freighter needs, but crews from other freighters had been sent over to the *Poelau Bras* so they could escape as well. The one hundred and fifty passengers were made up of army and navy brass and civilians who were essential to the oil production the Japanese coveted. These men, like Vader, were in lethal danger because they had all followed the "scorched earth policy," which meant they had burned what they'd left behind. The Japanese would not look kindly on their actions.

They were well out to sea when a Japanese reconnaissance plane spotted the *Poelau Bras*. It wasn't long before planes swarmed over them, stinging the ship with bursts of bombs. Shudders ran through the steel body, the motors stopped running and water gurgled in its bowels. Total panic ensued. The planes kept coming, diving and firing bullets randomly over the ship after they had bombed it.

Three of the twelve lifeboats made it to the sea. The others became inoperable as the planes mercilessly strafed the decks, and even the lifeboats and swimmers in the water.

A woman clutched Vader's arm. "Where are the lifeboats?"

"They're gone. Destroyed."

"What can we do?" she shouted.

"Jump overboard and swim!"

"We will drown. There is nowhere to swim to."

Vader looked at her and said, "Better to die trying than to surrender."

No sooner had he spoken those words than a pistol cracked near him. A Dutch officer slumped to the deck beside him, bleeding profusely. More cracks of pistols. Vader looked at his fellow officers, who had committed suicide or were about to do so. The ship was rolling and pitching. He vaulted over the railing into the sea.

The ocean was a lot rougher than it had looked from the deck. The lifeboats were tossing up and down in the high swells and so were the swimmers in their life preservers, who were desperately trying to reach the boats but were equally petrified they might be shot from the air.

The *Poelau Bras* was sinking fast. Her stern was already submerged. Now her bow pointed to the sky the way her masts used to do in better days. Then, while the ocean foamed around her like a bubble bath, the *Poelau Bras* slid backward and disappeared from sight. A black jet of water shot up high into the air, as though someone below had made a last effort to revive her. It died down to nothing more than a thin column of water that collapsed and fell back to the ocean that had swallowed her. The time was 11:37 a.m., March 1, 1942.

Vader swam away as fast as he could to clear the ship. Suction from a sinking ship was deadly, he had been taught. He had been swimming for a while when he noticed the planes had stopped coming back. The

Japs could be reasonably sure they had killed most people aboard, and any survivors would not live for very long two hundred and fifty miles from shore.

Debris floated on the ocean's surface, bobbing with the swells. The seascape was dotted with life vests holding the living as well as dead bodies afloat. Vader willed his fifty-two-year-old body to make a dash for his only chance of survival: the lifeboats. Some distance away he saw one of the three lifeboats that had made it. It was in danger of being capsized by swimmers who were frantically trying to get aboard, while those already inside were bailing out water that was pouring through a keel seam.

"Pull me in!" Vader shouted.

"We can't take you. We're leaking badly," was the answer he got.

"I'm Bozuwa. Captain Bozuwa. I'll fix the leak myself. I order you to pull me in."

All he had to prove his rank were the stripes on the epaulets of his wet shirt. One of the men aboard recognized him and convinced the others to take him on board. Vader fixed the leak and took command of a boat smaller than any ship he had sailed before, but more in need of his natural authority. When they finally managed to hoist the sail, he counted thirty-three persons aboard. Three of them were women.

They knew that reaching Australia was wishful thinking. The spot where they would most likely land was the large island of Sumatra, which was already in Japanese hands. But the Japanese troops couldn't possibly have occupied Sumatra in its entirety. Or so they hoped. Besides, what other options did they have?

They found six oars in the boat. Two men pulled on each oar. Every shift of twelve rowed for one half hour.

The machine guns had shot holes in the water tanks; one tank had lost all its drinking water, the other was half empty. For food they had ship's biscuits, round cakes that tasted like sand or sawdust. Most passengers passed them up. To ration the water required strict discipline. Every six hours half a cup was given to everyone.

The sun was no friend. It heated up the wood to such a degree that it burned the skin on contact. Their heads covered by a handkerchief or a piece of ripped shirt, their eyes closed, the passengers looked like roosting chickens on a hot summer day, as they sat on the gun wales. They learned about the doldrums, a region around the equator known for its lulls. Every morning the wind would die down completely, rendering the ocean surface as smooth as glass. In the evening the wind would pick up again, gently at first, then raging over them in gusts. In the daytime they suffered from the sun and heat, at night from sprays of seawater that made them shiver in their wet clothes from the cold. Even though they wanted very badly to jump in the ocean to cool off, they did not because they could observe the sharks at close range.

On the sixth day of this ordeal, they saw a bird. But the bird flew away and no land was spotted.

Then, early the next morning, they saw land. The sails were reefed, a line thrown overboard to sound the depth of the ocean. They heard the distant roar of crashing waves. They smelled sweeter air. Land? A beach? Blossoms? Tropical fruit?

The next morning, the sun did not climb out of the sea. It rose slowly from behind a dark line.

"Jungle!" they exclaimed. "We can hide from the Japs!"

What they saw was the southern-most tip of Sumatra.

On Friday, March 13, 1942, they dropped anchor, swam through the surf and threw themselves on the beach where palm trees, pregnant with coconuts, swayed over their spinning heads.

We looked at our empty dessert plates and coffee cups when Vader stopped talking. Beads of perspiration on his forehead reflected the light of the candles on the table. He threw back his head and took a deep breath. Father Gasson, I could tell, was dying to know what happened after that, but he had the good sense not to ask for more.

The next morning, when Vader came to breakfast, he looked very tired. All he said was, "Never ask me to tell that story again."

Chapter 20
Rosie's Store

I got into the groove of rural living in New England. Early in the morning, when I was making breakfast, the milkman walked into our kitchen and checked the refrigerator to see how much milk we'd consumed in the last two days. Then he brought our standard supply of three quart bottles up to date by leaving the difference. He did this whether I was in the kitchen on not, and many times I was there in my robe.

Every morning I walked to the post office at the end of the street, where Lois Pike, the postmistress, handed me the mail from box one. If there were letters from Holland, she waved them at me with a smile. When the monthly bills had to go out, she put stamps on all of them and kept a running account for the postage due.

Even the simple act of walking over to Wakefield's one and only store was an adventure, because it was so totally different from what I had experienced in Holland, where we only had retail stores, in the rural areas as well as in the cities. The bakery, the grocery store, the butcher shop might be tiny but they were separate enterprises. Rosie's general store stood on our side of the street, across from the Spencer house, with a gas pump in front of it. It wasn't really called Rosie's Store, but that's what Joan called it. Mr. and Mrs. Rose had recently moved up with their daughter, Margaret, from Massachusetts after Mr. Rose retired from the milk delivery business. Margaret started to work for Gijs and often babysat for Joan and Paul.

To keep Joan entertained, I would send her to Rosie's store on small errands. She'd saunter down the street with the small dog we'd bought for her at the Sandwich Fair, first by our white picket fence, then past the white clapboarded library and the original town hall, now used as "Treasure Shop" by the ladies of the church, and finally up the granite steps of the two-story building that was the store and had been for as long as anyone could remember. Sometimes it took her fifteen minutes to get there, having lingered to pick flowers or to talk to the librarian, Mrs. Lillian Brown. But once at the store, she'd hoist herself up on one of the fixed stools with red vinyl covers that stood in a row in front of the long counter, six in all.

Mr. Rose was a tall, lean man with a rectangular face, a jutting jaw filled with ill-fitting false teeth and friendly eyes behind dark-rimmed glasses; and Mrs. Rose was a tiny, sweet lady who usually wore neatly pressed slacks and a cardigan that hung unevenly over her back because she had a slight hump. They tended the store together and they sold everything from fishing tackle to chewing tobacco, bread—the factory kind in plastic bags that looked like whipped air and tasted likewise—suntan lotion, work gloves and canned goods. If it was practical, they carried it. Of course, they also sold candy. When Joan returned, she could hardly talk for the big fireball tucked in her cheek.

Men taking a break from work stopped by Rosie's store to warm up with a cup of coffee or cool down with a soda. Usually a few were sitting at the long wooden counter. Whenever I walked in from the bright

Wakefield Corner

outdoor light, the brown darkness of the wood interior would fall on me like a blanket. Before we emigrated we believed the American interior look was achieved with shiny aluminum and glass. That's what we'd seen in *LIFE* magazine. We'd expected bright colors but we didn't find them in New England.

One dreary March day, I walked into the store with Joan. Three men sat at the soda fountain. I recognized them as the hired help of Mr. Doe, the bulldozer operator. They'd been in our yard as the shovelers and the rakers, who cleaned up after Bob Doe had flattened the unsightly mound of granite blocks in our backyard. Their work showed on their boots, cracked with drying mud. Not too ambitious a lot, Margaret had told us. They spent a lot of time loitering at the soda fountain, she said.

I asked for some strong cough drops.

"I hear your husband's sick," Mrs. Rose said, and walked over to a rack behind the counter.

"Yes, he's feeling very miserable. He might have caught pneumonia," I told her.

One of the men sitting at the bar snickered. He winked at his pals, then turned his watery blue eyes on me and said, "Oh, come on, tell us the truth." His weak, pale face was filled with malice.

"That *is* the truth," I said.

I shouldn't have let him get to me, but I couldn't help it. My hair stood on end like a cat's. Bums, all of them, just sitting there slurping coffee. Not good enough to find decent work, but good enough to smear somebody else's reputation. I was about to tell them, with righteous indignation, that Gijs had a temperature of 103, and that, all the same, he was on the phone making arrangements for his patients. But I thought better of it.

"A little hung-over, right?" the man said, playing to his audience.

How did I handle this with dignity, I wondered. I felt woefully inept. Whatever you come up with, don't let him know he got your goat, I thought.

"That wouldn't have stopped him. Does that stop *you?*" I retorted, looking into his bloodshot eyes. Elsie Rose smiled and her eyes twinkled behind her butterfly-shaped glasses.

"Here are some strong cough drops, Mrs. Bozuwa," she said, handing me a box of Vicks drops. "I hope your husband gets well soon. You better keep him down!"

"Thank you, Mrs. Rose. Joan, say good-bye," and Joan ran behind the counter to be hugged. I cast an imperious look, the best one I could muster, at the men slouched over their cups at the counter.

There was a new dimension to being young, blond and blue-eyed, now that I was the doctor's wife in a small town. I'd been whistled at before when I lived in Holland, but in those days I could deal with it as I saw fit: stick out my tongue, ignore it, make a fresh remark like the sassy teenager I was. In Wakefield I was an extension of Gijs and he was six years older than I. The men who whistled at me—like the road crew did once when I drove by one sunny afternoon with my car windows rolled down—were his potential patients, people who someday might call me on the phone in distress. I had to build a bit of authority for myself. This came naturally to Gijs. His appearance was imposing and I teased him that his bald head helped; he was building a practice on it. His parents had groomed him for a position of authority, and the framed piece of paper on the wall in his office that stated he was licensed to practice medicine commanded respect. For me, it wasn't that simple.

In the middle of a wintry night, when our house was dark and in a deep sleep, furious pounding on our front door had awakened me. I jumped out of bed, opened the curtain and looked out. A car was parked at the curb. I opened the window. A man was shouting at me in a heavy accent. He wasn't asking for anything. He was commanding me to open the door and wake the doctor. His father was suffering a heart attack in the back of the car, he said.

"He's coming," I called down at him, and closed the window. I shook Gijs awake, threw a robe over my nightgown and raced down the stairs, over to the office, turned on the lights and unlocked the door. Immediately the car door opened and out tumbled two middle-aged men who supported an older gentleman in a silk maroon-colored robe, the kind actors wear on stage. The luxurious look of the shiny silk stood out in sharp contrast to the green dungarees worn by the men who were with him.

Gijs also appeared in his pajamas and a robe. A sensible woolen one, fit for an old farmhouse on a cold night. The minute he stepped into the examining room, all the men started to talk to him at once with unmistakable Italian accents. Gijs sent the younger men out of the room, but they kept drifting back, worried, wanting to provide background information. Papa was a disabled fire fighter from the city of Boston, a victim of WW I. "Gas, you know." Gijs looked at Papa in his silk pajamas and silk robe, and I could see him wondering who and what he was dealing with. A man this well-dressed, even in the middle of the night, was probably as well-connected in the Boston bureaucratic world as he was disabled.

But there was no question Papa was suffering.

The best thing I could do, I thought, was to keep the sons out of the examining room, so I asked them if they would like some coffee. Great idea, they said gratefully, and followed me as I walked into the house from the office. I had meant to prepare the coffee for them and bring it to the waiting room. Instead, they leaned on the counter that separated our dining room from the kitchen. Suddenly, our living quarters looked like a downtown bar, and I was turned into a bar maid, one dressed in a nightgown with a robe that parted at the knees, only barely covering them.

The eldest son, the one who had pounded on our front door, grabbed the one bar stool we owned and sat himself down as if it was the most natural thing in the world. When he saw an ashtray, he reached for his breast pocket in a routine gesture and felt around for cigarettes.

"Aw, shucks," he said, "I left them at home. You don't have a pack on hand, do you?"

I went over to a drawer, took out a carton of Winstons and handed him a pack. He reached into his other breast pocket and took out a fat roll of hundred dollar bills, casually peeled one off, put it on the counter and asked, "Got any change?" He noticed the incredulous look on my face, because he casually remarked, "Got lucky at the horse races."

"No, I don't have change," I said. "Never mind. You're welcome to it."

I shuffled back and forth on my sheepskin slippers between the sink and the stove and finally managed to produce some steaming cups of coffee. There was nothing more to occupy myself with after that. Should I go back to the office and help Gijs? Could I trust these men sitting around in my house by themselves? Words of wise counsel from my mother rang in my ears: "The more free and charming, the less trustworthy." Of course, I could tell them off, but they were under stress and in no way misbehaving.

"Do you live around here?" I asked.

"No, lady. We live in Lynn, but we have a cottage here on the lake.

We were up for the weekend doing some snowmobiling."

Finally Gijs walked in. He had called the ambulance.

"I'm going with him, Tiets. Would you go to the examining room and watch him while I get dressed?"

He dispatched the sons to the waiting room and I went in to see the patient. An oxygen mask covered his mouth and nose. He took my hand and squeezed it passionately, and I stroked his cold and sweaty one for reassurance. From barmaid to nurse, I chuckled to myself, and all this in my nightie. The sons walked in and wanted to take over the watch, but the father mumbled something in Italian to them and held onto my hand. Then he winked at me.

When the doorbell rang, one of the sons answered it. I could hear the undertaker's voice and the irregular beat of his footsteps because of his one stiff leg. Got kicked by a horse, he'd told me when I first met him. He'd been full of blustering stories then, but he was more subdued after Gijs had sent him away, the day before Christmas, when he came to the door with a half gallon bottle of precious whiskey, Chivas Regal, and a check for twenty dollars. "No way," Gijs had told him. He was an advocate for his patients, not for the undertaker.

The oldest son carried the oxygen tank out the door and down the path, and the father, who was attached to the tank, rested his arm on mine as we slowly made it to the black hearse that doubled as an ambulance. The sliding mechanism inside worked for coffins as well as for stretchers. The undertaker and his helper put the patient on the stretcher in a sitting-up position and slid him inside. The elderly man brought my hand to his oxygen mask for a farewell in an old-world gesture.

Back in the house, eerily quiet after the commotion, I opened the door to the children's room on my way back to bed. Their innocent faces, warm with sleep, grounded me again as a respectable mother.

On a Sunday afternoon in the summer that followed, Papa's oldest son stopped by. A visiting friend answered the door and came back to the lunch table, saying with a twinkle in his eye: "Gijs, there is a client for you."

Gijs didn't think of the people he treated as clients. Doctors had not yet started to retail their services. He charged five dollars for an office visit, and for that he treated the patient from head to toe. It didn't enter his mind to ring up his services like the check-out clerk at today's supermarket: so much for taking your blood, so much for bringing your blood to the lab, so much for bringing it back from the lab, so much for interpreting the blood test and so much for the treatment.

Gijs excused himself from the table and went to the waiting room. He returned with a greenback in his hand.

"Remember that Italian invasion, Tiets?" he said to me. "This was one of his sons. His father survived his heart attack, he said, and is doing well. The guy took a stack of hundred dollar bills out of his breast pocket like he'd done with you that night to pay for the pack of cigarettes. I told him the charge was seventy-five dollars and he put a $100 bill into my hand and told me to keep the change. He was much obliged, he said."

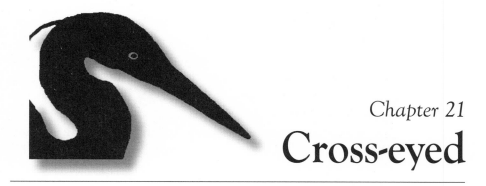

Chapter 21

Cross-eyed

"It stopped," Gijs said, "Listen, I don't hear it anymore."

Paul Hugenholtz and I jumped up from the couch in our living room and stood at the foot of the staircase, straining our ears.

"No, you're right!" I said. "My God!"

I looked at the frown on Gijs's face. We hadn't admitted it to each other, but we'd just been shooting the breeze while our minds were fixed on the one-year-old upstairs.

My heart pounded as all three of us ran up the stairs. We peeked into the room. Paul lay very still in his crib. Gijs put his hand on his son's back. It moved up and down in perfect rhythm.

"It worked," Gijs said.

"Is he out of danger now?" I asked.

"Sure. With the swelling down, the breathing is normal."

I felt exquisite relief.

It had all begun when my father sat next to me on the couch one afternoon while I nursed Paul, two weeks after we'd brought him home from Hanover. Pappie looked intently at his grandson.

"Tiets, have you noticed his eyes?" Pappie asked.

"Yes, they'll be blue, don't you think? Gijs says all babies are born with dark blue eyes and that it takes awhile for them to take on their own color."

"Yes," Pappie said. "They'll probably be blue like everyone else's in his family. But I mean..." And here he stopped for a moment. "I mean, have you noticed they're crossed?"

"Crossed? They're not crossed!" I said with indignation. Who but a

Paul with glasses

mother would know what her child looks like, from head to toe?

"Well, take a good look," Pappie urged.

As soon as I put Paul in his cradle upstairs, I tried to get his attention by moving a stuffed bunny back and forth. Paul responded by moving his whole head. My God, I thought, Pappie is right. I quickly finished pinning up the diaper and ran downstairs with the baby in my arms. Gijs was holding afternoon office hours when I barged in and a woman sat in the chair next to his desk. Gijs looked up.

"Excuse me," he said to the patient, and ushered me into the examining room.

"What's wrong?" he asked, and looked at his son.

"Pappie thinks Paul is cross-eyed," I blurted.

"Put him on the examining table," Gijs ordered.

He smiled at Paul while he took out an instrument with a little light at the tip. Paul tried to follow it. Gijs's smile faded. He repeated the test several times and then he turned to me.

"Your father's right. How could I've missed that? I can't believe we didn't see it ourselves."

Paul wasn't a little bit cross-eyed. His right eye almost disappeared into the bridge of his nose. Dr. Pete Goodall, an ophthalmologist, predicted Paul would have to be operated on several times. The first one had been performed two days before. During the intubation, the anesthetist misjudged the size of Paul's trachea. Quickly pulling the tube out and replacing it with the correct size had created irritation and swelling. Since the diameter of his trachea was probably not much larger than a pencil, very little room was left for air to go through. When Paul came out of surgery, I wondered if they had inserted a whistle in his throat. He sat on my lap the rest of the day and night, next to a vaporizer that spewed steam in his direction. My task was to reassure Paul, to prevent him from crying and squandering the energy he needed to get oxygen. By the next morning, Gijs decided we could do more for him at home in his familiar environment. He wrapped him up and brought him to his own crib. All through the house, even in the kitchen, we could hear his labored breathing. It sounded like the bellows at a forge.

Gijs came up with the idea of bringing him to the bathroom, to play with him while we had the hottest possible shower going behind the plastic shower curtains. We closed the door and stayed there till the wallpaper literally fell off the wall. We put him to bed under a warm blanket and he quickly fell asleep while we went downstairs and waited. There was comfort in the regularity of his labored breathing, in and out. As long as we heard the whistle, we knew he still breathed. Silence would mean one of two things: we'd either heard the first normal air intake or, God help us, his last.

Paul Hugenholtz had found us sitting like frozen statues in the living room, stopping by on his way to somewhere. Paul was always on a mission, or returning from one. Anytime he breezed through our doorway, I could taste the salt spray that had raged over his sailboat, or the thin, bracing air from the mountaintop he'd scaled. Mountaintops and rough oceans were his spiritual home, hospitals and medical conferences his battlefields. With a confidence that bordered on arrogance, he set his perimeters yards ahead of any man I knew. And when he wanted to, but only if he wanted to, he brought others to his frontiers and empowered them to believe they belonged there as well. That afternoon, he didn't talk about his latest mountain climb or exciting medical research. He sensed our mood and understood the odds. He was praying with us for his godchild. If Paul Hugenholtz were judged on his dashing good looks alone, or on the props he surrounded himself with, like the exotic dog he'd brought with him from Holland or the Jaguar he'd found sitting forlorn and unwanted in the Arizona desert, he could be dismissed as an excessively ambitious man, and he often was. But as he seated himself next to me on the couch that afternoon, his spiritual confidence was evident. It eclipsed his arrogance. I could understand why Loes had fallen in love with this man. Paul and Loes didn't, couldn't have children. Until that moment, I had viewed that fact as Loes's loss, but now I keenly felt that it was his as well. I really don't know if he viewed adoption as the way to fill this void in their lives. Certainly as a physician he had to be aware of the pros and cons. But in any case, he went along with it. A little girl was adopted and, a few years later, a little boy.

Joan made her entry into the living room, brought back home from a trip the babysitter had taken her on, so her parents could help her brother over his crisis. Already at four, she managed to command attention, and that day she was intent on getting her share. Her little brother with his eye operation had been doted on for several days now. At last, he was sound asleep and out of the way, so she could claim the limelight. She did so with calculated femininity by bringing in toys to lure her handsome uncle's attention. She got everything she clamored for. To get his undivided attention, she instinctively knew she had to manipulate him.

When I sneaked upstairs to check on him, careful not to wake him, I found Paul standing, smiling and rattling the sides of his crib. As though nothing at all had happened, he flung himself into my arms when I picked him up. A big bandage covered his eye but it didn't seem to bother him. The second I put him down on the floor he darted away.

When Paul was seven, and again when he was eight, Dr. Goodall operated on his eye under local anesthesia. Paul needed the fortitude to watch the needle that deposited the Novocaine come into his eye, and it required some mental preparation to keep a seven-year-old absolutely motionless. But Dr. Goodall had a way of instilling him with confidence. He asked Paul what his favorite book was. <u>Dr. Doolittle</u>, Paul said. The evening before the procedure, Dr. Goodall came to the hospital and brought him a new Dr. Doolittle book and read him a chapter. During the procedure Gijs, dressed in surgical clothes and covered by a mask, read the next chapter to him. And at night, after his office hours, Dr. Goodall sat by his side and read him a few more chapters. Eighteen years later, for Dr. Goodall's retirement party, Paul shed his torn blue jeans, put his long hair in a neat ponytail, donned a smashing blue blazer over neatly pressed slacks and gave a touching speech, remembering Dr. Doolittle and honoring Dr. Goodall.

With every subsequent operation, the errant eye muscle got shortened a tiny bit. Dr. Goodall predicted that, in time, his eye would straighten, but he warned Paul that later in life, when he was tired or drunk, it might temporarily turn in a bit. He was right.

During the years that he was still cross-eyed, Joan defended her little brother against the kids on the school bus, who teased him unmercifully. They nicknamed him Clarence the Cross-eyed Lion, after a TV show. If they were her own size, Joan clobbered anyone who called him that with her bookbag. If they were bigger, she only verbally abused them.

Chapter 22
American Citizens

When Gijs's parents came for a visit in the fall of 1962, we weren't aware that America was with one foot in a sea change. It didn't feel that way. It probably never does at the time. We look back and, only then, we see the signs. The mood in America was upbeat. It was a self-confident society with its attributes of shiny cars, its universities, its suburbs with homes on acres of space. It seemed like post-war America never met a problem it couldn't solve, and John F. Kennedy was the symbol of its youth and vigor. Filled with the best and brightest, his administration set a relentless pace of can-do, will-do governing. This in turn empowered young professionals to brazenly push out the old guard.

There must have been cracks, however, hairline wrinkles that betrayed underlying structural weaknesses, for a culture change isn't invented. It develops in reaction. I, for one, didn't see it coming. Everything American I became acquainted with in those years was new to me. There was no distinction between old or new. But before I could absorb America of the fifties, the protests of the sixties attempted to wipe out the established order I was getting used to.

We were jolted into the Cuban missile crisis. Gijs went out to rent a TV. Vader Bozuwa sat in rapt attention as President Kennedy informed the American people of what was happening and he didn't take it lightly. As a military man who had fought in two world wars, who had been taken prisoner by the Japanese on the island of Sumatra and liberated in Manchuria by the Russians in 1944, he realized how threatening the situation was. The Russians, he warned, could be brutal. That was his personal experience. When the Russians had arrived on horseback at his prison camp, they'd said to him, "We'll be back in two days. Do what you want." They meant: "Go ahead and kill the bastards." The prisoners put their captors to menial labor. The Russians rubbed their eyes when they returned and saw the Japanese guards on their hands and knees clipping the grass. "You'll never learn," they said, and packed the Allied officers off to the Philippines in a transport plane. Vader had little doubt about what they had done to their guards.

He looked at the footage of the Soviet ships plying the Atlantic Ocean with their loads of missiles and weighed the consequences of Khrushchev's move from a military point of view. He rated it as a tactical move, a strategic threat, but most Americans saw the Soviet the steaming up of Russian ships sailing close to their shores as a direct, personal threat. The recent wars they'd fought had been fought on other continents. Their blood had flowed into foreign soil. This was different. Khrushchev had touched a nerve. Something very essential in the outlook of Americans changed, even though disaster was quickly averted. The fifties had been lighthearted, secure after the murderous forties. Now a dangerous snake had slithered into the backyard. It hadn't bitten, not yet, but it could.

It was against this background that we obtained our American citizenship. One early November day we drove to Concord, New Hampshire with Vader and Moeder Bozuwa in the backseat of our red station wagon.

A respectful silence hung in the dark paneled courtroom as we filed in and took our seats among many foreigners. Like us, they'd followed the twists and turns of a red tape trail. This ceremony was the very end of that trail.

I tried to take in the vast space. Several brass lamps were suspended from a high arched ceiling. A standard holding the stars and stripes stood next to the judge's bench and an official portrait of President Kennedy, soon to be *our* president, hung on the whitewashed wall. We rose as one body when a clerk announced the judge who strode in, looking impressive in his flowing black robe. He talked to us like a stern father, extolling the virtues of the country we were about to become citizens of, reminding us what a privilege it was and what our duties were. Then he invited us to raise our hand and take the pledge. It demanded we "renounce and abjure all allegiance and fidelity to any foreign prince, potentate, state, or sovereignty." Just like that.

I didn't want to look at Gijs or Vader who stood on either side of me. The coincidence of his parents witnessing their son's naturalization was bearing down on my tear ducts. Vader, I knew, had devoted his entire career to serving and defending his country—our country—the Kingdom of the Netherlands. The defining moments in his life had been in defense of Queen and country. Moeder and Gijs had spent three years in internment camps in the Dutch East Indies. I tried to imagine what this moment said to them. If it was hard for me, how was it for them and for Gijs himself? Being Dutch had been life-threatening to the four of us during the war, and the hardships suffered as a consequence had only been endured because to bow to the dominance of another country had been as unthinkable as changing our given name. In my family, the proudest moment during our liberation had come when my mother took the Dutch flag out of the mothballs and raised it, wrinkles and all, even before the staccato firing of machine guns had faded from our ears.

So why did we do it? Why were we here doing such a hard thing? Could we foresee the consequences? Soon, during the Vietnam War, I would watch Dutch people burn the American flag in protest in front of the American Embassy in The Hague, Holland's seat of government. It was a wrenching sight. I had read about American citizens of Japanese extraction who'd been herded together and put behind barbed wire by the American government during WW II as suspect citizens. How had naturalized citizens from Germany fared? Was it likely that America and Holland would be, some awful day, at opposite sides of an argument, one that could lead to war? If Gijs had decided to emigrate to Russia instead, would I have gone along? Probably not. Even though the reasoning behind applying for American citizenship was mostly practical, as I suspected it was for most of the people gathered in that room, I could understand the American way of life, I could defend its democratic principles, its lofty goals, as they were laid down in the Declaration of Independence and the Constitution. Although I realized there was a difference between stated principles and daily existence, it was the American will to try hard to stick to its basic philosophy that impressed me. The checks and balances were in place to make it all work, even when human nature often made a mockery out of the carefully crafted laws.

The practical reasons for our naturalization were simple. Gijs could only practice medicine as a solo practitioner while he awaited U.S. citizenship. On the exact day we'd been in the country for five years—the amount of time it takes to naturalize—a letter from the New Hampshire

Board of Registration was in the mail. I found this reasonable. I also found it reasonable that we had to swear, when we were still back in Holland filing for immigration papers, that we would not kill the President of the United States. Both of us had been tested for tuberculosis. Some people viewed these regulations as indignities, but I could appreciate that the U.S. government wanted to protect its citizens, the ones who'd gotten to these shores before us. It was our privilege, not our right, to live in this land of opportunity.

For me, remaining a Dutch citizen with a green card was an option, but one I did not give much consideration. The war had taught me that in moments of crisis you must produce the correct papers or else, and I had a frighteningly clear and horrible vision of Gijs and me, at some devastating moment in time, standing at different sides of a barbed wire fence because we had differently colored passports. It had happened to others. It could happen to us.

We drove back through the late fall landscape in which the pastures were still green but the trees hemming them in were bare, revealing their naked structure like a woman who's taken off her jewelry at the end of a long day. This was the land I was a part of now, my land, my country. I have to love it bare bones, I thought. I'll have to trade the Queen's day for Independence Day; the Dutch flag for the American flag; Het Wilhelmus, the Dutch national anthem, for the Star-Spangled Banners. As of this day, I can be a participant with the right to vote. Or would I remain the observer? Would it be possible to be both participant and observer? How would that make me feel and how would our children view us? As outsiders? What price would we eventually pay for what we'd chosen? I was sure that somehow there would be a sacrifice. We pay for all we do, for what we choose, be it a religion or a mate, a profession, or the place we choose to live. Even when we fail to make a choice, there is a price to pay.

Gijs was stepping on the gas. We had to be in Wakefield before five, before the polls closed. On the very day we became American citizens, we had a chance to vote. The issue was important and we knew exactly how we would cast our first ballot: in favor of Wakefield joining a regional school system with Wolfeboro and other towns in the area. We'd heard all the arguments for and against and to us it made perfect sense.

Vader and Moeder waited in the back of the car as we ran up the granite steps of the Wakefield Town Hall, fifteen minutes ahead of closing time. The days were getting shorter and it was already dark outside. As Gijs reached for the door, a figure stepped out of the shadow of the granite pillars and moved to block him.

"Hi, Clarence," Gijs said to the man.

"You can't vote," Clarence said.

"I'm an American citizen now, Clarence." Gijs reached for the doorknob, but Clarence puffed himself up and placed himself against the heavy door. Even stuffed with air, his head barely reached the top button on Gijs's raincoat.

"You ain't registered to vote," Clarence said.

"We'll see about that." Gijs reached behind Clarence to open the door. Before I could follow, Clarence had worked himself in between us. He walked up to a wide table where two friendly ladies sat with large sheets of paper spread out in front of them. They were the keepers of the checklist.

"Doc here can't vote. He's not on your list," he said loudly so everyone within earshot could hear. "Rules are rules," Clarence said, "He and his wife ain't registered to vote." He looked defiant. Everyone present knew that Clarence was dead set against Wakefield joining the new school district. He wrote columns in the local newspaper and he'd worn out his pen producing arguments.

The women behind the table were lost for words. One of them I recognized by face. I'd seen her in our waiting room. She threw up her hands with a listless motion. Clarence had the letter of the law on his side; he had won and she obviously hated his hollow victory. Our first acquaintance with the law and order we'd sworn to obey only hours earlier was like a taste of vinegar. Gijs looked at the envelope in his hand with the documents that proved our American citizenship. He sighed and steered me out the door, back to the car.

We went home disappointed, dispirited and mad.

The school issue was narrowly defeated. The Wakefield children had lost out again.

Wakefield had a school system of sorts. It didn't include a nursery school or a kindergarten, and its high school students were tuitioned to Rochester and Milton, mill towns to the south. We hadn't thought much about education when we chose Wakefield to live. Our choice had been based on work. We frankly never made the connection between a place to live and its educational system. Our parents had lived where their work was. My father took over his father's pharmacy and continued to live in the town he grew up in. Gijs's father went wherever the navy sent him. Gijs had changed schools so often he couldn't remember how many he had actually attended. We had been naive to assume that all schools, no matter in what part of the country, worked with the same standards; naive to think it would be just like it was in Holland where every student had to pass the exact same tests to graduate. Those tests were sent under seal to all schools in Holland by the Department of Education on the very same day and opened at exactly the same hour and minute at every Dutch high school.

Three years earlier, on the seventeenth of March 1959, we had attended our first town meeting. Habitual complaints in Gijs's waiting room about the weather had taken a backseat to a proposed school addition, and we watched the momentum build up. Voters came out of the snowy woods, revved up for contention. Secretly, they looked forward to Clarence Martin's diatribes. They might shake their heads and laugh at him, but Clarence served as a convenient lightning rod for the vague angers that built up while the snow blanketed the ground. From Thanksgiving on they'd been cooped up inside, their minds turning into simmering pots. Winter was a time when most people stayed close to their wood stoves and gradually smoked their clothes with a sweet, slightly sickening pine pitch smell that permeated our waiting room. Heavy wool jackets patterned with bright red and black squares for the men; full-length wool coats over cotton dresses for the women. There wasn't much else to do but shovel snow till the sap started to run and maple syrup could be made. Skiing was a crazy thing that was done up north by the rich. Some ventured out on snowshoes. Not for a sport, but to get the firewood inside. Men went ice fishing or were content to sit home, stoke the fire, read the paper and aggravate their wives, down one pack or more of beer and wait for the snow to melt. Work came to a grinding halt if you were a laborer, and the majority of the men in Wakefield worked with their hands and with machines.

Trucks and old cars lined High Street as Gijs steered our car down the steep hill to the base where the brick town hall stood, the tallest and biggest building in town. Town meeting had already started when we entered. Mr. George Wentworth, the moderator, had his hand on the gavel, ready to pound it. He looked august up there on the stage behind a wide table, his half moon of gray hair gleaming with reflections from the dim overhead lights. For the occasion, he had hoisted his bulky frame into an old-fashioned dark blue suit, one of the few worn in the hall. Next to him sat the clerk, Elden Richards, with thick books spread out in front of him, pen in hand and his head slightly tilted back so he could look into the hall through his glasses.

Below the podium sat the voters of Wakefield on rows of stiff wooden chairs linked together with a rod, fumbling with their Town Report booklets and ready to mark the votes with a pencil in the margins, as Mr. Wentworth steered them down the list of articles on the warrant.

The second item on the warrant, "To see if the School District will vote to raise $128,000.00 for the construction of a seven-room addition to the Paul School," was read aloud. We'd come just in time. This was what everybody had been waiting for, what they had come out of their warm homes into the cold night for. One of the school board members seconded the motion.

Clarence Martin didn't waste a minute. He hopped up from his seat and started right in, but Mr. Wentworth stopped him.

"If you want to speak, you have to identify yourself first."

A collective chuckle rippled through the hall, but Clarence could stand any kind of abuse. He was used to it. He had the floor, he had the voters' attention and that was all he cared about. His voice became louder as he walked up the middle aisle from the back of the hall. Heads turned to see him, and what they saw was a short body in a soiled, homespun wool cardigan, with sagging side pockets that came down over his knees and left less than twenty inches of his brown pants showing. He was like a bird, I thought, a predatory bird, deliberately approaching his prey with only one thought in mind. You wouldn't compare Clarence to a mammal. A fox wouldn't make as much noise to achieve his objective, and other animals I could think of, though equally intent on killing, were too large or too sleek in body to qualify for the comparison. With his head cocked back, his eyeglasses high up on the bridge of his sharp nose, his slight body dancing up and down, he resembled most of all a bantam rooster.

"Folks," Clarence started, raising his index finger, "if you vote for this, you'll sure's hell get taxed off yer land." He touched a nerve. Men in dark green wool trousers, upheld by wide suspenders, some with their red-checkered hunting caps still on, shifted around on the hard benches, their bodies betraying the agitation they felt, the agitation Clarence could verbalize for them.

"Next thing, we'll have the state coming in telling us how to run the school. Our own school! Kids these days have everything they need. Things we didn't have when *we* were kids. Tell me now, honest, didn't *you* go to a one-room school? Up here on the hill or over in East Wakefield? And you had to walk to it, even in the winter, didn't you? Snow or no snow! Right? None of these fancy school buses! Take a look at yourself! You did all right, didn't you? Folks, we don't need no fancy big school. We have zero population growth. What do we need a bigger school for?"

"Isn't he a little pepper pot?" a lady in front of me chuckled to her husband.

Whatever pot, Clarence was stirring it. He was correct about the zero population growth. In the rows in front of me, beside me and behind me were people who'd seen their fiftieth birthday come and go a while back. Only a few young faces were interspersed in the crowd like fresh daffodils in a wilted bouquet of irises. These older people had probably been educated in one of those small one-room schoolhouses that, like old wood signposts by the roadside, marked time gone by. Their children had moved elsewhere. Gijs spent a good deal of his time on the phone to the relatives of his gray-haired patients. They seemed to be scattered over the entire map of the United States. When they came home for the funeral of their old man, they told Gijs there hadn't been anything to keep them in Wakefield, what with the railroad collapsed and farming not a way to make a living but a sure way to die: all that strenuous labor and no rewards. They buried their fathers with regret for their hard-lived rural lives, took their mothers with them to their promised lands or parked them in the county home. Then they put the farm up for sale.

Many of the voters around me were the ones who'd held on to the ways of their fathers and did part-time what had been done full-time before. I recognized Ed who also drove the school bus now; and Bill who headed the road crew but came home every winter night to a barn full of sheep, and who drove by our house in the summer on his green tractor to hay the fields of Marie Saunders down the road. There was Russell, who'd started a grocery store. That store and Rosie's store, plus two garages and Norman Poisson's fish and tackle shop, formed Wakefield's only visible commerce. Real estate dealers began to hang out their shingles here and there to sell the fallow land, feeding like crows on what fell by the wayside and turning one man's disaster into another man's paradise. They sold

Wakefield's physical beauty, its untouched shores that circled its seven lakes. The real estate dealers, together with help from the state in the form of aggressive advertising in urban newspapers, lured folk from the city to come and restore an old farm or build a cottage by the lake. It was a new enterprise that would change the character of the town, and Gijs and I had arrived just in time to see it happen.

"Mr. Moderator, I am Allen Clark. May I have the floor?"

"Granted."

Heads turned to look at the man who spoke with a Boston accent, a voice that carried authority. He sat off to the right of us, in the same row.

"Who's that?" I whispered to Gijs. I assumed that by now he knew everyone in town.

"That's Reverend Clark. Retired. Lives on Stoneham Road," Gijs whispered back.

I looked into the face that went with the voice. His light blue eyes, the upturned wrinkles around them, his silvery hair and sensitive mouth synchronized to convey a reassuring impression. This man had no fears, no mean bone in his body by the looks of him.

"I would like to remind the voters of their responsibility toward the children in this town. The world doesn't stand still and Wakefield shouldn't stand still either. If we take the attitude that what was good for us should be good enough for our grandchildren, then this town will be left behind, and I'm sure our grandchildren won't be grateful for our lack of foresight. Let's not act out of fear! Let's not just think about the money! There's more at stake here. We should have faith in our children and give them the tools they're entitled to."

Allen Clark, Gijs told me on the way home, had recently bought an old farmhouse and remodeled it. Instead of running a church, he decided to write a weekly sermon and send it to lay people in remote areas that had a church building but lacked a minister. "Home Prayers," he called his service. Allen Clark and his wife Doris, Gijs said, had tired of the suburban life around Boston and wanted to return to basics, to the values of the farming life. A growing number of people, like the people we'd met in Woodstock, Vermont, shared their outlook, but the locals privately resented these retirees who had the money to live the life they themselves had to quit. Likewise, native sons who'd done well elsewhere and came back to their inherited homesteads weren't always as popular as they thought they had the right to be. It rubbed the locals the wrong way to see them live on the land without the toil that was breaking their own backs. They knew full well that when these "sons come home" started a vegetable garden or put a heifer in their backyard, they were just playing a game. There would still be money left in their banking accounts when they'd paid for the heifer and the seeds, and they didn't even have to offer their produce for sale.

Reverend Clark's words gave courage to a woman who looked to be in her thirties. Age wasn't easy to tell here in winter. The body shapes were hidden under shapeless woolen coats, and I ended up interpreting body language. If they didn't move their bodies around, I tried to judge the characteristics of the only part of them that was exposed: their faces. People didn't seem particularly preoccupied with fashion or with their own looks, except when they went to church. To be comfortable and protected was the reasonable objective. But the women did care about their hairdo. Sometimes they came to the office in curlers.

"Are you on a trip to Mars?" Gijs would ask them.

When they finally got it, they would defend themselves by saying, "No, Doc, I'm going out tonight, kick up my heels with my hubby!"

And Gijs would retort, "Aren't you out now?" They got the message. They would take their curlers out before they went to see this new Dr. Bozuwa. He seemed to care how they looked.

"Do we need all of them school buildings all over town?" the woman posed. "It's wasteful. Six schools for one little town and some are falling apart! It's gonna take more money to keep them from goin' to pieces than buildin' a new one. Have you ever peeked inside them? Thirty-eight kids in a room! That's what you'd see. How would *you* like to keep that many kids in line and teach them something?"

A while back, I had been asked to give a talk and slide show about Holland to eighth graders, so I knew what this woman was talking about. The plaster looked crumbly, the windows were set high into the walls so the only connection with the outside world was the sky, and the clanging of the radiators had provided unsolicited accompaniment for my slide show. When the bell rang for break, I could hear a thunder of leather shoes hitting the wooden floors and staircase, as if a herd of buffalo had invaded the building.

"Nonsense," an older man piped up. "We have six schools because people live spread apart. This is the Town of Wakefield, but we are really the villages of East Wakefield, Union and Sanbornville. We don't want to spend extra money carting kids around in busses. Let them walk to school. Good for 'em."

I began to lose track of who said what. The heated arguments circumvented the central truth: people were not willing to pay for a better school. Not the retired people who'd recently moved up here because they felt they'd paid their dues. Not the locals who either didn't see the need or who were afraid they'd be taxed off their land. My mind drifted off. The people who rooted for good education were definitely in the minority. For what I could understand, and it wasn't easy to grasp the New Hampshire twist of the tongue, it wasn't a likely prospect that Wakefield would improve its school system soon. The previous year they had voted down a proposal for an eighty-thousand-dollar building project, we had been told, and they would do it again tonight.

After the negative vote, people filed out and divided into clusters. Their voices blustered into the damp March evening as they rehashed what had transpired, weighing their failed or victorious strategies, and gearing up for the next round. It would take one long year to gather more ammunition to hurl at their opposition. Both sides' heels were dug in. I looked at Mr. Everett Brazier, the Superintendent of Schools, as he passed by with a stack of papers tucked under his arm. He avoided eye contact with the voters. I had read the barely veiled warnings in his annual report that, like it or not, change was bound to come. Better to do it now willingly than to be forced into it later.

How could we give our children a good education? I was a Montessori kindergarten teacher and had been fortunate enough to work very close to the source. Dr. Maria Montessori, the Italian doctor who had evolved into a famous educator, made her home in Holland, and when I came to Amsterdam to study she was still alive. I worked with her grandson, Mario Montessori, a psychologist, and with Miss Nettie Luytjes, principal of the school where Dr. Montessori tested her revolutionary methods. When Gijs came into my life, I was teaching at that school in an experimental classroom for two– and three-year-olds.

A more energetic woman might have turned the obvious void in Wakefield into a career opportunity and started a school introducing the Montessori method. I saw the need, but being a doctor's wife in a strange country absorbed my energies. It took all my wits to learn bookkeeping and decipher the strange codes on medical insurance forms. I asked Vic, our wonderful carpenter, to help me create some of the resources of the Montessori Method: the pink tower, the brown staircase, the red sticks, each with ten elements so the decimal system would be subconsciously absorbed by a child's sensory system. I painted the blocks the colors that matched my memory of the classroom tools I had used day in and day out in Amsterdam. Joan was fascinated and quickly grasped how to use them, but it was not enough to keep her sociable nature satisfied. Neither was a mother-teacher, though I was better than nothing. She needed interaction with other children. I called Diana Hopewell, whom I'd met at Admiral Thomas's cocktail party. She had a daughter exactly Joan's age and I wondered what solution she'd found. Martha was enrolled in a small private nursery school in Wolfeboro.

On a back road, in a ranch type house, Dot Auderer had transformed her large basement into a magical children's world. This transformation had sort of happened to her, she explained. When the neighborhood kids seemed to gravitate to her home, she made them play in the cellar, she said, and it grew into a school.

Dot was a perky, sweet woman, and her personal qualities largely made up for the lack of daylight in the basement. Gijs brought Joan to school on his way to the hospital and I took her back, a twenty-minute ride each way. And when Gijs was caught off schedule by an emergency, there were two nice ladies who worked at the Wolfeboro Bank to take her. It all worked out beautifully. So far, so good.

But was it really so good, I wondered. What would the people of Wakefield, who'd taken out silver dollars from under their mattresses so we would stay, think of our sending Joan to a nursery school in Wolfeboro? These people who had pride in their community, did they feel judged by two uppity immigrants? Patients who hold a grudge would have little trust in their doctor. That was one cause for concern, but a more cutting reason was that I wanted to be liked. For that to happen, the label "outsider" would have to come off eventually.

What it all came down to were choices. In some things we had little choice, like our accent, a dead giveaway and impossible to erase. We worked on enriching our vocabulary, but adopting different customs, even tastes, went deeper. Once, invited over to the home of a couple in town, we were offered a drink in a tall glass. I had a hard time not spitting it out with the first sip.

"What's in it?" I asked cautiously.

"Ginger ale and bourbon," was the answer.

The unfamiliar taste made me feel oceans away from home. On our first trip to America, I had cheerfully tried to swallow anything that was put in front of me. But now that I knew we would live in this country permanently, strange foods and different customs had the effect of making me homesick. At that party, the men had gone straight for the kitchen and lined the counters, helping themselves to booze and swapping stories about serving in the Korean war or the last baseball game, while the women sat primly in the living room, swapping recipes or stories about their kids.

Gijs got funny looks when he wandered over to the ladies in the living room. It reminded me of our Hanover days when he hung Joan's laundered diapers on the line. "Don't do that again," the young fathers had said to him. Gijs had kept on hanging the diapers. He followed his own rules. For example, he dressed the way he always had: soberly. His necktie never got loosened for relaxation and blue jeans weren't the first thing he reached for after a long day's work. He dressed the way a professional man from Holland would. In America, I discovered I had to relearn how to judge people by the way they dressed. While weeding the front garden one day, I saw a middle-aged man come down the street in baggy khaki pants, a red plaid jacket and a slightly soiled, cotton cap with a visor. A farmer, I judged. On his way back from the post office he stopped and greeted me. I looked into a face with fine wrinkles, a city face unweathered by the elements, and into intelligent eyes that were at once kind and authoritative. He extended his hand.

"I am Frank Heck," he said. "We're up for a week."

My God, I thought, this man is the world famous authority on hematology from the Mayo Clinic, the man who married Dr. Louise Paul, who'd been the local doctor here before the war. I had totally "misplaced" this man. In my Dutch experience, I had never met a professor in khaki pants. I couldn't have. That was not part of the dress code in Holland. I had a lot of "translating" to do. His simple self-introduction of "I am Frank Heck" was impressive in itself. Never, ever would a Dutch professor, or any other Dutchman, use his first name. That was reserved for the intimate few. He wouldn't even use it to sign his name. F. Heck. That would be all.

The customs these people grew up with were different from the ones that had been drilled into us in little Holland. Not better. Different. It was one thing to visit another country and come home with your observations like, "Did you know they have zippers for a fly on their pants in America? That's right, no buttons!" Or: "Americans eat corn. They consider it food for a summer's feast. Can you imagine?" Those observations you could toss off, entertain with and forget about. It was quite another to make them your daily customs and felt like deliberately taking your comfortable clothes off and exchanging them for someone else's, which weren't even what you would have bought for yourself. The color louder, the fit not quite right.

Choices! We had to make choices. We started eating corn gingerly; it was considered pig fodder back home. At first we found it a boorish sight to watch the other bite into an ear the way Henry the Eighth tore into a beef chop in the movies, but we developed a taste for it gradually. Gijs bought slacks with a zipper for a fly and discovered it was a handy invention. Bit by bit we incorporated such great unknowns into our diet as swordfish, scallops, broccoli, zucchini, iceberg lettuce, baked potatoes and bacon for breakfast. None of these had been staples in our mothers' kitchens. Gijs drew the line at peanut butter and jelly sandwiches, though, and I stopped at baking pies.

The trick was not to lose our Dutch identity in this process of assimilation. With what tongue would we speak at home? So far we spoke Dutch, but from the day Joan entered nursery school she came back with English, a little bit more every day, and passed it on to Paul. I remembered the book I had read before we left about the effects of language on immigrants' children. Could we teach them both languages?

Joan made friends at her little nursery school. She got invited to friends' homes in Wolfeboro. Her sixth birthday was around the corner. A decision had to be made: Wakefield or Wolfeboro for first grade? Since we'd only seen negative votes in our own town on the school issues, Wolfeboro was more appealing because the citizens there had voted for the new regional school district and were busy planning and building for the future. We put her onto the Wolfeboro school track and she didn't get off till her sophomore year. Paul followed in her footsteps. We paid for their tuition from nursery school through high school. We owed it to them for taking them to a rural area.

Looking back, I think that Gijs and I were probably more sensitive to the issue of school choice than the people in town ever were. We struggled to belong. Most immigrants do, I think. We are faced with a choice: we can hold onto our own language and customs, seek our own company, be eccentric and feel we still belong to where we came from; or we can embrace our new home, adopt its ways, drop our mother's tongue and lose our old identity. Probably the best way lies somewhere in the middle.

Chapter 23

Our Barn: Stage and Stable

J oan's world expanded. She found out there was more to Wakefield Corner than the church across the street and Rosie's store, because on the other side of Rosie's store was a house filled with kids. Two of them were girls her age, the Doe twins, whose father had bulldozed the granite blocks out of our field. The three girls got wind of each other and started to play. Joan came home all excited about the Does' living room with a big TV in it that was going all the time. The twins had two older brothers and, together with Joan and Paul, they were the only young children on the whole street. Peter Brown, the one who had driven Gijs home when he broke his leg, was a teenager.

On our street, only Bob Doe, Gijs, Sam Paul—the plumber—and Reverend Calvert made their living in town. Reverend Calvert, the minister of the church across the street, was a painfully shy man who herded a small and ancient flock. When Paul was born, he had dutifully made the two and a half hour trek to Hanover and back. He'd sat next to my bed and said, "I suppose he'll be called Junior," and left. I was impressed with his brevity, but it seemed an awful long drive to deliver one sentence.

There were several empty houses around us. Either their owners had recently died of old age, or they had been inherited by descendants who made their living elsewhere and just came up for the summer. The Elmwood Inn, a three-story giant, had been silenced by bankruptcy, its glory faded after many years of service to travelers on their way to the White Mountains in post coaches, and later to vacationers who came by train.

From its high crest of thriving agricultural days, Wakefield had fallen to a low ebb. The cows, the sheep, the chickens, they were all gone. Their living quarters still stood, like the rails that wound like double ribbons through the woods and were resting now from carrying the weight of the passenger trains. On one end of the street lived the two Pike brothers, who tended what was left of their farm business. On the other end lived Rollins Brown, who spent his days in a comfortable Oldsmobile, selling mutual funds throughout the state to people like Gijs. Both the Browns and the Pikes were of old Wakefield stock. Most homeowners had a blood link with Wakefield that went back to its early days.

Joan and Paul developed a romantic notion about their street. Look, they said, we have a plumber, a doctor, a farmer, a lawyer (he practiced in Boston and only came over on summer weekends), a businessman and a contractor. And we have a store, a library, a school, a church and a post office. "We are a real town, Oma," they would tell my mother.

Wakefield Corner looked like a thriving farm community with its white farmhouses, and its luscious green fields falling like a full skirt about her. But it was make-believe. The one-room schoolhouse served as a museum, the inn was closed, the library open three hours a week, the church on life support, the post office on its last legs, and after Mr. Rose died, his store stood empty. It didn't look at all like Beaver's neighborhood on the TV show that Joan watched at the Does'. We heard about hippies, drugs, the pill, war protests, the civil rights movement, all these earthshaking trends that were radically changing the face of America, but we didn't see any sign of it where we lived. No black people lived here. We saw no men with hair to their shoulders, no rock'n'rollers, just an occasional short skirt.

Wakefield looked like the past, but it was *our* present-day stage and on it we created our own reality. Gijs came up with the idea of buying a pony from a patient who raised them as a hobby in his retirement. I was aghast, but Gijs thought it would add some jazz to life.

"Do you remember a horse by the name of Louisa, by any chance?" I asked him.

"Sure, I do," he said, "but this is not a big horse from the race track, Tiets. Reuben says he'll train the pony for us. He can make a cart and teach it to drive. It's a totally different proposition."

We paid a visit to Reuben Lang's small farm on Lovell Lake. A stooped man answered the door. We were invited to the barn's basement down a dimly lit staircase. He went down first, placing his ankle-high boots with care, and resting his cane on each tread. Curious eyes turned to us from behind thick manes that hung like curtains. Seven-year-old Joan pulled back a bit when she felt a wet nuzzle on her blouse, but Reuben told her not to worry, that's just the way horses say hello. Next to the standing stalls was a box stall. The delivery room, Reuben said.

"Now, you kids stand back, because the mother will be distrustful. I'll call Myra, she can hold her."

Reuben removed a shovel from a rack and pounded it against the ceiling. Moments later a woman in a faded cotton housecoat walked in. She was shy when she shook our hands, but there was nothing shy about the way she grabbed the mare by her halter. Reuben motioned Joan and Paul—who was four—to come closer and they shrieked when they saw a black bundle lying in the straw. Reuben stooped over and patted it. The mare snorted ferociously, but Myra had a good hold on her. Joan and Paul kneeled down, carefully stroked the black hide and fell in love. What could I say? It was a deal. The pony would be theirs in the fall.

I had never forgotten Louise. It had been five years since she had ruled the barn, and me. Yet there was hardly a trace left of her, not even the smell. The box stall had been taken over by leftover lumber. Joan went to Vic right away and asked him to build a house for her pony. What kind of a house, Vic wanted to know. Just like the one he's in now with his mother, Joan told him. He went with her to look where her pony lived and promised to make something even better.

It was a beautiful fall day when the pony arrived. Joan was seven, Paul four. My parents were staying with us at the time, and my mother asked if the pony had a name.

"Sambal," Joan said. "Like the Indian hot stuff Daddy puts on his rice."

Reuben would bring the pony on his pickup truck after Joan got out of school. She had alerted the Doe twins and they were waiting with their brothers and cousins. They lined up on the sidewalk, necks craned in the direction of Lovell Lake, as if they were waiting for the president to come by in his limousine. We heard the put-put of an aging engine chugging up our hill. There was Reuben's red truck with something that looked like an ice-fishing house strapped to its truck bed. The truck stopped at the curb in front of our house. Reuben, in red suspenders over a white T-shirt that had seen better days, rolled down his window.

"Your pony's back in there!" he said to Joan. "You just wait a minute till I get out of this thing." He lacked agility, but not courage. His spine was crooked with arthritis and it had reduced his tall frame to child size. His fingers were clenched into a frozen grip, but he tackled any job and was master of his animals.

"Myra," he called to his wife, "hand me that rope."

Sambal stood pressed against the opposite wall, lonely and vulnerable. I worried that he might jump out before Reuben got a good hold of him, but Myra climbed up the ramp and prodded him down the planks.

"Well, here's your pony, kids!" Reuben said, and handed the rope to Joan, who took it without hesitation. Paul held onto Sambal's tail. When my mother watched the procession moving over the lawn toward the barn, she said, "Your dream come true, Titia!"

My mother watches Sambal's arrival

Twenty years too late, I thought. But I had to admit that the scene had a fairy-tale quality to it, the way the low autumn sun raked over the lawn and turned Paul's and Joan's blond hair into blobs of gold that moved like fireflies in the mild air.

Sambal's shiny coat glistened in the sun and outlined the muscles he had developed in his five-months lifetime. He seemed more curious than afraid. The big opening in back of the barn, fit for a loaded hay wagon, dwarfed his tiny body.

Joan opened the stall door and led the pony into his bedroom.

Reuben had taught her a thing or two over the summer months, and she moved around the pony with ease, which lent her an air of authority that went unchallenged by the twins and Paul. Sambal was given more hay than he could eat in a week and fresh water in his bucket.

"Who will clean the stable?" my father asked during dinner.

"I will," Paul said.

"Have you looked at that shovel Daddy bought? It's bigger than you are," Joan said.

"I can do it," Paul said.

"You'll take turns," I said, and goaded them to the bedroom they shared. When I went to tuck them in after Mammie and I had done the dishes, Paul had already fallen asleep but Joan's bed was empty. I checked in the barn. There she was, sitting on a stool in her pajamas, reading a book to Sambal who rested his head on the stall door, as if listening to her every word.

"I'm reading a story to him," she said. "I thought he would be lonely without his mother and all the other ponies. I would be lonely if I had to sleep in a barn all by myself."

I kneeled next to her and asked what she was reading to Sambal.

"_The Velveteen Rabbit,_" she said shyly. "Well, I didn't really _read_ it, but I showed him the picture of the Skin Horse." The book was open to the page with an illustration of a well-worn toy horse on wheels and a stuffed bunny rabbit propped up in a chair.

"Remember the Skin Horse, Mammie? I told Sambal he would become _REAL_ and that I will _REALLY_ love him."

Joan liked to read stories. She couldn't read all of the print, but that didn't matter. She filled in the gaps with colorful details from her own imagination. Red Riding Hood made many side trips on her way to her grandmother's house that weren't on the page. Paul would sit next to her on the couch, transfixed by the words that fell out of Joan's mouth. Sometimes, I pretended to write letters at the dining room table so I could listen to Joan's fabrications and Paul's questions. He didn't buy into everything she said, I noticed. Once, she told him a story she'd heard in her Sunday school class about God. He asked her where God lived.

"In the sky," Joan said.

"I know! But where in the sky?"

"Nobody knows."

"Then how can you say he lives in the sky?" Paul came back at her.

"That's what Jesus said. I don't know what God looks like, but I know what Jesus looks like," Joan said, "because I saw his pictures."

"Where?" Paul asked.

"There's a picture of him in the church. He has long hair," Joan said, and then to me, "Mammie, I wonder why he had long hair."

I thought quickly, too quickly probably. "Because they didn't have scissors in those days."

"Did they have hammers and nails?" Joan asked.

"I don't know."

Joan reads to her brother

"Well, they must have had them, because how could they have nailed him to the cross otherwise?"

"Did he die?" Paul asked, and immediately after, "I don't want to die!"

"But you *have* to die!" Joan said.

"Just imagine," I said to them, "you would live on and on. You would be so old, aching all over, your body wouldn't do what you wanted it to do, and all your friends would have died. You wouldn't enjoy life at all!"

"Yes, but there's always the world around you," Joan said. "You can always enjoy that!"

"I don't want to die," Paul said.

Two weeks before Christmas, Joan came back from the library with a book under her arm about the birth in Bethlehem. She showed it to Paul and gave her own understanding of how Joseph and Mary had looked for a place to sleep and how they'd ended up in a barn.

"See, just like in our own barn," she said, then was quiet for a minute.

"You know," she said slowly, "we could do the Christmas story right here. We have a barn and animals!"

Paul was lying on the rug in front of the open fireplace and studied the colorful illustrations in the book.

"Look, Joan," he said, and pointed at a picture. "There's a little horse there. It looks just like Sambal. And there is a dog like Princess. "

That's how it started. The next two weeks we were out straight planning a pageant. Joan got everyone involved. The librarian said she could keep the book a little longer so Vic could make a manger exactly like the one in the book. I was given pen and paper to write a script. Familiar carols would string the scenes together, we decided. That way nobody had to learn lines by heart. There wouldn't be time to rehearse them anyway. Gijs promised he would clean up the barn, and the children made sure he would put their bicycles and toys in the loft, because people didn't have things like that in "those days."

Joan and Paul looked very carefully at the illustrations in the book and counted how many people were involved. There had to be kings and shepherds and an angel. The innkeeper got skipped over. They thought hard about how many kids they knew. Joan gave herself the role of Mary and then started to think about the rest of the cast. Steven Doe would be her husband, she said. He was shy, but he wouldn't have to say a word and she would know what to do in case he forgot anything. The twins could be the kings. When I reminded her there were three kings in the story, she chose Tinker Curtis who went to the second grade with her in Wolfeboro. And Tinker had a little sister, Cassandra, whom Paul often played with. Those two could be shepherds. Now an angel. She had been torn between being Mary and the angel. She would have liked to be both, because we had put in the script that the angel would make a dramatic appearance from the hayloft with one of my photofloods shining on her. Joan gave the job to Martha Hopewell, though reluctantly. I emphasized it was an excellent choice, because Martha's theatrical qualities were obvious and that's what you needed for playing that role. Paul said two shepherds wouldn't be enough. The book showed a field full of them. How about Mark DeWolf, the son of Gijs's nurse? Good idea, Joan said, and then she remembered Martha Hopewell had two little brothers. They could also be shepherds.

The pageant was *the* topic at our dinner table. Gijs wondered if they'd thought about an audience. Actors needed an audience. Paul and Joan thought hard. There was no question that it had to be on Christmas Eve, but who would want to spend their Christmas Eve in a cold barn, Gijs asked. The parents of the children in the pageant, of course, and Vic and his wife Rose. How about Reuben and Myra Lang and Donna, our cleaning lady? And would Sarah of Sarah's Spa be too old? It also happened that we would have houseguests then. Ton Vreede, a Dutch surgeon, who worked in New York City, and Nora van Steenwijk, who was a Dutch operating room nurse in Montreal, had been invited to spend Christmas with us. In the end, everyone who was involved with Joan and Paul's daily lives was put on their list. Dr. Paul let us borrow the costumes from the time when enough children lived in town to put on a pageant in the church.

Ton and Nora arrived a day early. Both single and working long hours in hospitals, they were looking forward to celebrating the holidays with a family in the country. They didn't know what they were in for. Ton and Gijs put on snowshoes to find greens in the woods for decorations, which they strung into garlands to hang from the barn's cross beams. Nora helped me set up a dressing room; Joan and Paul dragged hay bales to an open space across from Sambal's stable and arranged them in a semicircle. That's where the guests would sit. The hay would keep their bums warm.

Christmas Eve we were too busy to stop for dinner. Gijs and Ton left to pick up the actors by car. The parents would come separately. Nora and I started to work on Joan and Paul.

"Sit still," Nora said to a squirming Paul while she fitted his headpiece. He giggled.

"I want to see," he said.

"We should have a mirror here," Nora said to me, "They'll all want to see themselves."

When I brought it in, Joan immediately took a look in it. Nora had wound a sheet around her body and draped a shawl over her head and shoulders that perfectly matched the blue of her eyes. The rest of the cast got dumped on us all at once. Nora was a Godsend. She managed to have them stand still long enough to make the necessary adjustments to their garments in length and width. We went through two boxes of safety pins.

"I should have lipstick!" Martha said.

"No, silly," Joan said. "They didn't have lipstick in those days!"

"Actors have makeup and lipstick," Martha insisted.

"But you're not an actor. You're an angel and angels don't wear lipstick," Tinker said while Nora fitted her into a king's cape. Martha took a look at Tinker's golden crown and quickly reached for her wings and asked me to attach them to her back.

"I'm the archangel Gabriel," she said dramatically while I struggled with the wings, "and I have good news!" She raised her hands slowly in front of her.

"Stand still, Martha, or this pin will stick into you instead of your dress."

Mark DeWolf came in wearing a real Arabian headband. His grandfather, a theology professor, had brought it from Jordan. Everyone was deeply impressed. The children stood in a circle around him. Mark stared at the floor.

Ton came to the door and said all the guests had arrived. They were in the living room drinking sherry. How long should they be kept busy? He didn't want to get them smashed before the pageant. I looked around and figured we were as ready as we were ever going to be.

"Where's my doll?" Joan shrieked.

"Your father hid it under the hay pile, Joan," Nora said.

"Do you have Princess with you, Paul?" He would be heartbroken if Princess missed out on the pageant. She's a shepherd's dog, he had reminded us.

Ton returned and said they were ready. I grabbed Joan's recorder and started to play "Silent Night," while the children and Nora followed me into the barn. A hush fell over the audience. Gijs started to sing *Silent Night* and everyone joined in. Sambal raced around his stable and the cat jumped down from the loft with a thud. Joan and Steven walked around the barn, knocking on the walls, saying over and over, "Do you have room for us?" It must have dawned on Joan, right then, that she'd forgotten to put the innkeeper in the script, because she finally said to "Joseph," who

Sambal at the nativity scene

was following her around with a deadly serious face, "We'll have to sleep here, I guess." She stopped at the cradle and looked anxiously at the hay pile next to it, looking for the doll. She reached her hand in it, quickly withdrew the doll and put it in the cradle.

The shepherds had positioned themselves on the floor, pretending to sleep, and Princess lay at Paul's feet. Martha had climbed the ladder to the hayloft while the attention was focused on Mary and Joseph. She wanted her part to be a surprise, and it certainly was when Ton switched on the photofloods. Martha was ready for him. She scared the little kids on the barn floor below her out of their wits as she dramatically announced herself, raising her arms in a slow and deliberate gesture. I had attached some patches with fluorescent paint to her dress with the unwanted result that she looked more like a ghost than an angel, but her voice made up for it. She announced with perfect diction that she had "Good News."

The shepherds rubbed their eyes like they'd been told to do and moved to Sambal's stall. Princess stuck close to Paul's side and lay down next to the manger. For Paul it had been the highlight of the evening.

I struck up on Joan's recorder *We Three Kings from Orient Are* and Tinker, moving slowly with a regal tread, came walking in, carrying her mother's silver teapot. The twins were content to have Tinker lead the way.

All that anticipation and now it was over. The barn hadn't burned down, in spite of all that loose hay and the hot floodlights; the kids hadn't fought or refused to carry on. It was a miracle.

Someone started *Silent Night* again. Gijs lit a candle and held a cold fire rod in it for each of the children and coaxed them back into the house in a sparkling procession.

"Will you do it again next year?" the guests asked while they sipped hot wine back in the living room.

"No," I said. "This was a once in a lifetime performance."

They tried to talk me into it, but I knew that very few things in life are perfect and this evening had been perfect. I believed more in precious memories than in dutiful traditions.

Chapter 24
An Interrupted Vacation

"When Harry walked into the shed, there was Joan, holding an ax over Tinker's head," Penny Curtis said.

"Oh, my God," I gasped. "Was she serious?"

"Dead serious," Harry said.

"I didn't know Joan could get that angry. I mean that's pretty extreme. An ax!" I said.

"They didn't give each other an inch," Harry said, and I detected a hint of admiration in his voice. "Don't ask me what it was all about!"

"I'm sorry you had so much trouble with her."

I had come to pick up Joan and Paul after a vacation Gijs and I had taken in Florida, and we were sitting in the Curtis's kitchen, having a cup of coffee. They'd recently moved to Wolfeboro from Philadelphia and had bought an old colonial house that sat on top of a hill with a sweeping view of Lake Wentworth, Lake Winnipesauke and the Belknap Mountains.

"Don't worry," Penny reassured me. "They didn't fight all the time! But one thing I know: your kids love their own home, Titia." She laughed. "One day, they packed their suitcase. I saw them walking down the hill. Joan was holding their suitcase in one hand and Paul's hand in the other. Can't you just see it? Really, it was the cutest thing. Of course, I knew they would come back. They just wanted to make a statement."

What a gracious woman, I thought. I was concerned, though, that Joan had reached for an ax. She must have been blind with anger. I questioned her about it on the way home.

"Tinker is so bossy, Mom," she told me. "I like Cassandra much better."

"That's still no reason to raise an ax, Joan. Did you make up with her?"

"Sort of. She really gets me mad. She knows everything better and lets you know it. I can't stand her."

It wasn't hard to imagine that these two would irritate each other because Tinker was very smart, I had noticed, and just as willful as my own daughter. But an ax! I scolded her, but decided not to come down too hard, since I hadn't been a witness. Three girls had probably been one too many.

"When is Daddy coming back, Mom?" Paul asked.

"I don't know. It depends on how Opa Bozuwa is doing."

"Will he die?" Paul wanted to know.

"I hope not," I said.

I'd put Gijs on a plane to Amsterdam in Miami. He'd looked pale and weak when he'd turned around to wave at me. I worried about him. He was determined, though. The Bozuwas weren't sentimental, but when something happened to one of the four of them, they dropped everything and went to the rescue. Doing less wouldn't be honorable.

This time it hadn't been as easy as dropping everything. The call came halfway through our vacation. The first days had been glorious. We'd driven in wonder over roads lined with tall palm trees and inhaled the sweet aromas of orange blossoms in temperatures that reminded Gijs of the tropics. The random roads we took funneled us onto the Keys. We recklessly rented a cabin on a beach that was part of a swank resort, for a "late season" rate. We had time to swim, to sleep in late, and to make love with the sure knowledge that the phone wouldn't ring with a patient on the other end of the line.

We thought we'd landed in heaven until Gijs ate some fish that made him so sick to his stomach, he couldn't keep anything down, not even water. After a few days of this he was near dehydration and I helped him into the bathtub, so at least his body could absorb fluids through the skin. An ophthalmologist who stayed in the next cabin helped me take care of him. Gijs couldn't stand up, he was that weak. Stay a few more days, the doctor/neighbor said, but we were cruising on our last dollars. We should never have stayed at such an outlandish place.

I emboldened myself and walked up to the impressive front desk of our resort and explained my dilemma. My new friend, the doctor, backed me up in saying that my husband was too ill to travel for at least two more days. Our cabin had already been spoken for, the man behind the desk said, but he had a room available for us on the third floor of the main building. I expected a maid's room for the low rate he quoted, but instead, our new quarters were three times the size of our own bedroom at home. It even had a balcony. Gijs immediately slid into the luxurious softness of fine percale sheets after the exhausting walk across the parking lot. Outside, the surf played its rhythmic game with the beach, rolling off and on, and the rustling palm trees nearby sounded peaceful and tropical. In this exotic setting the telephone rang and disturbed the induced feelings of bliss. Vader Bozuwa had suffered a heart attack.

The next day we were back in Miami. Gijs staggered into the first travel office we caught sight of. It had one clerk and one desk.

"Hello," Gijs said, "I am Dr. Bozuwa." Using the doctor's title might give him more heft in what he expected to be difficult negotiations.

"We're here on vacation," he continued, "but I just got a call from Holland that my father had a heart attack and I need to get over there as fast as I can."

"Well, I think I can help you, Doctor," the man said. That title did it again, I thought.

"I hope so, but first let me tell you the worst part," Gijs said. "I don't have enough money with me."

"Do you have a credit card?" the travel agent asked.

"I applied for an American Express card, but it hadn't arrived yet when we went on vacation."

"Do you have a check with you?"

"No," Gijs said.

"Well, that's all right. I can have you sign a generic check if you give me your bank's name."

The man was most accommodating, but I shook my head. Since I did the books I knew there wasn't enough in our account to cover a check for airfare to Holland. We lived hand to mouth.

"There's not enough in the checking account right now, I'm afraid," I said. "But I'm sure there will be more than enough when I get back. I sent out bills just before we left. There should be quite a few checks in the mail."

I was painfully aware how phony this sounded, but it was the God's honest truth. Why did Gijs even think he could walk into a travel office and expect to walk out with a ticket to Amsterdam? I'd told him so on the way over. He'd been in tighter squeezes in his life, he said, and you never know unless you try. Well, we tried. Gijs didn't say anything. The travel agent didn't say anything either. He sat behind his desk, rubbing his gray moustache a few times and resting his chin between his thumb and index finger. In his sixties, I estimated him.

"You know, Doctor," he said slowly, "I came from Buenos Aires. I was a dentist there. When I came here, I couldn't practice dentistry because my license wasn't recognized. I had to struggle those first years and then my mother got ill and I didn't have the money to go. She died and I didn't get there. I've always felt terrible about that."

"Yes, I can imagine," Gijs said. "That's when you wonder if you did the right thing by emigrating." Where was this was leading us?

"It won't happen to you!" The travel agent stood up abruptly. He placed himself in front of us, looking directly into our eyes. "I'll get you there. Just be sure to send me a check when you get home."

We left the office with a ticket in hand, profusely thanking him.

"Hurry up now," he said with a smile, "or you'll miss your plane, for heaven's sake!"

The first thing I did when I got home, even before picking up the children at the Curtis's, was to go through the mail, deposit the checks I found and send off a check to the travel agent in Florida who had his heart in the right place.

Vader told his son to get back to work after ten days of hanging around the hospital. Then he went ahead and died the day after Gijs flew home. He was to be buried on Joan's eighth birthday, April 29, 1965. That morning Gijs left early to make hospital rounds and I drove with Joan and Paul to Boston to see The Sound of Music, as I had promised earlier to do for Joan's birthday.

As our station wagon sped over smooth highways, I tried to imagine how, on the other side of the ocean, a mournful procession moved at a respectful pace over brick roads between Rotterdam and Dordrecht. In the back of my station wagon, two Bozuwa children played tic-tac-toe. In the back of a no doubt spacious black limousine, two Bozuwa women— mother and daughter—followed a hearse that preceded them through the flat Dutch landscape. At this very moment, Vader's body was on its way to the place where he was born. Grazing cows in meadows would silently witness his last journey. It could have been very different.

In both World Wars, Vader narrowly escaped a seaman's grave. In WW II, his body could have been thrown into a makeshift grave in Manchuria, had he succumbed to death in the Japanese POW camp. Vader had survived odds most of us don't have to face. Yet his body would make it to the cemetery intact, not eaten by sharks in the Indian Ocean, not riddled by bullets, even though he had been condemned to death and brought before a firing squad because he'd blown up the airfields on Java. He'd had the presence of mind to tell his executioner that, according to the Geneva Accord, the executioner didn't have the right to condemn him, because Vader outranked him. And this day, Dordrecht would receive him after his heart gave out at the age of seventy-five. A natural death. It was an incredible feat.

The road ahead of me was straight, the driving easy and automatic. So were my answers to the children's occasional questions. My mind was far away, following the coffin to its resting place in Dordrecht. I thought of how Vader had grown up there, the son of a contractor; how he had played soccer in the meadows on the winning team; how he had been sure he wanted to go to sea, and just as sure he wanted to come back to marry his high school sweetheart, Rietje van Strij. I wondered how it felt to Moeder to return, after all those years, to that small city that she had worked so hard to get away from. Vader's Navy career had been brilliant, and Moeder had played her part by shedding the provincial ways. They had come from hard-working people who set high standards of integrity and self-discipline. Lowered into his grave, everything said and done, Vader had more than lived up to his stern upbringing and passed that outlook on life onto the next generation.

I imagined Moeder walking through the neat rows of grave stones, upright, well-dressed and controlled, at the most giving into the comfort of her daughter's arm for support. She might even have the will to speak at her husband's grave. Moeder, it seemed to me, was capable of doing almost anything she put her mind to. If it were necessary and just, then Moeder would rise to the occasion. This was how I viewed her. Not that she was a stone without blood. Her feelings were intense but measured, and they surfaced more in her actions than on her face. Although brought up in the Victorian age where men ruled, Moeder had discovered she could rely on herself and that she had a great talent for making people get along with each other.

I stood with the children in line at the movie house near the Boston Commons, and soon we were swept up by what we saw on the wide screen. The camera zoomed in on Julie Andrews who sang exuberantly while running through meadows in the spectacular countryside of Austria. I had a hard time reconciling my thoughts about a funeral in Holland with the vibrancy of the voice that filled the space around me. Yet, like the novice, Vader Bozuwa had been the epitome of courage, though in very different ways. The novice knew she didn't belong in a monastery and had the courage to get out. Vader knew he would die if he stayed on a sinking ship and had the courage to jump overboard.

Joan and Paul were engrossed by the fabulous nun on the screen who could sing and make naughty children behave, while I was mixing these vivid images with memories of a very different life that had ended just a few days ago. I had only known Vader for ten years, and most of those years had been spent on opposite sides of the Atlantic. Yet, as Maria von Trapp waltzed by the side of the Danube River, another part of my brain clearly saw Vader sitting in the apartment in Rotterdam, in the tall-backed chair that suited him so well in style and size. I saw him clean his pipe with a small silver instrument he took from his vest pocket, and tamp the aromatic tobacco into the bowl with his index finger. He would perform these rituals, calmly and deliberately. I could see the blue spirals of smoke surrounding his strong face, the face of a man who had made tough choices in his life and who was at peace with them. Not because they worked out so well for himself (they didn't in some ways), but because they had been the only right thing to do at the time.

On the screen before us, Captain von Trapp, now remarried to the novice, was reluctantly singing with his family on a stage in Salzburg, while plotting an escape from his beloved country. A man of principle, he would rather leave his comfortable lifestyle than serve under the Nazis and dance to their tune. It looked like a defining moment in his life and in that of his new wife and children.

Vader Bozuwa had made a similar decision at the end of the war. After the Russians liberated them, Vader and the group of officers he had spent the last three years with were flown to the Philippines. Once there, he got embroiled in a political power play. The British decreed that the Dutch military could not return to the Dutch East Indies for fear they would recapture their colonies. If the British were going to lose their colonies, then so would the Dutch! There was only one way for Vader to find his wife and children on the island of Java and that was to return as a civilian and forego the rest of his naval career. That decision could not have come easily. Most of the top brass in the colonies had made it out of Java in time and had spent the war in Australia. In the motherland, the Navy had been reduced to a shadow of its proud past. There wasn't much room at the top and there wasn't much left to command. Officially, Captain Bozuwa had drowned in the Indian Ocean. The surviving Navy brass had already sliced up the pie. If he were going to have a piece of it, he would have to hurry back to Holland, to the capitol. He decided he had served his queen and country honorably and as best as he could, and sent a telegram of resignation to Her Majesty. Then he set out to rescue his family. According to the Red Cross, they were still alive. He boarded a ship as a civilian that took him to the islands where he'd once been in command of the Dutch Naval Air Force. He rescued his family from the angry natives who wanted their country back.

On the return trip from Boston, Joan and Paul were not content to play games in the backseat of the car. Their minds were spinning with "Sound of Music" images.

"Did Vader Bozuwa wear a uniform like Captain von Trapp's?" Joan wanted to know.

"Yes, he did!" Paul said with great conviction.

"How do you know? He always wore a suit!" Joan said.

"I saw him in his uniform," Paul said. "It was dark with lots of buttons and stuff."

"I don't believe you," Joan said.

"I did too," Paul shot back. He was stubborn and to this day he maintains he saw his grandfather in uniform, which I doubt. I think he saw a picture of him in uniform. But, just maybe, Vader had put on his uniform's jacket to please his grandson.

Joan shifted focus. "What did that black cross mean, Mammie? You know, that one on the red flag. I mean, why did it make Captain von Trapp so mad?"

"Because he didn't like what the flag stood for," I answered. "His country was being taken over by its neighbor, Germany. There was a man there, named Hitler, who wanted Germany to be the boss of all Europe. So, he was really mad. Just picture him holding an ax over his neighbors. That mad!" As I said this I looked in the rearview mirror. Joan caught my eye. She grinned.

"It would be like Canada coming into America," I continued, "and saying: Move over, we're your boss now. Do as we say! Do you think Reuben Lang and Vic Bezanson would like to do what the Canadians told them to do?"

Joan laughed. "No, I don't think so. Daddy wouldn't either. Was Captain von Trapp in the same war you were in?"

"Yes," I said.

"Was Daddy in the same war?" Paul wanted to know.

"Yes, it all happened at the same time," I said, and the whole way back from Boston to Wakefield I tried to explain what it had been like. As I compressed the happenings of five years of German occupation and four years of Japanese internment camps into images that were palatable to an eight-year-old and a five-year-old, I was aware that I gave them a good guy versus bad guy version of war. Hitler was bad. The Japanese were bad. Vader Bozuwa was a hero. As children of WW II victims, Joan and Paul entered the Vietnam era with the conviction that it is honorable to fight a war and to wear a uniform.

Gijs didn't talk much about his father's death. What was the sense? You take a loss and you go on. That's what life had taught him. His family had lost everything they'd ever owned when they left the Indies, except the silver spoons Moeder had carried from prison camp to prison camp. When they returned to Holland, they bought themselves what they needed to dress up a house with Vader's back pay, and had fun doing it. Vader came out of the war a civilian without a job, but he became director of a government agency, The Royal Dutch Meteorological Institute, in Rotterdam. Life goes on, you do the best you can and you don't look back.

Yet I noticed Gijs began developing a terrific backache after his father died. It was the riding lawn mower's fault, he said, when I asked about it. The lawn was too uneven after the winter's frost had worked up the rocks; that was the other thing. He stubbornly kept going, trying not to complain, but grimacing every time he got up from a chair. He got terribly constipated. That was the backache's fault, he said, and kept going. He developed hemorrhoids. That was the constipation's fault, he said, and he kept seeing patients.

The hemorrhoid grew to the size of a crab apple. He had it lanced in the hospital after he'd made his rounds. I put a soft pillow in his office chair when I couldn't talk him into canceling his office hours. After his tenth patient, I went in under the pretense of bringing some tea and noticed that the pillow I'd put in his chair was soaked with blood.

"That's enough!" I said. "You can't do this to your patients."

"OK," Gijs said with a sigh, but he actually looked relieved. He didn't have to go on proving that the son could endure the pains the father had suffered.

A few weeks later, we attended a party at the Hopewells'. Gijs could stand up straight again without grimacing. He was having a good time, allowing the whiskey to bury the miserable winter. Suddenly, I saw him in the center of a group of men who put their arms around him, as if they had to support him to remain standing. I rushed over. "He's all right," a friend said. "It's about his dad."

Gijs was crying. It was a strange sight. I had never seen him cry before. I looked at his friends who seemed totally at ease with this big man who cried the way a child does when it knows it's safe to let go. All of them had been pilots in WW II. They hadn't known each other during the war, yet they'd seen the same thing: death. The pilots had mounted their planes, day in and day out, wondering if they'd come back alive. They'd lucked out. Many of their pals had not. Gijs, in those same war years, had taken care of people in the makeshift prison camp's hospital, day in day out. More often than not, he had to help bury the man whose bedpan he'd emptied the day before. There were no words to remember these happenings by. A slap on the shoulder said much more. Yes, buddy, I know. I've been there. I've seen my friend get shot out of the sky. I don't understand it, but I've been there.

Unlike Gijs, I looked back. I went into the darkroom to print a negative from a picture I'd taken during Vader's last visit to us. I'd asked him to sit on the edge of a picnic table and Gijs to sit on the picnic bench below. I put Paul on a little child's chair. Moeder stood in front of them, out of my camera's range, and held their attention long enough for me to take a picture with the three male Bozuwa heads lined up vertically. I had made them go through this exercise for my Famous Photographers' School course assignment: arrange three objects into an effective composition. Why not people, I'd thought.

I put the negative in the carrier, turned off the lights, exposed the paper and put it in the tray with developer, rocking it back and forth gently. After thirty seconds the outlines of the three heads, stacked above each other, emerged. I rocked the tray some more and saw the father, the son and the grandson under the safelight. Even though the heads were lined up in a straight line, it looked like a perfect circle. The circle of life.

Three generations of Bozuwa men

Chapter 25
The House
Next Door

In the mud season of 1965, Sam Paul walked up the driveway and opened the bulkhead doors to our neighbors' cellar to let the dampness out. Melted snow had risen a foot high over the cellar's dirt floor. He did this every spring for Esther Tripp, a retired schoolteacher, who owned the house but lived in Providence, Rhode Island. She had inherited the old Colonial, dating back to the late seventeen-hundreds, from her father. Every year she came up in June to spend the summer months with her housekeeper Ivy, who was cross-eyed, and with her good friend Miss Tulip, who lived in West Hartford, Connecticut.

If I were looking for Joan and Paul and couldn't find them in our yard, I would find them with the ladies next door at their big round dining room table. Miss Tripp and Ivy knit, crocheted, pasted and glued things for the Christmas Fair of their church back home, and the table was often covered with construction paper, scissors, pots of glue and all colors yarn. More than once I found Joan and Paul cutting out Christmas cards, or sipping iced tea with the ladies on the swinging sofa in their small front yard, which looked like a green blanket hemmed in by a white picket fence. It was the only piece of land that went with the house. Or so I thought.

On this cool day in early April, I watched Sam from the kitchen window while I cleaned up the breakfast dishes after Gijs had left with the children on his daily trip to Wolfeboro with the dual purpose of making hospital rounds and dropping the kids off at school. Sam Paul wore his usual railroad cap that was a cross between a baseball cap and a chef's hat with its striped cotton material gathered and puffed up on top.

Sam had attended the University of New Hampshire ages ago, and come back to his hometown to be the local plumber and insurance agent. He was the moderator, senior deacon and janitor of the church across the street, as well as trustee of the town's libraries, and God knows what else. On Sundays he wore a dark blue suit, but the rest of the week he was in overalls and a denim jacket. He didn't move fast, but he was always where he was needed, and never without the butt of a cigar on his lower lip.

After he had opened the bulkhead doors, Sam lingered in the driveway that separated the two houses. He looked up and down, reached into his pocket, took out a piece of paper and a measuring tape. He ran it from the side of the Tripp House toward ours and looked on the piece of paper as if to check something. He did this in several places along the gravel driveway we had put in after our first winter in Wakefield, because getting into our barn with the car had become quite a trick. More than once the car had gotten hung up in muddy ruts, clods of wet soil flying around from our spinning tires. Miss Tripp hadn't objected. Good idea, she'd said.

I was curious, so I walked out, still in my robe.

"Good morning Sam! What are you doing?"

"Good morning," he said, and swung the metal tape off the gravel driveway. With a ring of finality it recoiled into its casing. He stuffed it back into the pocket of his denim jacket, carefully removed the cigar from his lips, looked at it thoughtfully and then said, "Esther Tripp died last week."

Sam looked down again at the butt of his cigar that had no sign of fire in it, and twirled it between his thumb and forefinger.

"She left the house to the church and the library, but she stipulated that her friend, Miss Tulip, would have the use of it as long as she lived," he said after a long pause.

"This is all bad news, but I'm glad to hear that Miss Tulip will still be around. She's a very nice lady."

"She was," Sam said.

"What do you mean, Sam? Was?"

"She died an hour after Esther died."

"What did you say? Were they in a car accident together?" I asked.

"No, nothing of the kind. Miss Tripp died in Providence, Rhode Island, and Miss Tulip died in Hartford, Connecticut. Both of natural causes."

"I've never heard of such a coincidence."

"I'm checking the property lines. On this side of the house it comes out to here," Sam said and drew a line in the gravel with his black ankle boot. I looked up to the road along an imaginary line. There was only a strip of a few feet left on our side. If Sam was right, it meant we couldn't get into our own barn from the road. The Tripp house had been wedged between the inn and our house on a tiny plot of land.

By the time Gijs came back from the hospital, the Tripp house had crowded me out of my own house. Its hemmed-in condition had reversed itself: it was spewing sewerage on my land; screaming kids ran all over; my car stood buried under snow in the street, ready to be scooped up by the town's snow plow. Our privacy had evaporated!

Gijs listened patiently to my projections.

"We'll have to buy it!" he said.

"Are you crazy? Where do you think we'll find the money?"

We had just recently got a loan to remodel his office. I could just picture the face of the loan officer at the Wolfeboro Bank!

"We'll have to find it elsewhere," Gijs said. "It's worth a try."

"OK. Just imagine you would find that pot of gold. What would we do with another house?"

"We could do what the Burwells at the Cape did: use it as a guesthouse."

"Those people are well-off! We can't put ourselves on a par with them," I said, but I could feel the prospect creep into my blood. Just imagine! Pappie and Mammie living next door. Joan and Paul going there for tea after school.

"No matter how we swing it," Gijs said, "it will be better to control that property, or we can forget about parking our car in our own barn!"

Sam Paul was the best source of information. The church deacons and the library trustees—Sam was one of each—were in agreement to sell the property, he told Gijs. They were in the process of having it appraised.

The house was appraised for six thousand dollars. I considered that the end of it. I was brought up with the notion that you pay as you go. Having a mortgage on the house you live in was one thing. Taking out a loan to improve a place you work in was reasonable. But buying a house you didn't need just because it happened to be next door was quite another.

Gijs looked mysterious when he went out the door soon after, and he looked downright triumphant when he came back. He'd gone to a friend, a Dutchman who'd recently moved into our town to retire. He was a generation older than Gijs, with a colorful past that had brought him to the Dutch East Indies in the twenties, back to Holland in the thirties, escaping from there to fight the Germans in WW II and, when the war was won, to New York in the late forties. Karel ter Weele was an adventurer, an entrepreneur and a savvy businessman. And, what's more, when Gijs walked into his house that day, he happened to have a check for six thousand dollars sitting on his mantelpiece. He waved it in front of Gijs after he'd heard his story and said, "You're welcome to it. I just sold some stock and I was wondering, just this morning, how I would reinvest it!"

I threw out my doubts and decided to go with the flow. Gijs's intuition had brought us to Wakefield, and I'd begun to think that was not such a bad idea after all. By nature and through experience Gijs was more given to taking risks than I, and if he saw this as a good opportunity then why hold him back? We could always sell the house, he said, if it became a burden, but then we could redraw the property lines to fit our own needs.

Miss Tripp's death seemed remote to Joan and Paul. They hadn't seen her since the previous summer. They were sad, but when we were allowed in the house as serious buyers, they sniffed the place out like dogs, the barn first of all. It's where Miss Tripp went on what had seemed to them a mysterious mission. She would get up from the dining room table, they told us, to go "somewhere" in the direction of the barn. When they wanted to follow her, Ivy would hold them back. Now they found a door, painted a sickening shade of green, sitting kitty-corner at the far end of the barn. After they peeked in, they turned back quickly, their fingers pinching their noses, but they were curious enough to step into the darkness of the outhouse. I could hear them giggle and whisper. A moment later they dashed out with expressions of discovery, disgust and childish delight that I envied.

Miss Tripp's house, it turned out, was modestly equipped. It had one faucet in the kitchen and a one-holer in the barn and, needless to say, no septic system. When we climbed up the rickety staircase to the barn-loft, we found a door with a lock. One of the keys in the bundle Sam had given us opened it up to a shoe shop that looked as if the owner had just gone out for lunch and forgotten to put up a sign saying he'd be back in twenty minutes. From the things we saw hanging on the walls and sitting on the benches, we could tell he'd gone out for lunch forever in the previous century. Wooden lasts sat in racks on the pine-planked wall and tin cans filled with tiny wooden pegs lined the crudely boarded counter. Freeman Pike, Sam told us later, had worked there as a shoemaker. Dr. Louise Paul, Sam's sister, bought the entire content and donated it to the Historical Society to place in the schoolhouse museum down our road.

After Joan had inspected every inch of what she viewed as a welcome expansion of her territory, she remarked that Miss Tripp's house was built exactly like ours. The staircase was built the same way, it had five fireplaces, and a barn attached to the house.

"They are twin farms, Dad," she said. "Just like the Doe twins."

"Twin Farms, that's what we will call our place, Joan. Good idea," Gijs said. It rang in my ears with a sweet sound and my mind saw many possibilities.

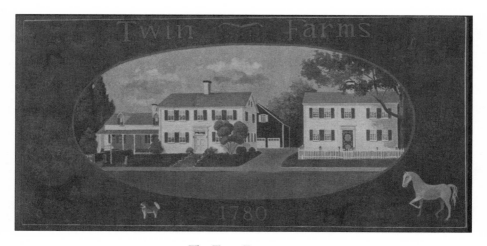

The Twin Farms sign

Chapter 26

Dutch Students

A troop of musicians who played gypsy music and called themselves *Tzigane* were our first guests in the Tripp house. They studied at the University of Utrecht, Gijs's alma mater, and my cousin, Tjalling Ament, was the link. In the spring of 1966, he wrote us that *Tzigane* had booked passage on a student ship to the States and wondered if Gijs could be their impresario for the month in between crossings. Gijs didn't waste a minute. He bought an old station wagon for three hundred dollars from Bob Duchano, our local second-hand car dealer, arranged for a U-Haul to carry their instruments and secured engagements for them through various Dutch Consulates. But first they would play for us in Wakefield. Tjalling would come ahead to pick up the car, drive it back to New York and bring his buddies up north. Gijs wrote them they could all sleep in the Tripp house.

We hustled to get ready. Vic was in the last stages of putting on an addition to the office. Three days before the guests arrived, the lawn was still strewn with asphalt shingles, the new roof wasn't completely on and the clapboards not painted. Gijs told me not to worry, he had several patients he could think of who wouldn't mind working off their unpaid bills. The next day, twelve men materialized with hammers, paint brushes, rakes and lawn mowers, and they buzzed around like bees in a clover field.

It had taken a year to pass papers on the Tripp house. In May, an auctioneer had hauled out the old chairs, beds, mirrors, picture albums and dishes. He could conveniently display them on the lawn of the bankrupt inn. Gijs and I picked out some small items to bid on, like chamber pots and a big wooden chopping bowl. Paul, barely six years old, bravely bid on an upright desk he'd seen Miss Tripp write at all the days of all the summers he could remember. He just had to have that desk! When the crowd of antique dealers noticed that a little boy had set his heart on it, the bidding stopped. The hulky auctioneer helpers brought the tall oak desk with a flip-up front to where he sat in his own little chair. He guarded his prize possession like a faithful dog and didn't move away until it was time to go home with it.

Without its furniture and artifacts the Tripp house looked worn and stripped. I wondered if it had sagged over its one hundred eighty-five years, or if it had been built that way. Vic told me they didn't bother much with levels in the old days. When Paul and Joan played marbles on the bare floors, they inevitably ended up in the fireplace, the lowest point, as if the house were a hammock. I looked at the faded wallpaper and the peeling paint and wondered how I could create a new identity in just a few weeks time. The bare bulbs that hung from the ceilings in each room looked like Edison himself had manufactured them. Folding cots with sleeping bags in the upstairs rooms would have to make do, and I put the chamber pots from the auction under them. Vic fashioned a table out of a door and I bought chairs for it at a yard sale. The students, who had come to America as we had nine years earlier, with *LIFE* magazine pictures of shining steel in their minds, would probably be astounded when they were shown their quarters. An outhouse? A chamber pot? Are we in America?

Fifty guests were invited to the Wakefield performance, more than half of them Dutch. The year before, Gijs had organized a Netherlands-American Medical Society by placing an ad in the American Medical Society Journal. It would serve as a contact point between doctors who'd been trained in Holland and could provide support to and among its members. When the response was overwhelming, he planned a party aboard the flagship of the Holland-America Line, the *ss Rotterdam*, when it was moored in New York's harbor that very spring. Never lacking in imagination, he invited the Dutch Ambassador and the Dutch Consul in New York for the inauguration. We'd met many new people then, and when we invited them for a garden party with *Tzigane*, they accepted immediately, even the ones who lived in New York City and Connecticut.

On the day of the party, the skies were the color of lead as we hauled folding chairs and tables across the street from the church. I kept a prayerful eye on the inky clouds as we set plates down for fifty people to dine outside. The musicians hadn't shown up yet, but the guests from out-of-town had begun arriving. It seemed as tight an organization as when we arrived at Idlewild Airport in 1957 without a day to spare to come in under Eisenhower's Special Immigration Quota.

Looking out over our yard, I marveled at the feminine curves of Moose Mountain in the hazy distance. Two black ponies drank from the trough in the field; dark blue delphiniums rose majestically against the barn boards. It looked like a movie set to me. After the war was over and American movies could be screened again, my brother Herman and I used to sneak off to matinees and gazed at the fanciful homes, the luscious gardens and the space-without-end that Diana Durbin and Bing Crosby waltzed through. Wakefield, New Hampshire, wasn't Hollywood, the homes not quite as fanciful, the people not quite as good-looking. Yet that day it felt as if I owned the movie set we had so admired then. That space-without-end was all around me.

Mary, the caterer, was unloading her car, and brought in large pans with cold ratatouille, a pre-sliced ham, a succulent roast beef. Joan and Paul followed her around and helped carry in the fake silver trays.

"We're the servers tonight," Joan told Mary who managed to look delighted. "A Dutch lady is coming and she'll bring us costumes."

Kin Cullen, a new Dutch friend from Jackson, New Hampshire, appeared with two authentic costumes from the island of Marken. She spirited the kids to our bedroom and transformed them into genuine Dutch stock. Paul came down the staircase backward, very carefully placing his wooden shoes on each tread and wearing baggy black pants that bloomed out at the hips. Joan was close behind in a wide vertically striped skirt with a black apron over the front of it. They were quite taken with themselves.

Meanwhile, the brass hands of the clock moved dangerously close to the magical hour. Still no students! Could something have happened to them? Had Tjalling even made it back to New York to pick them up? I walked over to Gijs.

"They called," he said. "They'll be a little late. The car overheated."

"Oh God," I groaned. "Where did they call from?"

"Not too far from here," he said vaguely.

I panicked. They might not show up till tomorrow! I never wasted time on in-between scenarios. My mind went straight as an arrow to the worst possible one. The party would peter out when our guests realized the major attraction of the evening, that haunting gypsy music they remembered so well from their Dutch student days, or that they looked forward to because we had talked it up, was not to be.

From the window in the dining room I watched Loes Hugenholtz, who looked aristocratic in her floral summer dress. The sun highlighted her enviably thick blond hair, which she had twisted into a bun. Her head was always slightly pitched forward, ready to listen, ready to react. She'd told me countless times she was shy and detested cocktail parties, yet she projected the opposite. I wondered if she ever felt the awe she inspired in others. The mere length of her, those penetrating eyes, the vivid interest with which she listened, turned heads. But she wasn't an easy conversationalist. Loes expected to hear the truth and gave back the truth, pleasant or not. It was a rubbing point between Gijs and Loes.

"You're hypocritical, Gijs!" she'd once told him. When he asked her why, she said, "You don't say what you think!"

Gijs was brought up to be diplomatic.

"If I am hypocritical," he had retorted, "then you are egotistic! It's more important to you to feel good telling your truth than to protect people from your truth."

Loes disdained formalities as much as she disdained the title she was born to. To her mind, Gijs just applied the good manners he'd learned. Nothing more. They irritated each other with the different ways they expressed the same underlying quality: care for others. Loes as the social worker, who could listen well and had superb intuition; Gijs as the physician who gently steered his patients and had a knack for diagnosis.

Loes put trays with tiny sandwiches to Joan and Paul and sent them off in the direction of a small group that had strolled over to the pasture.

"Go tell them about your ponies," she said.

"What shall I tell them, Tante Loes?" Paul asked.

"Well, you know, that they are half brothers and that you know how to drive them or something like that. Most people come from the city."

"Don't they have ponies in the city?" he asked.

"Not in their backyard!"

"I'm glad I don't live in a city then."

Loes reminded him that his real mission was to get food to the guests, and he set out very slowly, unaccustomed to the wooden shoes that wouldn't bend, balancing the tray that was twice as wide as himself.

Paul Hugenholtz stood at the nucleus of newly arrived guests and he had grabbed their attention. Unlike his wife he relished gatherings. His dashing looks helped him win over women almost instantly, and men, especially his peers, viewed his jaunty arrogance as a welcome challenge. The ambitious pace of his life stocked his treasure trove of stories, and he handed them out like colorfully wrapped candies. The males around him soon felt it was Paul they had to measure up to. He simply viewed their posturing as a deserved compliment.

But there were some other big egos walking around on our lawn that night, and IQ's to match them. These men had great hopes for themselves. There was Rients, a thoracic surgeon from New York City, a head taller than Paul Hugenholtz, his large frame awe-inspiring and telling of physical strength and boundless self-confidence. He talked in clipped phrases that were like well-aimed arrows with a cynical slant. Yet when his dark brown eyes smiled, I knew I would hand him my heart if it needed mechanical fixing, convinced he would see me through the ordeal. Paul handled him with respect, fully aware that Rients, a few years older, was already near the top of his career, while he had still a lot of steep climbing to do.

There was Co, who'd trained with Gijs in the same hospital, in Rotterdam, and was now in Boston with his family to fulfill a few years of residency at Massachusetts General. Co didn't hide his ambitions. He would take any opportunity to outline the career he had in mind for himself. He would go back to Holland, shake up the medical world there, wake up the antiquated educational system and tell the professors to move over. President Kennedy was his hero: young, ambitious, fast-paced, and attractive to women. He even wanted to die young like J.F.K., but that part of the identification he didn't manage, though he would fulfill most of his other dreams.

Joan walked by with an empty tray on her way to the kitchen. Minutes later, she stepped down on the flagstone terrace, restocked. She headed straight for the animated group that had formed in the middle of the lawn and nudged her way into the circle, her blue eyes within her tanned face shining with mirth and a hint of flirtation. Her costume drew attention and she rewarded her admirers with filled mushrooms and warm sausages. If she was shy she hid it well. She lingered just long enough to force others to take her into account. Many of the men in the circle would become her favorite uncles, models for "the ideal man." She got to know them well over the years as frequent guests in the Tripp house.

When Hansie Mead alighted from the terrace door, all heads turned to look at this striking young woman with hair so blond it was almost white. Her eyes were only slightly darker than robin eggs. She probably had thrown together the cotton summer dress she wore the night before. It didn't matter. She could have worn a burlap bag and it would not have made any difference in the spectacular effect she created, covering her body that had already brought forth four children with flowing, pleasing lines.

"They think I'm Dutch," Diana Hopewell said to me with a laugh. Somebody just gave me a whole dissertation on something, and I just nodded. It was too late to say 'I don't speak a word of Dutch!'"

The women around her were exchanging the number of children they'd had.

"We were too late for the pill," said one woman who was closer to forty than thirty. "You young ones have it easy!"

"Bob and I want to have lots of children. We create good protoplasm. I think what the world needs is quality control!"

"I love babies," Hansie said, smiling. "What could be more wonderful than those small, pink bundles? I just love them!"

"Gijs and I were at a dinner party the other night," I broke in, "Our host hailed the pill as the best thing that ever came along. We had a heated discussion. That night I had a nightmare about date rape and pornography."

"We don't know exactly what effects the pill will have," said Nel Greep, who, like her husband, was a doctor. "But it could very well create a culture shock. Our daughters will have to make choices we didn't have to make, and that may not be as easy as it looks."

"I don't think this would have been a topic of conversation among our mothers," Mrs. Fredericks from Wellesley said. "They were more concerned with how to survive the next air strike, or where the evening meal would come from!"

"They didn't have any choices," I said. "My mother's brothers were sent to the university, but not she. She had to go to a household school!"

"True, we had the choice to study," somebody else piped up. "But what did we do with it? We found husbands!" We all laughed.

"And now we can support their careers!" said Nel.

"Oh well, at least we're intelligent mothers," Hansie said.

We didn't know it then, but we would be the bridge between Victorian housewives and career women in power suits.

A car was loudly honking its horn. Joan and Paul set down their trays and ran around the barn. When Gijs and I got to the driveway, we saw the doors of Bob Duchano's old Ford station wagon open. The contents poured out like foam from a bottle of beer that's been shaken too much. Steamy young men in sticky shorts stepped out on the gravel, shook themselves loose, and looked around.

"We must be in the right place," one of them said, eying Joan and Paul in their costumes.

My cousin Tjalling introduced us to his fellow musicians. Then he pointed at the car.

"We brought you a surprise, Gijs," he said with a secretive smile. A man in his fifties sat in the back seat. Gijs stuck his head inside and exclaimed, "My God, what are you doing here?" He grabbed the man's hand and pulled him out of the car. "How are you?"

"How do you do?" the man said to me shyly. "I am Everwijn," and I remembered that the servers at the student club were never addressed by their own names, but were given medieval names like Hardewijn and Everwijn. We spent part of the evening explaining to the non-Dutch guests that university life in Holland is organized quite differently from the United States model, especially in Utrecht where customs and traditions found their roots in what happened centuries back.

"The gentlemen offered me this trip because of thirty years of service," he said to Gijs, "They enrolled me as a student in math so I could go on the student boat. Do I look like a math student, Mr. Bozuwa?"

"You look like a professor, for God's sake!"

"The gentlemen told me this was meant to be a vacation for me, but I want to make an exception for you. I'll take care of the bar tonight!"

"We have no time to stand around here," one of the students who'd been introduced as Erik said. "Everybody clean up. I give you fifteen minutes at the most!"

"Maybe we'd better move the piano first," Gijs said. "I bought one for only fifty dollars, but all the same, it looked like it might rain this afternoon, so we didn't put it out on the terrace yet."

The pianist in the group looked doubtful at the mention of fifty dollars. Gijs reassured him that he'd paid as much to have the relic tuned. When they expertly lowered it onto the flagstones, applause rose from the lawn. The students bowed and turned on their heels, and then reappeared within half an hour in black trousers and wide-sleeved satin shirts that were gathered at the wrist. Gasps of awe went up when Everwijn stepped out of the kitchen door in dark blue livery, complete with red braiding and many brass buttons. Against the backdrop of a New England farm he looked outlandish. Yet Everwijn seemed as comfortable in his livery as a local farmer would be in his coveralls. He walked over to the long table stacked with wine bottles and glasses and started to take orders.

Erik and Tjalling came around the barn, carrying a cimbalom between them as carefully as if it were a basket with eggs. It was a prized

Tzigane

possession they had diddled out of some Hungarian gypsies in Utrecht with sly manipulation, because the iron curtain had sealed off the source of these instruments. The legs were quickly screwed under what looked like a dulcimer in a table frame. It was placed prominently on the terrace as the centerpiece of the little orchestra that further consisted of two violins, a viola, a bass and a piano. Our backyard took on the atmosphere of a concert hall just before the director steps onto the podium. Dissonant sounds of tuning string instruments filled the mellow air.

Their tuning completed, Erik took up his violin and said "Hascha!"

The alumni from various Dutch universities raised their glasses of wine and cried out, "Hascha!" With that war-cry Erik lifted up his right arm with a grand gesture, tucked the violin under his chin and slid his bow over the strings with a long, sure pull that brought out a soul-wrenching sound. It was the signal for the other musicians to join in. Roel, the cimbalist, took up his mallets and started to strike the strings on the cimbalom, up and down, to the left and to the right, extracting a rhythmic sound against which the sensual violin could play its haunting melodies, much like a drummer does for the saxophonist in a jazz band. The cimbalom is the heart and the violin the soul of gypsy music. A hush fell over the guests. Visually, it was a sight to behold. It seemed like these young men used their entire bodies to play their instruments. But it was the eye of memory and imagination that caught the most tingling images: the sounds and swells of the violin produced visions of horsemen galloping over tundras; of couples swooning under an arbor of grapevines; of people mourning people; of celebrations, of making love, of living the full measure of life. There was no end to the emotions that rose along my spine as the silk sleeves moved and shimmered in the late afternoon sun, which had broken through the threatening clouds two hours earlier.

Joan abandoned her job as a server and brought out a chair from the house. She placed it to the side of the cimbalom and sat there for most of the evening, entranced by this strange music that seemed to make everyone around her so happy. During dinner, she brought out another chair and hauled it over to Everwijn so he could sit as well, while everyone else was seated. We had told Joan and Paul they could stay up as long as they wanted to. It was almost midnight when we caught them dozing off, but not willing to admit to sleep. They were surrounded by an aura of light from the candles that Gijs had set around on the terrace and in the flowerbeds.

The neighborhood was a deaf audience: the library, the old town hall, the church and the bankrupt inn stood unmoved, as silent witnesses. The gypsy music rippled over the surrounding fields until the early hours, until finally the young students had reached their climax and stumbled up the creaky staircase of the Tripp house, to their field cots with the chamber pots underneath, and all the guests had taken their leave.

Chapter 27
Tzigane Leaves

"When the man reached in back of him and pulled out this dark thing," Erik said, "I thought 'Oh my God, this is the end,' and I told everyone to stay in the car!"

We were sitting around the breakfast table, sipping tea, two days after *Tzigane* had arrived. The night before they had played at the Bittersweet Inn in Wolfeboro, and on their way back a man in a beat-up car had stopped them. Wearing khakis and a sleeveless home-knit sweater over his shirt, he'd stepped out and commanded, "Get out of yer caaar."

"I turned the window down an inch and asked, 'Who are you?'" Erik said, stirring his cup of tea. We had just finished a hearty breakfast of pancakes with maple syrup and bacon, as an example of New England cuisine.

"The man was furious," Eric went on. "He reached into his back pocket and took out a police badge."

"Erik told us not to get out of the car," Roel said. "We couldn't see the man very well, but when Erik turned his window down a little farther, we heard a waterfall of words. We didn't understand his accent. Not a word of it."

"I thought the best way out would be to say we were Dr. Bozuwa's guests. Then it dawned on him that we were foreigners. He immediately changed his tune." Erik laughed and took another sip of his tea. "The man profusely apologized and explained he'd stopped us because the light over our rear license plate didn't work. We were let go."

"Two minutes later, we were stopped again," Tjalling said.

"Why was that?" I asked.

"Would you believe he asked us to come home with him and have a beer?"

"Oh, so that's what happened!" I said. "I got a call from his wife after you left there."

They had followed the car and soon found themselves in the tearful embrace of the policeman's wife, who'd already downed more than a few beers. Two years ago to the day, she had told them, their almost-blind son had been killed in a car accident. He'd been the passenger in his brother's car. Erik and the others were full of sympathy and, after some more beers, they went to the car and unpacked their instruments—the cimbalom, the bass and the violins—and played in the kitchen of the constable and his wife. Mary Katwick had called me after they'd packed up their instruments and gone on their way.

"I had your darling gang here! Such nice boys! No long-hair jobs," she said. She couldn't get over her good luck that these boys had played their special music for her. I had been totally mystified how *Tzigane* had landed itself in a house in Brookfield. I tried to recreate the picture: the cimbalom next to the black wood stove, the beer bottles on the checkered linoleum of the kitchen table, the boys in their satin blouses and red vests bowing up a storm, the sounds amplified by the low ceiling of the cape the Katwicks lived in.

"Would you like another pancake?" I asked. Eric reached over to take the platter from my hands. I looked at his: finely boned, slender hands with agile fingers. Cradled around the neck of his violin they had moved rapidly over the fingerboard with sure intent, extracting the most stirring melodies. The fingers and the face worked together. It had been hard not to sit and stare at Erik all night, drinking in his intense animation.

Joan sat in Tjalling's lap. The conversation among the seven of us was in Dutch, and she followed every word. All of a sudden, Dutch wasn't just a funny language anymore, a language only her parents used, or her grandparents or the people in a faraway country who spoke it to each other. These young men, who could not only play the most sweeping music she'd ever heard but who also had wonderful stories to tell, were in her house right now and she reveled in their presence. English had become Joan's language after she'd started school, but now the "Dutchness" around the table excited her. She wanted to be a part of it.

It was late Monday morning. Gijs was back in the office. Patients came and went. For *Tzigane* and me it was a day of rest. Swimming.

Fishing on Kingswood Lake. Letter writing. Everyone went his or her way. I cooked a big pan of chili for their last evening with us. When Gijs came out of the office at five-thirty, he found a sedate group sitting in his living room. Not for long. In no time he had Everwijn preparing drinks, the students looking at pictures of his own days in Utrecht, and after supper we stood around the piano on the terrace, belting out familiar songs, a mixture of the patriotic and the idiotic. We ran out of whiskey and wine, and started on a bottle of Southern Comfort. Gijs went inside and came back with candles and set them out around the terrace and on the piano. Everwijn laughed and said, "Mr. Bozuwa, you always wanted candlelight at your parties. And a carriage ride afterwards."

"Nothing has changed, Everwijn," Gijs said. "I will take you on a carriage ride. And this time you won't have to phone the livery stable. I have my own. Come on, Tiets," he said to me. "Let's get the ponies!"

"You must be kidding, Gijs. Now? They're in the field. It's pitch dark!" I said, but I could tell there was no stopping Gijs.

I quickly rounded up some flashlights, two leather halters and leading ropes. A half moon hung in the dark sky above the tree line. It provided a measure of light after my eyes got adjusted to the darkness of the pasture. I stood at the gate and called, "Sambal, Brandal!" I didn't see any movement, but the ground underneath my feet trembled with hooves that rapidly moved in my direction. Two furry bodies, black as the night itself, stood before me, snorting. This was going to be a lively ride, I thought. Good thing I refused that sweet Southern Comfort stuff. I would have to keep my wits together.

I brought the ponies into the lit barn. The two sulkies stood ready. Paul and Joan were asleep. I briefly considered waking Joan up. She was pretty handy at harnessing her ponies, handier than seven Dutchmen filled with wine and whiskey. But I thought the better of it, at this late hour.

Sambal and Brandal stood perfectly still, subdued by all the people around them, and let themselves be fitted into the various straps of leather that had to be attached to the carts in a precise order or it would all end up in a tangle, as hard to undo as a ball of wool. Gijs and I each took a carriage and drove it around the barn to the terrace where Everwijn had stayed behind, stretched out on a lawn chair. The Southern Comfort had taken its effect, or maybe we shouldn't have wondered why we'd run out of whiskey so fast?

"Here's your carriage, Everwijn," Gijs said, and took him aboard on the narrow seat beside him. Erik joined me. The ponies were fired up by the excitement and moved right along, their irons beating a staccato rhythm on the pavement. They knew exactly where to go, guided by the moonlight. At the end of the road they veered onto a dirt path, and Everwijn almost fell out of the sulky. All the swaying and motion had made him feel the effects of the Southern Comfort even more. When we came back into the yard, Gijs and all the students hoisted him out of the sulky and carried him to the Tripp house, singing, *"Utrecht, Utrecht, die oude Bisschop-stad, daar heb ik van m'n leven toch zo'n lol gehad."* With each refrain of their club song, they pushed him up a few more treads of the staircase, until they had him on the landing. There they lifted him up and gently put him on his cot. The next morning, no mention was made of this scene. Everwijn appeared, fresh and shaven, his suitcase packed.

The rain that had threatened on the day of their arrival had postponed its downpour until the day of their departure. Gijs, Joan, Paul and I stood on the front lawn under a black umbrella to see them off. One by one, they came over to say good-bye, holding their own black umbrella over their head. Thus we stood across from each other, trying not to poke each other in the eye with the sharp rods that stuck out every six inches of the black cloth, while we spoke parting words and received grateful kisses. Everwijn reached out his hand, said he'd never had such a good time in his life, then, as an afterthought, grabbed me and planted a kiss on my cheek, gingerly, while a tear rolled down over his. Erik was last. I cringed at the thought of him leaving. I knew I would never see him again. And I haven't. I had fallen in love with this lean, vivacious young man, ten years my junior. It wasn't just his artistry, his good looks and his intense blue eyes under the shock of wavy blond hair. He had awakened aspects of the life I had left behind in Holland, aspects I had buried, because they were too hard to live with in Wakefield. I was living the practical life now: gardening, cleaning horse stalls, cooking, remodeling an old house and sending out bills. It was mostly a non-contemplative life, lacking in artistic stimulation. What Erik had brought out in me were memories of my boyfriend, Jan, who had been an assistant curator at the Rijks Museum in Amsterdam, and who could while away an entire evening telling me about a single exquisite print by Rembrandt. Like my mother, he had a way of making me feel a part of a vibrant world of the arts that was now out of my reach. My new life circled around children, managing an office, digging up weeds, harnessing ponies.

I cried when I walked back into the house. Not for a lost love but for a lost way of life.

Chapter 28
Discipline

Joan loved Paul, Paul loved Joan, and they beat on each other every chance they got. They giggled together, conspired together, they turned on each other and defended each other. Joan had the upper hand being three years older. Although initially it was easy for the big sister to bully the smaller brother, Paul fiercely defended himself when his considerable measure of patience overflowed. At times, I had to pull the two of them apart and bring them to their senses.

In the spring of 1966, I took Paul for a visit to the school that Joan had already been going to for two years. In September, he would be going there every day. As we entered the handsome brick building his little hand slipped into mine. He gripped it hard, but he kept walking, taking in the high-ceilinged hallways and looking up at the big kids who walked there matter-of-factly, books under their arms. At the end of the endless corridor we knocked on a classroom door and looked into the curious faces of twenty or so first graders. Still quite cross-eyed and vulnerable, Paul stood in the door opening, waiting for a miracle that could safely shove him over the threshold, but before the teacher could get to him, two children suddenly cried out, "Hi, Paul." His sweaty palm relaxed in my hand. Kids from the Reading Hour in the local bookstore had recognized him. I quickly turned away. Paul came back on the yellow school bus with his big sister, beaming.

For the next ten years, Gijs took his children to school every morning at 7:30 on his way to the hospital. It was a thirty-minute drive and in it he taught them the multiplication tables. Once they knew those by heart, he embarked on the more complicated stuff like addition and subtraction with multiple digits. Joan wrote the numbers on the windows she had steamed up with her breath so she could impress her father with rapid answers, while he had his eyes on the road and she sat in the backseat. It was important to impress her father. He was the one to please, the principal in her school of life, where I was the teacher involved with her daily lessons and chores.

A mother who felt she had to act for two when her husband was at sea had brought up Gijs with strict codes of behavior. A sister, five years older than he, had dominated his life, and thirty women who'd crowded into their house when the Japanese soldiers forced them to, had told him what to do, even though he was already sixteen years old. He was actually relieved when he was summoned to go to a man's camp on the day he turned seventeen. Gijs was used to following orders and expected the same of his children. And if there were one thing he couldn't stand, it was conceit. If Joan showed only a hint of it, he lectured her, and if she showed more than he liked he sat her down and made her write "I am an egotist." Thirty times.

"Stop crying," Gijs commanded when she cried after he had disciplined her. Of course, she couldn't, because she was mad. Her pride hurt, how could she stop? Paul, wisely, would sit very still and stare at the food on his plate.

Outbursts like these usually took place at dinnertime. Gijs would come out of the office after a long day. Joan and Paul would have been hanging around waiting for dinner, after a day in school, topped off by an hour-long ride on the school bus with rambunctious, teasing kids. It was like a bad recipe: parents and children both at their low point; add a slight provocation and the sauce curdles. Joan, quick and verbal, could push her father just a little too far, over the edge of his good nature, and like a thunderclap Gijs would explode. Afterwards nobody could remember what had started the upset in the first place.

Usually, I knew how to uncurdle the sauce by adding a measure of quiet logic, drop by drop. Only once did I have to use a more drastic remedy. Joan hadn't fed the ponies before supper, as she was supposed to, but she wasn't about to admit to it and gave some sassy reasons for why she could do it just as well after supper. She took a stand. Gijs was fed up. He chased her around the dining room table. Paul melted into the woodwork, petrified. I looked at my husband and my daughter chasing each other, both out of control, Joan scared to death, Gijs beside himself. A drop-by-drop solution wouldn't do. I grabbed a tall glass and threw it at the wall. It sailed over their heads and crashed dramatically against the wall, just as I had planned. Everybody was stunned, including myself. I had never done anything quite so calculated and spectacular. But it worked. Gijs and Joan stopped. Paul's eyes opened wide. After the noise of shouting voices and shattering glass, the silence was deafening.

"That's enough!" I told my stunned audience. Gijs and Joan looked like two balloons that had been punctured by an arrow. Limp and exhausted, they leaned over the back of their chairs. Paul ran to the kitchen closet and fetched a dustpan to pick up the broken glass.

Joan and her father

"OK," Gijs said. "Let's go out for supper."

We all piled into the car and went to the Pine Hearth restaurant. How do they do it, I asked myself. Twenty minutes ago a thunderstorm threatened to put an end to life as we'd known it, and here we were joking and laughing. Joan told her latest elephant joke—"What time is it when the elephant sits on the fence? Time to repair it!"—and Gijs sipped his beer while savoring his daughter's considerable gift for story telling. Gijs, Joan and my mother were like traffic lights. They went from green to red, and back again, without warning. Most of the time their lights were on green, which made you forget they also knew how to operate red. When I was a child, I did what Paul did: shrink, dodge and get through it somehow. I had learned not to pile more oil on the fire. While Mammie lost control,

I would hang on to my own. But secretly I admired their innate quality to let it all fly. They lived spontaneously, driven by their impulses. It made them a lot of fun to be with, however unpredictable.

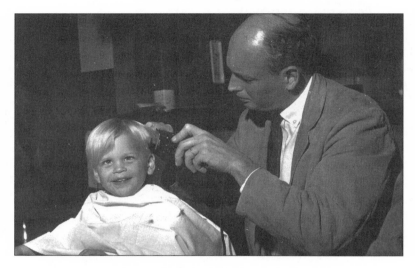

Paul gets a haircut

Paul was more adapt at creating smooth waters than Joan. He looked at his older sister and, early on, saw the pitfalls of provoking his father into a righteous mode.

Joan absorbed the strict rules, but she also listened to Gijs's stories of defiance, which made for good conversation around the dinner table: lively images of Gijs, a student, climbing up the ancient circular staircase of the Gothic cathedral in Utrecht, to the very top of the tower where the carillon hung. There he rang the huge bells in the early morning hours, waking up Utrecht's sleepy citizens as well as the police. He was arrested and released after he explained he'd done it to announce the birth of a royal princess. Joan was apt at retrieving such stories when confronted with Gijs's strict rules of behavior, and she tried to throw her father off-stride with them. But Gijs was not easily thrown off course, and usually Joan quickly backed off. Not Paul. He didn't find himself in opposition to his father's will very often, but if he were, he would hold out to the bitter end. It was a memorable sight to see our shy and amiable five-year-old turn into a stubborn fury, crying but unwilling to say "I'm sorry" if he was absolutely certain there was nothing to apologize for.

Chapter 29

A Widening Circle

W e loved the New Hampshire winters when the familiar outlines of the flower borders and the fenced-in fields faded away under layers of snow, the sky turned cobalt blue and the air felt like bubbly champagne.

My childhood winters had been damp and raw. An ever-present wind drove the cold over the flat landscape and lashed me in the face as I biked over a heath on my way to school. We traveled like a flock of geese, taking turns at being in the lead. Bundled up in raincoats, woolen shawls and heavy sweaters we pushed down on our pedals with grim determination to stay warm. For sport we skated on the canals.

When Gijs and I first came to Wakefield, skiing was just for "flatlanders," as far as the locals were concerned. But a group of young entrepreneurs transformed Moose Mountain—the one we saw from our dining room window—into a ski area. The farmers' offspring was intrigued and rented equipment to try out this new sport. The old guard thought it was a useless activity to be pulled up a mountain by a motor, only to hurl down it on two flat wooden sticks moments later. To what end? But the younger generation didn't think of usefulness. It was out to have fun.

We could practically ski in our own backyard. Gijs, like me, had only skied once in Europe. We were rank beginners. Nevertheless, Gijs offered himself as a ski-patrol. What he lacked in skill, he made up for in guts. Together with other members of the ski-patrol he would come down the mountain holding the ropes of a toboggan that carried an unlucky skier. Joan and Paul were in awe of their father, and we all skied for free as long as Gijs was at the mountain every weekend.

Now that we had a mountain to ski on in our backyard and an

extra house to receive guests in, we became a favorite destination for the doctors we'd met in New York City when Gijs launched the Netherlands-American Medical Society. Every weekend was booked. Our new friends drove north from Connecticut and Boston with young children who were mostly Joan's and Paul's ages. All of a sudden, we had a new circle of friends. It was like working in America during the week and going to Holland for the weekend. Only it was better, because in Holland we would have sat around the stove and here we were skiing as if we were on vacation in Austria.

The Dutch language bounced off the walls of the old farmhouses,

Sambal pulls Joan and Paul through our street

and the barrier to speak the funny language of their parents was lifted for all the children, not just ours. It became cool to speak in their parents' tongue at Twin Farms.

Saturday nights were spent around our big fireplace drinking French wines and Dutch gin, brought as hostess presents. Together we cooked traditional Dutch meals like *boerenkool met worst*, with kale bought at the Italian open market in Boston and a smoked sausage that somebody's mother had sent over from Holland. Some of our guests had spent their youth in the Dutch East Indies, like Gijs, and together they prepared spicy rice dishes.

Not all of these Dutchmen had come to America as immigrants. A few were here as residents or fellows at the great teaching hospitals of Boston, and they knew they would return to Holland. Most of us though were trying to find our way in a different culture. Would we succeed, we wondered, in bringing our children up to be Americans?

Congregated in a New England farmhouse, eating Dutch food, speaking our native language, we compared notes on how we dealt with two cultures that were not total opposites, yet still different. The American way of life was more laid-back and informal, we all agreed. How many times had we not been told by our parents that "You just don't do that," or "You can't wear that." When we'd asked why it almost always came down to differences in class. Table manners were of utmost importance. We ate with a knife in the right hand and a fork in the left. Putting one hand under the table was rude. Formalities and codes had been invented so the lines could be sharply drawn. Our mothers wouldn't dream of being addressed by their first names, unless they'd given express permission, and all of our parents adhered to a strict dress code. No jolly plaid shirt for my father or slacks for my mother.

We weren't altogether sorry that we'd escaped that stifling intensity. It wasn't hard to make people's acquaintance here. We marveled at American generosity, how helpful they were. Each of us had experienced an incident where an American had showed, with endless patience, the way to do the things we didn't know about, be it getting up on water skis or tying on snowshoes. In Holland that wasn't always the case. Americans were great coaches, but they were also ruthlessly competitive. And we didn't like it that these mostly amiable people sued each other if bad luck befell them. Was misfortune always someone else's fault?

Looking back forty years later, I think that the immigrants who'd come before us had taken to heart the part of the Declaration of Independence that states that all people are created equal. The barriers they'd known in whatever country they'd come from were gladly broken down. We were the superficial ones by putting so much emphasis on class and feeling protected by the unspoken rules of our parents' generation. Interestingly, in the intervening years, Holland has grown closer to America in its social structure, its customs and its taste, and the other way around. Unfortunately, in political ideology the two countries have grown further apart.

The children, who darted around us while we brainstormed, blended the two cultures without a thought, switching from English to Dutch and back again in the blink of an eye. They were just as happy to roast marshmallows in the fire as eating *speculaas* cookies. Joan, at almost eleven, was the oldest. The rest of the group varied from the diaper stage to the lower grades of elementary school.

My mother, who missed having grandchildren close by, regularly

Joan with her Grandmother Wetselaar

schemed to have Joan come over to Holland, starting when Joan was five. When I questioned her sanity at suggesting such a young child undertake a transatlantic flight by herself, she simply refuted my arguments by describing how she had traveled, alone and by boat, from the island where she was born to the mainland. An uncle had met her. A wonderful adventure, she wrote, and it had probably taken as long then as it would take now to fly over the Atlantic Ocean.

I said *no*.

But my mother didn't give up easily. The following year, she wrote that a friend's granddaughter, whose parents were in the diplomatic service and stationed somewhere in Africa, had traveled alone to Amsterdam without a hitch. If diplomats' children could do it, then why not Joan?

My imagination went wild with kidnapping scenes, or with Joan stranded in London on Heathrow Airport after she'd missed the connection to *Schiphol* Airport. I was just frantic contemplating it. But Mammie had no qualms. Just hang a sign on her chest, she wrote, that says, "I am on my way to Amsterdam." Like Paddington Bear!

When Joan turned eleven, Mammie reminded us that a child under twelve could still travel for half price. Joan got wind of Oma's plans. Without saying a word about it, she started to save money for the trip. She was confident that whatever she was short would be forthcoming from Oma Wetselaar. It was a determined gesture that could not be ignored. Luck would have it that two of our new Dutch friends, Jos and Ine Ceha from Connecticut, were taking their family to Holland that summer, and they offered to take Joan along.

For the three weeks she was gone, it was eerily quiet in our house without her jokes and swirls of motion. Gijs and I met her in Meriden, Connecticut, at the home of the Cehas. A stunning waterfall of Dutch words fell from her mouth. Non-stop.. She pronounced the names of the villages and cities she'd been taken to without a trace of an accent. Exuberant as a puppy, she told us about all she had seen, the many boats on the canals, how on one trip she had counted forty bridges. She had visited the farms around my parents' country house and described how, when she stood at the living room window, she had watched the cows being milked by hand in the pasture next to the house. So close by, she could see a jet of milk from the cow's tit foam up in the steel bucket underneath.

Holland had been like a precious perfume to Joan. She had inhaled its very essence. Was it the way she had picked up the language? Was it the sense of family? Was it her delight in Dutch foods, like *poffertjes, friten, taartjes, ijs met slagroom, en drop*? Or was it her delight in the things they do, like riding their bikes everywhere, walking to the stores with a big leather shopping bag on their arm, riding the train, or the way they center their lives in their homes, small as those might be?

Whatever it was, Joan had absorbed it. She radiated it.

I felt blessed that my child had experienced Holland. No flowery description could have painted a truer picture of our homeland. At the same time, though, I realized that she now had attained dual citizenship. One of our Dutch friends, a psychiatrist, called that status by a different name: transatlantic schizophrenia.

We didn't become friends with only other Dutch immigrants, though. A blizzard in the winter of 1967 brought the Avery family into our lives. Gijs had to venture out in the deep snow to make a house call in Brookfield. I laid a fire and sat Paul in my lap to read to him. Gijs did not return alone. The patient's wife drove behind him to get the medicine—Gijs kept a small pharmacy in his office for situations just like this—and they came in together through the barn since the path to the office was buried under five feet of snow.

A slender woman—in her thirties, I guessed—with closely cropped hair came into view. She knew she was interfering in a domestic scene and told me to stay put when I made a gesture toward her.

"Sorry I had to take your husband away," she said to me. "Flagg has to go to Tennessee tomorrow. I don't want him to go, but he's determined."

"Didn't we meet at the lake, at Dr. Sawyer's house?" I asked her. "I seem to remember you and me running after toddlers on their lawn!"

Mary laughed. "Yes, I remember."

She looked around the room with disarming frankness and I saw her taking notice of the Dutch clock. She examined it closely, drinking in the blend of New England and Holland.

"Do you have horses? When I came into the barn, I thought I could smell them."

"We have two ponies," Joan answered quickly. "They're half brothers."

"Well, I'll have to take a look at them on my way out. Do you ride?" she asked me.

"I did when I was in Holland," I said, skipping over the experience with Louise.

"Then we'll have to ride together this summer! I'm bringing up two horses. I'll give you a call at the end of June when we come up to the cottage, and we'll make a date."

True to her word, Mary called me when the snow had melted. She rode early in the morning, she told me, before too many mosquitoes were out to pester the horses. I dove into the trunk where I had put my riding breeches in mothballs nine years ago and hung them outside to air.

I was more than a little nervous. I didn't know this woman. Our first meeting had been a controlled affair. Flagg Avery's parents, who owned a summer home close to the Sawyers, had been invited to an afternoon tea, and I was sure Mary had been there because she'd been told to be. I pictured Mrs. Sawyer, who was anxious to keep us in town, saying to the Averys, "Come and meet the Dutch doctor and his wife. They're new in town."

What would this Mary Avery be like? She was probably a college graduate. The address given for sending the bill for the house call was in Weston, a Boston suburb. If she could spend the summers in their cottage by the lake, and bring two horses, she had to be well off. I didn't hold that against her, but it put her in a different category than most of the young, struggling women I knew, of which I was one. Would we have anything in common? Being from a different country might be interesting for the first few hours, but after that?

On the day of our ride, I woke up to a beautiful sunrise. I put on

Mary Avery

my breeches, riding boots and a short-sleeved blouse. On the drive over, I pumped myself up with confidence. There was more to me than just being my parents' daughter or my husband's wife. I'd begun to gather some credentials of my own. My command of the English language was improving. I'd mastered the hocus-pocus of medical insurance billing. I'd served as president of the Hospital Aid Society in Wolfeboro and done a passable job. Our Dutch friends called me Santa Titia because I was superintendent of the Sunday school across the street. Best of all, I was making progress in photography. One of my pictures had been chosen for exhibition in Cologne, Germany, at the Foto-Kina, a photographic industry show.

Two horses stood in a paddock by the side of the driveway that led down to an unpretentious barn-red cottage. Mary Avery walked out of the house the moment I turned off the motor. Her children were still asleep, she said. She'd brought a dependable teenager with her for the summer to watch over them. Obviously, Mary had supreme confidence she would return. I couldn't help thinking back to my one and only ride on Louise when I'd almost not come back. I prayed the horse Mary had brought up was not a leftover from the racetrack.

We walked up the hill to the paddock. I was way overdressed in my boots and wool breeches next to Mary in sneakers and dungarees. Thank God I'd been smart enough to leave my black riding jacket at home.

Mary had an easy way of showing me how to tack up the Appaloosa without making me feel like a complete idiot. She was a born teacher and had a lot of knowledge to impart.

The horses slowly woke up, making contented noises as if clearing their air passages after a good night's sleep. The steady rhythm of their four hooves hitting the rocky path had a quieting effect. I actually had time to look left and right, where delicate ferns poked their heads through the debris the previous fall had left behind.

Mary talked about spending her summers in New Hampshire as a child, at a farm where she had a pony and a cart. It was a dream come true to now own a horse. She kept her Morgan gelding in a paddock behind their house in Weston. The Appaloosa I was riding belonged to a friend who went to Cape Cod for the summer and couldn't keep her horse there.

As she spoke, the words falling as naturally as water flows through a brook, I looked at her small, straight back. It was like listening to a talk show on the radio. She had a third son, the eldest, twelve years old. His name was Linc. He would be coming back from a summer camp in

Maine in a few weeks. The other two were about the same ages as Joan and Paul.

By the time we were ready to trot, Mary knew why we'd left Holland, how we'd found Wakefield, how much I missed my mother. She had a way of zeroing in on the essence of my past and present. Her questions were well chosen. Not the standard question of how I liked it in the States, which would force me to give a standard reply.

It was a ride I would never forget. It opened up a part of New Hampshire I thought I knew but didn't. From my new vantage point in the saddle I could take an intimate look at the woods that I passed by at fifty miles an hour in a car. We went over paths normally used only by hunters and loggers. The child in me was transported to the days I spent watching the Dutch cavalry exercise around my parents' country house, before the war. Since we lived at a three-way intersection, the officers would get out the maps they carried in leather pockets attached to their saddles. It had intrigued me so much that I asked my mother for a large piece of paper and crayons so I could map out our entire neighborhood of farms, fields and woods.

After we untacked the horses and sponged off their sweat, Mary handed me a bathing suit. I dove into the clear water of Kingswood Lake. When I came up for air, a fairy tale world of shimmering water with reflections of the mountains in the distance surrounded me.

The day was still young. As was I. This was America. I was an American. Lucky me!

Chapter 30
Honduras

My mother had suggested that we look at the future in chunks of five years, to keep it manageable and not too overwhelming. She'd dropped this piece of wisdom in 1957, when she came over for Joan's baptism and we'd been in the States for not even half a year. Now it was 1968 and Gijs reminded me, pointedly, that eleven years was twice as long as he'd spent in any other place in his entire life. He had changed nationalities, and working in a rural community with a great need for medical care was satisfying and exciting, but was that all there would be to life? Just Wakefield, New Hampshire?

Obviously, his state of mind was ripe for the stories he heard from other doctors in the Netherlands-American Medical Society. One of them, Rob Meyer, told about how he spent his vacations in underdeveloped countries as a volunteer with Care-Medico. Even though the residents of Carroll County were relatively poor—with a few exceptions like Mrs. Burwell and other summer guests—they were not as needy as the patients Rob described. Rob treated malnutrition. Gijs treated obesity.

In the early spring, Gijs took off for the highlands of Honduras to work on a medical team in an outpost named Santa Rosa de Copan. There he spent a month treating the kind of diseases most doctors only know about from textbooks, and worked in a primitive hospital where one bed held two adults or four children, head to foot. Santa Rosa was cut off from the world without even as much as a telephone.

I moved into the Tripp house with Paul and Joan while Vic enlarged our kitchen at home. We received the first letter from Gijs after ten days. Joan and Paul hung on every word. Some of it they couldn't understand because it was too medically technical, but they latched on to the stories about the children in Santa Rosa who were infested with hookworms.

"Are they like the ones from the garden, you know, the kind Uncle Bob uses for fishing?" Paul asked.

"No, not that big. But however big they are, they're not good for you."

"What do they do to you?" Joan wanted to know.

"They eat your blood. Those poor kids have hundreds of them aboard."

"How do they get the worms inside their body?" Joan asked.

I told them the worms get inside through contaminated food. They had a hard time imagining how poor the people in Honduras were, and how remote the villages where they lived. In Sunday school they'd heard about hungry people, seen pictures of emaciated children on the envelopes for "One Great Hour of Sharing" that they put money in from their allowance. Now their father was there. It brought the suffering close to home.

"When I was as old as you are now, Paul," I told him, "I had worms, because we were in a war and we didn't have enough food and hardly any soap. When a war is going on, or you're very poor, you get sick faster and more often."

Suddenly, their worldview expanded to what it means to be poor or to be in a war. That their parents had gone through WW II had not really registered with them yet. They began to ask questions. Had I been hungry when I was their age? Not until the end of the war, I told them. The food didn't taste very good, because we didn't have enough sugar and practically no meat. How about Dad, they wanted to know. When I told them he'd been a prisoner, they wanted to know who'd put him in prison.

"The Japanese soldiers. Everyone with a white skin was driven into certain parts of the city. Then the Japs put a fence around them. There was no chance to escape because all the people outside the camp were colored."

How about Opa and Oma Bozuwa and Tante Janneke, they asked, and I told them as much as would be useful for them to know about their father's background without unduly worrying them. They were at an age where they would forever remember what I told them about their grandfather who'd spent the war years in Manchuria, and about their grandmother and aunt who'd had all the people who lived across the street move in with them.

"They were with forty people in that house!" I said. "Can you imagine? It would be as if our whole neighborhood came to live with us."

They hung on my words as I told them that when their father turned seventeen he was sent a notice that he had to go to a man's camp. He was allowed to take one blanket, two sets of underwear, two sets of clothes, a toothbrush and that was it. Books and writing material were forbidden.

"He couldn't read or write all that time?" Joan asked.

"That's right. But Dad told me that once, when he and some other prisoners were told to move a billiard table for the camp commander, they dropped it on purpose and then they took the pieces of slate—that's what a billiard table is made of—and used them to write on."

"Cool!" was Joan's reaction.

They wondered if Dad had been hungry and I retold the stories I'd heard Gijs refer to many times. The Japanese hadn't given their prisoners much food. For breakfast they got tapioca. For lunch they had a soup made of cut-up gut that was left over from the animals the Japanese guards ate. At night they got a little block of rice. They'd been hungry all the time.

"But your Dad had a great idea," I said. "He knew the natives lived on the other side of the fence. They had free-ranging chickens. He could see them through the barbed wire. He saved up some rice and laid a trail of kernels from the other side of the fence to a spot on his side where he'd put a basket upside down, held up by a stick. He attached a rope to the stick and held on to it while he hid in the bushes, waiting for a chicken to take the bait."

Gijs had told me he'd had to wait a long time but there was nothing else to do anyway. Finally, a chicken strayed in his direction. He whispered "Tok, Tok, Tok" to the chicken, and sure enough, she found the rice, got to the basket and puff, he'd pulled on the rope and the chicken was trapped.

"What did he do with the chicken," Paul asked. He kept chickens, sold their eggs, and wouldn't allow us to kill his hens.

"What do you think, silly? He ate it, of course!" Joan said.

Why didn't the people in Honduras have enough to eat, she wondered. Was there a war going on?

"No, there's no war. They're just very poor."

"Some kids in my class are poor." she said. "One boy in my class and his family must be very poor. His clothes are funny looking and he's dirty. But I like him. I think I'll marry him."

"Just like that? Marry him?" I asked.

"Well, then I can teach him to dress right and how to keep himself clean, talk right so he can get a good job. And then I'll divorce him."

When Gijs returned, he had lost sixteen pounds. Joan noticed it right away. He answered many of her questions. It wasn't a war that made the people in Honduras suffer from poverty and malnutrition, he told her. It was the system of government. He asked her to recite the pledge of allegiance, like she had to do in school every morning, and to think about the meaning of those words.

"Liberty and justice for all is not what the people of Honduras enjoy," he told her.

Gijs felt that going to treat patients in the back country for a month had been only a tiny drop in a very large bucket of needs. It had brought temporary relief, but it hadn't essentially changed conditions. For that to happen, the political system needed to be transformed. As long as a privileged few held all the cards, no amount of outside help from volunteers would alter the lives of the workers under their thumb. The Care-Medico people and the Peace Corps workers he'd met brought compassion, but each one was painfully aware they hadn't, and couldn't, effect a metamorphose. When they shared a beer at night on the terrace of their modest inn, they said to each other, "They don't need doctors here. What they need are plumbers."

The Honduran doctors had been hard to work with, Gijs said. They were only in Santa Rosa de Copan to fulfill a one-year obligation to the government. They accepted the very aspects that were repugnant to Gijs. They'd witnessed it all their lives: the poverty, the feudal system. Most of them had but one wish and that was to become a doctor in the United States.

It was a political problem in the end, he said.

Joan remembered his remarks and confronted him a few years later with his own words, when the course of her own life was threatened.

Chapter 31
A Visit from My Parents

A conspiracy had been plotted while Gijs was working in Honduras. Or was something floating in the air that affected Dutch doctors practicing in America? Whatever it was, I was stunned to find out that every Dutch doctor we'd befriended over the last few years and who'd stayed with us at the Tripp house, would be returning to Holland during the course of 1968.

Paul Hugenholtz was offered a professorship in cardiology in Rotterdam where he would set up a brand new cardiac center. It was an offer he couldn't refuse. He took Nora van Steenwijk, the crack operating room nurse from Montreal who visited with us often, with him. We'd known all along that Bob and Annelies Koumans would return, since Bob was in Boston on a fellowship. But Jos Ceha, a psychiatrist, and Jan Pameyer, a dentist, had come to the States with the same expectations as Gijs. They were going to build a life here, become a part of America.

If our friends found reasons to leave, then what were ours for staying? Each one of these highly specialized doctors was headed toward a bright future in medicine, and indeed, each of them eventually became a professor at various universities in Holland. The wives had no problem with returning. Life in America had been an exciting interlude, they said, but they were Europeans at heart. It was hard to define exactly what the differences were between living on the North American continent and the Western European one, but in broad strokes it had to do with the history of civilization that you felt all around you in Europe, even if you weren't looking for it. Then there were the ties with family and friends. It was so much easier to live where you feel you belong, they said, and if it was good for their husbands' future, then so much the better.

We were sailing into treacherous waters. My mother's five-year plan had been a stabilizing influence, but I saw the writing on the wall. The very fact that Gijs had even considered going to Honduras was an indication of restlessness. What would he think of next? What opportunities would there be in Holland for Gijs, who had not specialized? Had conditions improved in Holland for a family practitioner? If they hadn't, what would be the point? Would we even want to live in Holland again?

I was baffled by my own reaction. I, who had found leaving my country such a trauma, was now questioning if I wanted to return. Our parents would love it. Uncles and aunts who didn't have children themselves would dote on Joan and Paul. There would be college reunions to go to, friends to reconnect with. I had no difficulty imagining how it would be.

Yet something was holding me back. When I lived in France, in 1952, holding down a job as an English instructor at a small private school outside of Paris, I had come down with a terrible case of bronchitis and nothing worked to get me over it. I was run-down. My father advised me to get on the train and come home. He was disgusted with the kind of ancient treatments the near-blind old pastor, who was the headmistress's father and who lived on the third floor of the school, administered: a bag with hot mustard seeds on my chest and a ritual of putting cups on my back to extract "the bad fluids." But I refused. I had contracted for the whole school year. In the end, my mother solved the problem. I will never forget the sound of the creaking gate and the footsteps on the gravel path that made me get out of bed to see who was there. I couldn't believe my eyes. It was my mother, determined as always, with a handbag filled with powerful antibiotics and vitamins. Out of bed before dawn, she'd taken the train to Paris and braved her way to Montmorency. The *Ecole Joyeuse*, where I worked, was a long walk from the train station. But Mammie was determined because she knew that going home mid-term wasn't an option I would consider.

The more I imagined going back to Holland like the others, the more I got depressed. Gijs didn't talk about it much. He was either too busy catching up with his patients after a month of absence, or he was brewing on a plan. I didn't rock the boat. First, I had to figure myself out. The same thoughts kept chasing each other round and round, till I began to notice that each time I ended up resenting the idea of returning. It had been hard work building a practice in a rural area, becoming American citizens, and bringing up two children with a heritage that wasn't allowed to put their American experience in its shadow. A balancing act that took careful stepping around in the maze of choices. If we packed up, the last eleven years could be chalked up on life's calendar as "an interesting adventure." Putting it in those terms was repugnant to me. I had made the switch in my mind. I had sworn allegiance to the American flag and considered it a life-changing act. Unless Gijs, like Paul Hugenholtz and some of the others, could claim that he would make a valuable contribution to science and medicine in Holland, I would see going back as nothing more than opportunistic.

That Loes Hugenholtz would be leaving moved me to the core. She had become my best friend. When Loes talked, she painted with words. With fine brushstrokes she layered the familiar with the poetic. She had a way of turning a backyard into a magical world, a kingdom of gnomes where mushrooms turned into tables, broken sticks into a cathedral. Walking in the woods behind our meadow with Joan and Paul, she made them see how this land had been used for hundreds of years by pointing out the old apple tree that nourished the bears, the small strawberry plants the blue jays were after, the stone walls the first settlers had built as they turned the woods into meadows. She was always the first one to see deer tracks on the banks of the stream that ran through the woods. And when the crows screeched high up in the trees, Loes told the children that the birds were warning the other animals in the woods that humans were intruding their domain. Joan and Paul had walked those woods many times before, but they'd never seen what they saw when they walked there with Loes.

Loes had a micro way of thinking that set her apart. Unlike her husband, she didn't need mountaintops to conquer or oceans to sail in gale winds. What Loes longed for was a little house and a small yard, a bookcase with the world's best literature, a spade and a hoe. That way she would nurture every living thing under her care in a world apart from the world. She fascinated me and made me stop and look at myself. After remodeling our own house and then the Tripp house, I had embarked on remodeling the barn to accommodate the two horses we'd bought after my riding with Mary Avery the previous summer. There was always that next project, as if I was afraid to be without one. And the continuous activity was generated as much by Gijs as by myself. Loes was content just to be, while we put our energy into broadening a platform on which to build a life.

After all the Dutch friends had left, it was a blessing to have my parents in the Tripp house in the fall. September was their birthday month, and this trip was my father's seventieth birthday present to himself. He had sold the pharmacy and now was ready to enjoy his retirement. Mammie was exhausted from the upheaval of having to divide herself over remodeling our modest country house for more extensive summer use and outfitting a city apartment for winter living. She was ready for a break.

My parents eat breakfast in the Tripp House

During their one month stay, she established her own routine in the Tripp house. Plants appeared in the sunniest window. Each school day, Joan and Paul ran over to the Tripp house after the bus dropped them off, knowing that Oma had a special teacup for each and cookies in the closet. Oma would listen to their events of the day while mending a pile of clothes I had gleefully handed her. It was déjà vu watching her sit at the dining room table, surrounded by a sewing box, a pile of clothes and the teapot and tin with cookies.

When I went over early in the morning, after Gijs and the children had left, I could count on her sitting at the dining room table next to the teapot with a cozy pulled over it, waiting to have breakfast with my father who was a late riser. She poured me a cup of tea, buttered a piece of toast without asking me if I wanted it or not. Of course, although no longer a child, I was still her child. That would never change. But now, except for feeding me toast with more jelly than was good for me, she treated me more as friend than child as she allowed insights she wouldn't have before. The past year of preparing for my father's retirement had taken a toll, I sensed. Handling the closing of the pharmacy had brought out fundamental differences between my parents. Mammie had advocated more retirement provisions for his personnel, but Pappie had teased her that she was a "salon communist." His assistants would have a job at another pharmacy after his own closed, but they weren't provided a pension plan while some had worked for him for many, many years. I found this curious. My grandfather, who had sympathized with the Nazis and who had had to pay a big price for that poor judgment after the war, had originally been attracted to Hitler's laws of providing health care for everyone. He had personally fought for better social provisions as an alderman. That's what had got him on the wrong track of becoming a member of the Nationalistic Socialistic Movement. Was the son rebelling against the father at a late age?

Mammie's gift for creating harmony was often upset by Pappie, who had a gift for upsetting the predictable life his wife preferred. He lived by impulse. He got up when he woke up. He went to bed when he was tired. The times varied at both ends of the day, but the hour was always late. Oblivious of the tempo that the world at large adhered to, he lived in his own rhythm. My brothers and I had learned to step around in the minefield in our home, forever alert for an explosion when one parent caused the other parent's bucket of patience to spill over. The grandchildren learned to do the same.

When Joan was three, Paul just a baby, and the trains were still running from Wakefield to Boston, Mammie's patience ran out one night during their first visit to us. Pappie had jammed the movie camera when he tried to take out the film for developing. He looked exasperated and utterly defeated, as if the world had done this to him. His mind had never grasped the inner workings of modern apparatuses. Mammie, in front of Joan, exploded and snatched the camera from him to have me take a look at it. I couldn't budge the bowels of the thing either. Disgusted with both of us, she took up the phone and called Pim Visser, whom she'd met the weekend before. Pim had impressed her with his ability to install a hi-fi system in our living room. In a controlled and pleasant voice she asked if he might be able to fix the movie camera, and she arranged to meet him at his office in Boston the next day. She wrote down the address and told him she would take the train early the next morning. Then she turned around to the three of us who stood in stunned silence and said, *"Ziezo, dat is geregeld."*

Pappie told her she was out of her mind. How would she ever find an office in Boston with Pim in it? While her grandparents quarreled, Joan sat as quiet as a mouse in her high chair.

At dawn, Gijs brought his mother-in-law to the train, and after supper I took Pappie and Joan to the station downtown to pick her up. The train was chugging around the bend as I pulled up to the platform. There was Mammie, looking radiant and elegant in her Dutch linen suit, her round face framed by a jaunty summer hat. The conductor helped her down the high steps of the train compartment. Joan, who'd been visibly apprehensive about meeting Oma with a last memory of her as a ball of fury, took a careful look before she ran up to her. Mammie stooped down, put her packages on the pavement and pressed her granddaughter to her bosom.

On the way home, sitting in her lap, she listened eagerly to how Oma had found Pim in his office near South Station. He had taken the camera apart during his lunch hour and fixed it. She had toured the city in a sightseeing bus and visited the State House, Bunker Hill, Paul Revere's house, the North Church. And she'd even found time to buy slippers for Joan at Filene's. Pappie sat next to her in the backseat and held her hand while his wife regaled us with her keen observations

In 1968, the trains weren't running anymore from Wakefield to Boston, or to anywhere else. Paul had turned from a baby into an eight-year-old and Joan was close to becoming a teenager. But Opa and Oma hadn't changed a bit. They had a way of providing moments of bliss as well as tension, each one memorable.

One day, Paul decided that he wanted to show Opa the small fiberglass rowing boat he'd bought with the savings from his egg route. It was kept at the Averys' cottage. On one of those splendid warm September afternoons, I drove my parents and Paul over there. I carried two aluminum folding-chairs to the deck near the water while Paul rowed his super-light blue boat over to a spot where it would be easy for his grandfather to get in. His blond head bobbed back and forth as he rowed, my father facing him, an English tweed cap topping his head. When they neared the dock, Paul steered his boat parallel to the dock and as near to it as he could. Pappie grabbed the ladder, pushed off to set his foot on the first rung, but the boat, light as a feather, drifted away from him and he fell backward into the lake. Paul looked stricken. Soon, my father's cap emerged, his head still under it. There was much splashing about and we heard gurgling sounds from his throat. Pappie had never been an enthusiastic swimmer, less so with his clothes and shoes on.

Paul jumped overboard to help his grandfather up the ladder, and then quickly retrieved his boat before it could drift off to the middle of the lake. Moments later, they stood before us, dripping wet, their clothes clinging to their bodies in sharp pleats. They looked at each other and burst into laughter. But their smiles froze when they turned around and faced my mother while a puddle of water formed around their feet. In the overwhelming sudden silence, I could hear the trickle of water from their

My parents in rare form

shoes hit the water below as it fell through the cracks of the deck.

"*Gerard!*" my mother screamed. "For heaven's sake, how can you do such a stupid thing? Look at your beautiful leather jacket. It is ruined. It will be all water stains. And we have to go to the Hopewells for dinner. We'll be too late!"

Paul stole a look at Opa.

"It was my fault, Oma. Really."

Oma ignored him. She gripped the armrest of the deck chair, preparing to get up. It was a major effort to propel her stout body out of the low chair. Its aluminum frame creaked under her weight. Then, a moment later it gave and collapsed. Paul's grandmother landed with an impressive thud on the wooden boards and lay spread out on the deck, on her side with the hem of her skirt way up her thighs. Paul's eyes widened. He didn't know what to do.

I saw a gleam in my father's eyes, but he didn't say anything. Mammie lay still for a moment, stunned by this turn of events. Before I could get to her, she'd straightened up and sat looking at her exposed thighs. None of us knew what to say. We'd seen the dark look in her eyes moments before she fell.

Mammie glanced up, saw Paul in his soaked clothes, her husband with a widening ring of water around his shoes, all eyes fixed upon her, and she got the giggles. What a relief! All four of us doubled over laughing, and I packed everybody, wet or not, into the station wagon to bring them home. It made for good conversation around the Hopewells' dining room table that night.

It was a dream come true to have my parents live next door. I could cross the driveway any time I wanted and see my father nestled in the comfortable wing chair Mr. Lewis had donated when we first arrived in Wakefield, with a pile of books and magazines next to him. My mother was either tending the plants or she sat at Miss Tripp's desk that Paul had bought at the auction, writing lengthy letters to the family back home. In her clear, rounded handwriting she made comparisons about the weather— so much warmer, even in September; the vegetation more prolific though the seasons were shorter by at least two months; and about going to the church across the street where people were cheerful and forthcoming but the sermons less profound than she was used to.

Mammie engaged Paul and Joan intellectually. Not just interested in their grades, she wanted to know what books they read, if they were taught more than one language, how they spent their days at school. Joan, in turn, challenged her with her own questions. Being all of eleven years old, she'd begun to criticize teachers and ministers. At the church, ministers had followed one another in swift succession, and none of them had been intensely involved with the Sunday school curriculum or how the children were brought into the ranks of believers. Coloring pictures of sheep and their shepherds seemed to be enough for them, and I wondered sometimes what would happen if I taught communism down there in the church's basement. Not that I wanted to, but I was sure the minister would never find out. Recently though, our church had attracted a new minister, a woman, whom I respected. Joan, however, didn't take to her.

"Oma, who was the first person to have the idea there is a God?" she asked. "I tried to look it up in the encyclopedia but I couldn't find the answer."

"That's the wrong place to look," my mother answered.

"Where should I look then? Oh, I know. You're going to tell me to look in the Bible!"

"Well, that's one place to look. What is it exactly you want to know? Why is it important to you to know who the first person was who thought there was a God?"

"That would prove that somebody dreamed it all up," Joan said. She thought she was being very smart and she knew she was challenging her grandmother.

"Don't you believe there is a God?"

"Nobody can prove it!"

"Because you can't see God?"

"Yes." Some hesitancy was creeping into her voice. "I mean, the minister is always reading from that big book. But those stories were written a long time ago. That was back then. They don't make me believe there is a God."

When my mother reported this conversation, I remembered thinking the same way as a child, but at her age I hadn't dared voice such thoughts.

"I understand," my mother said to Joan. "Just remember this: we don't see God. We feel God."

The next day, Mammie walked over to the library next door and asked Lillian Brown to show her the children's section. When Joan and Paul came home from school and ran over to the Tripp house for their tea and cookies, Mammie sat them down on the couch, herself in the middle, and read the book by Irene Hunt she had checked out. It was nicely illustrated and Paul especially liked the upside down saucepan Johnny Appleseed wore on his head. Both listened intently to how he helped the people migrate to the West from New England by giving them healthy seeds. Mammie put special emphasis on the last pages where a young girl, whose life had been saved by Johnny Appleseed, wept when she heard of his death. "How can you say he's dead," her brother had said to her, "when all through the Ohio Valley there is this morning a trail of apple blossom?"

"This is how you can think of God," Mammie said to Joan. "You can think of Johnny Appleseed as Jesus. His father had taught him how to grow apples. He gave the seeds to others and taught them how to tend an apple orchard. He spread the message. The apple orchards multiplied until nobody could remember who'd given the seeds or who had taught them what to do with them."

Two months after my parents returned to Holland, Paul's Labrador got run over after she jumped off a snow bank and landed under the tires of a passing car. Gijs cancelled his evening office hours and we all piled into the car to take the dog to the vet. Paul was sad beyond words. His dog was in shock, breathing with great difficulty. It lay on a folded blanket in between the children on the backseat. Paul sat like a statue, but Joan was all action, stroking Jip's soft fur. The vet thought a tire had gone over her pelvis. He got a reaction in her hind legs, but her tail was broken. No telling what organs had been damaged. He would keep her overnight for observation.

On the way home, Gijs prepared the children for an unfortunate outcome. He gave Jip a 10 percent chance for survival. Paul and I were in tears, but Joan scolded us for not having faith. She made Paul kneel beside her in front of his bed, next to the chair that wore the imprint of Jippy's body from the nights she slept there curled up into a black ball.

"Thank you God," Joan prayed out loud, "for having Jippy live a happy life for eight months. Please make her better. Amen."

Jip survived. Joan wrote her grandmother about the accident. She ended with, "I was the only one, Oma, who had faith that Jippy would get better, and she did!"

It was wonderful to see how my children indulged in being grandchildren. Joan put a tennis racket in my father's hands and begged him to teach her how to play after she learned he'd made it to the national semi-finals in Holland before the war. The Averys had a tennis court near their cottage on the lake, and Joan was impressed with Linc Avery's ability to play tennis with his father. Pappie showed her how to hold the racket, how to swing it for maximum effect.

Their visit was timely. With practically all of our Dutch acquaintances and good friends gone back to Holland, I was trying to regroup. Could I live here without that Dutch connection? The Hopewells were also going to leave soon. Bob would be working for Outward Bound in Colorado.

I knew I could count on my mother to put my life into perspective. Mammie gave me heart. She warned that we shouldn't idealize Holland.

"Don't think you could have a practice like this anywhere in Holland, Gijs! A doctor in a rural area in Holland doesn't have the freedom you have. And I doubt he would have two horses and two ponies in the barn with enough meadow to let them roam in."

Mammie also pointed out that we shouldn't think just of ourselves. Joan and Paul would have more opportunities on this side of the ocean. She was impressed with how they learned at school to have confidence to speak in public by having to give oral reports. And if I thought the teaching wasn't always in depth, then I should supplement their learning with my own effort.

"You can create your own world, Titia. Don't underestimate what you have to offer them," she said. "If you read books, they will read books. If you are interested in history or art, they will be interested in history and art. If you speak more than one language, they will want to do the same. Trust yourself. My father taught me how to play the piano when we lived on the island where nobody else even had a piano."

Chapter 32

Saying Good-bye to Vic Bezanson

"So, who will inherit Vic Bezanson's estate?" the librarian asked me two weeks after Vic died.

I looked up from the children's section where I was hunting for a book on horses for Paul. The question, one I'd been brought up never to ask of anyone, jolted me. The tone of voice suggested she already knew, or in any case suspected, who would be Vic's heirs.

"Vic had a sister with two children," I said, "and Rose also had a sister, I believe. And they were close to a friend on the North Shore, where they came from. The friend's daughter is married to a minister. " This was all I told her.

I checked out the book for Paul and left. As I walked the few yards back to our house, I felt I had been pumped for information. As I often was at the hairdresser's. But there, at least, I expected it. A doctor's wife must know a lot about the people in town!

Yet the reason the librarian asked me who would inherit from the Bezansons, and why I was defensive about it, had little to do with what I knew as a doctor's wife. After Rose, Vic's wife, died in January of 1969, Vic was desperately lonely. He proclaimed all over town that the Bozuwas were now the only family he had.

When the Spencers sold us "the Roberts place" in 1958, Vic had practically come with the deal. Every morning he showed up in his green Chevy, a faded Stetson on his graying hair, a cigar with a plastic mouthpiece clenched between his false teeth. Soon he moved his table saw into our barn. He was an amazing worker, quick as lightning. Over the years he built us a kitchen, an addition to the office, closets, bureaus, cabinets, and he did it all by himself. After our home was transitioned from a farmhouse of the past to a doctor's house in the sixties, he started on the Tripp house. He pointed out its authentic qualities, and we deliberated at great length about how to put in heating ducts without cutting through the old timbers.

But what gave him the most pleasure was building things for the children. Vic and I often went into cahoots to plan their birthday surprises. Right under their eyes, in the barn, he built beds for them with drawers for their toys underneath, and he took childish pleasure in dreaming up fibs when they asked him what he was making. "Oh, just a chicken coop for myself."

Another year, he fitted a dollhouse inside the unused fireplace in their bedroom. The greatest surprise had been a little store. While they were away at school, I painted it red and green and Vic put the letters "Joan and Paul's Country Store" on it in white. It had a counter, shelves, a child-size door and a roof with real shingles. He'd made it so we could take it apart and bring it to the Hospital Street Fair in Wolfeboro, where it was every child's envy as Paul and Joan doled out cones with crushed ice and syrup, selling them for a quarter each.

Joan and Paul's country store

It made for a lot of fun to have Vic around, but it wasn't always easy. If you were his friend, he put you on a pedestal, with the ever-present danger that you might find yourself crashing down from that lofty height. People who moved to the area would ask us who was doing the carpentry for us. Vic would go over, work for a while, but then something inevitably happened and he quit. Never would he go back there again. No, sir! One of our new acquaintances was a Dutch opera singer who'd bought an old farm for a summer place. Vic's linear thinking was no match for her artistic will to accomplish perfection. She had great vision but lacked understanding of how a New England wooden house differed structurally from a Dutch brick one. "That woman is crazy," Vic said, "She better find somebody else to cut her house up. I'll be damned if I do it!"

He wasn't angry but very hurt when another friend, who'd hired him to do some work, took him to task about religion over a cup of coffee. Vic was no match for Harry's debating skills, which had been honed at the best schools on the East coast. Vic was a faithful member of the Episcopal Church, and he enjoyed going there, all dressed up and proud of the beautiful woman at his side. Harry, who was in active combat with God, challenged Vic unmercifully. Vic came straight to our house afterward and looked upset, beaten and diminished. I tried to calm him down. The most important thing, I told him, was to have a faith and know how to live that faith.

I had no difficulty imagining what had gone on in Harry's kitchen. I'd seen Harry debate the same points over dinner when Paul and Loes Hugenholtz stayed with us. Gijs, Loes and I gave up after a while, but Paul stood his ground till the early morning hours. Paul simply stated, over and over again, that he believed in God. You either believe or you don't, he said. It was a memorable night, and, to his credit, Harry called up the next morning to say he knew he'd been beaten. I thought it an interesting term. Paul hadn't had any desire to beat Harry. He just wasn't going to be made to say that it was unintellectual, not to say stupid, to believe in God. I would never forget the utter calm with which Paul listened and made his own point clear. Needless to say, Vic did not want to work for Harry after that.

Vic's life pivoted around his wife Rose. He walked beside her in awe. Rose made him look respectable. She came to our office dressed for the city, in a mink stole over a silk dress, her hair impeccably done up in a French roll, her hands soft and elegant with diamond rings. She carried herself well. They had moved up from Marblehead, an upscale town on the coast. Vic had built up a good business there. During WW II he'd

served as a navy officer on some islands in the Indian Ocean, building
airstrips. Those had been heady days, and he showed pictures of himself
to Paul and Joan, looking dapper in a starched white uniform, standing
in the shade of palm trees, his officer's cap cocked jauntily on his head.
He'd contracted malaria, but other than that he'd enjoyed himself, he
said. In the mid-fifties he'd sold his business and bought a piece of land
in Wakefield with a view that led the eye over sloping meadows toward
Lovell Lake, with Mount Washington looming spectacularly in the
distance. But after building his house on it, he was too much of a worker
to sit idly at home.

Vic with Paul

Vic and Rose didn't have children and there was no evidence of
family, except for Vic's vinegary father who had come to live with them.
The only other relative I was aware of was his sister, equally cantankerous
to live with, Vic said. He had broken off with her long ago.

The attraction of working at our house, Vic told me, was having
young children around. Paul carried Vic's tools around and spent hours

watching him sawing, hammering and fitting. Paul knew what "plumb" and "level" meant by the time he went to first grade. It made as much a difference in Vic's life as in mine when Joan and Paul started school. He felt lonely eating his lunch by himself, not sharing his sandwiches sitting on a sawhorse with the kids in the barn. Rose had become involved in the children's lives indirectly by carefully choosing extras for them in Vic's lunch box. I speculated that Vic told Rose how Joan and Paul had liked that special milk shake she made, with honey and a raw egg, because soon his thermos held enough for the three of them. Paul and Joan also got money for good report cards and pennies to buy candy with.

Vic talked about Rose as "Grammy" to them. Joan lifted her eyebrows when he first introduced the idea of calling her that.

"My grandmothers live in Holland, Vic. We call them 'Oma,'" she said.

"I know," Vic said quickly, "but Rose is your American grandmother." Joan looked at me for help.

"That's like *Tante* Loes Hugenholtz, Joan," I said. "She isn't really your aunt, but you call her that because she feels like family to us."

Oh," Joan said, but she never called Rose "Grammy." Instead, both children called her "Mrs. Vic," and Vic remained Vic.

Rose had a heart attack in January of 1968 and a year later she died. Vic tried to get on with his life. The miniature poodle he'd given Rose to keep her company while she was sick, and whom she'd named Duchess, received an overload of affection. Duchess ate hamburger for breakfast and ground tenderloin for dinner. He took her everywhere. Joan's collie shepherd, Princess, and Paul's Labrador retriever, Jip, towered over this curly, furry ball of energy and they ignored her precocious barking. When they got enough of her, they growled and moved to a quieter spot.

Paul, who at nine still held my hand when we crossed the street in Wolfeboro and didn't care if his schoolmates saw him do this, and who still crawled into bed with us every morning to watch Captain Kangaroo and Mr. Green Jeans on TV, sensed Vic's need for affection. They played cards together and built saddle racks in the barn. Joan, approaching thirteen, had discovered the teenage shell to crawl into. Hours on end were spent in her own room upstairs. Paul felt left out from the space she was creating there for herself with magazines and posters of The Partridge Family on the wall, and he announced he didn't want to become a teenager. He spent time with Vic instead. Try as he might, Vic's old trick of giving the kids pennies didn't work on Joan. She wasn't for sale and she politely ignored him and retreated into her expanding, internal world.

Vic shrank his workload after Rose died. Just a few odd jobs here and there. We noticed he was slowing down, coughed a lot, but then, he always had a cigar in his mouth. He showed up daily, Duchess under his arm, the cigar with the white plastic mouthpiece between his lips. I began to anticipate the slow crawling of his green Chevy over the gravel on our driveway. He had a special way of rapping on the door that led from the barn into our sunroom. One hard rap, three short ones, followed by a long one. It sounded like an S.O.S. sign, a command as well as a plea. No matter what I was doing—paying bills, writing letters, doing dishes, answering the telephone, making appointments for patients—Vic would not wait for the door to be opened. He was part of the family and by walking in he proved that fact, that wish, again and again. He unloaded his burdens of loneliness. The children were at school, Gijs made rounds at the hospital, and I listened to Vic and watched helplessly as he hurtled himself toward the end of his life. His lean body was getting ever leaner, his cough more persistent, his strong will to live buried alongside his Rose.

When I came back from a trip to Holland in September—my mother turned seventy, and my brothers had me come over as a gift to her—Vic beamed. During my absence he had concocted a plan with Gijs to make a riding ring in the meadow as a surprise. From his car parked in the field he had called out his instructions to Gijs, Paul and Joan on how to dig postholes, cut lumber and hammer the rails to the posts. The four of them couldn't wait to have me view their handiwork. Joan and Paul tacked up my horse and handed her to me. Never mind that I had just completed a transatlantic flight, or that I wore a skirt. I had to mount my horse and ride around the new riding ring. Vic in his car, Gijs leaning against it with the children, wore a look of immense satisfaction.

It was the last construction job Vic tackled.

I think he already knew, before Gijs took X-Rays and ran blood tests, that he had lung cancer. Once the fact was proven, Vic approached his demise in the same way he had tackled construction jobs: with total dedication, planning and haste. He was alone in the world and dropped strong hints that he wanted us to act as his son and daughter. I began to take a hand in his daily life. I could see that Vic hadn't done any of the housework Rose, who had been a meticulous housewife, used to do.

A film of dust covered the mahogany furniture, hiding the lustre of the well-appointed living room. Vic passed the time in the den where he sat dressed in his old work clothes because he thought they wouldn't show the egg yolk drops he spilled on them, or the ashes from his cigar. The TV ran nonstop without being looked at, just for the noise it made and the sound of a human voice. The dishes grew mold in the sink, dirty clothes lay in a heap in the corner of the bedroom and his bed wasn't made. I couldn't bear it. We had an extra house; we could take care of him.

When we told him of our plans, Vic was like an engine on the verge of collapse, letting out one last, loud bang. He immediately packed me in his green Chevy and drove us to his lawyer in Rochester; to appoint Gijs and me as his guardian who could handle his affairs, I thought. Once there, it became obvious that Rose and Vic had decided, even before Rose became ill, that they would leave their earthly belongings to Joan and Paul Bozuwa. I protested. Clear in my memory were stories in the Dutch newspapers about a certain Dr. Adams who lived in a seaside resort in England. I think it was Brighton. Dr. Adams had been so very, very kind to old widows in town, taking tender care of them until their death, the story read. When the numbers began to add up, of the dead widows and the estates they'd left Dr. Adams, it became evident that he had relieved them not only of their earthly possessions, but of their lives as well. So, I worried how it would look in a small town like Wakefield if the local doctor tended a couple till their deathbed and then was left their estate?

The lawyer sat quietly behind his impressive oak desk. He was an older man with wise eyes behind his metal-rimmed spectacles. He listened patiently to my fearful objections. This had been the will of Rose as well as Vic, he observed. It would give Vic peace of mind, he said, if he could leave this earth with his affairs and belongings in the hands of people he had respected and trusted. I told him I had to think about this for a moment. Vic, next to me in a roomy leather fauteuil looking as thin as a matchstick, exuded urgency. He hated his sister with a passion, he said. He didn't have children. Was there a cause he was passionate about? I asked him. Yes, he said. I care about your children's future.

"It's hard to accept," I said. "I'm flattered, obviously, and grateful. But on the other hand, I struggle if we can accept this from you."

"Why would you struggle when Rose and I want Joan and Paul to have it? It could pay for their education."

"Because I don't want Paul and Joan to grow up expecting to get things from others. They should be who they are without being calculated about it."

"They didn't ask for it. You didn't ask for it," Vic said. That was true. Vic had been the one doing the asking. He had always desperately wanted the children to love him.

"This might sound ungrateful and disrespectful," I said, "but promise me one thing: never, ever mention the word inheritance to the children. They like you a lot. You've been a part of their lives as long as they can remember. Let's not get their feelings for you mixed up by such a big gift."

By the time we left the lawyer's office, my signature was on Vic's savings account. I felt very strange putting it there. Was I a good actress in the lawyer's eyes, a manipulative mother, out to get the best for her kids? After years of settling estates, he might be cynical enough to have such thoughts. But if that was so, he didn't show any of it. He'd made no effort to steer Vic onto another course.

I don't know if the Wakefield librarian ever found out who inherited from the Bezansons, but I suspect she did. It wouldn't have been hard to put her ear to the ground and hear a voice more willing than mine to inform her. Vic had told Sarah, from Sarah's Spa, exactly what he planned to do and why, which was as effective as putting it in the paper since the Spa was the center of town, the place where you would find the plumber, the carpenter or the information you needed. If there was anyone with evil suspicions we never heard about it, directly or indirectly.

We installed Vic in the Tripp house, in a small room downstairs with his TV set at the foot of his bed, a basket for Duchess on the side. A bottle of household ammonia stood on the nightstand beside him. Whenever he had trouble breathing, which was most of the time, he held it up to his nose and took a deep sniff. This was his own invention and it seemed to work for him. Gijs reassured me that it couldn't harm him. If Vic was rugged enough to take it, then let him do it and believe in its temporary relief.

Paul walked straight to the Tripp house after the school bus dropped him off, let out Duchess and kept Vic company, playing a card game or watching TV with him. At five-thirty Joan went over and coaxed Vic over to our house to have supper, holding his hand while he slowly progressed, step by step, over the gravel of the driveway.

Vic was losing ground rapidly, but he didn't complain. He was firmly focused on the last bend in the road ahead. He was going to enjoy his grandchildren now that he'd taken care of his affairs. One last thing we had to do for him. While he was parked in the driveway of his house, he instructed us what to do with the stuff we hauled out. He'd made his funeral arrangements. He was ready.

I wasn't surprised when Paul said to me, "I don't blame Vic for wanting to die. And you know what? It makes it easier to accept that he's going to."

In the spring of the same year we'd lost one of the ponies. Brandal had cut himself in the groove of his jaw on barbed wire. It had become infected, went too long unnoticed and, one evening, Gijs and I found him dead in his stall. We got him buried before the children woke up the next morning. It had been a sad, tearful day. Joan put the American flag in our backyard half-mast. It was their first real loss. They were incredulous that one day their pony could have been running through the fields, munching on the very grass that covered him the a few days later. Joan had put herself on a stool next to Sambal's stall, as she had the day he'd arrived in our barn, and talked to him to console him. The inevitability of death had penetrated their young minds.

Vic spent his last day a week before Christmas. The night before his funeral a foot of snow fell. The people Vic and Rose had worshiped with arrived in galoshes and filled up half of the church. I was touched to see Harry's wife slip discreetly into a pew in the back. The sun penetrated through the stained-glass windows at its low December slant, illuminating the coffin before the altar. An American flag, its colors of white, red and blue brightening the otherwise sober church interior, covered it. Military pallbearers stood next to the coffin and, at the appropriate time, folded the flag with great ceremony, one fold at a time, until it was reduced to a small triangle. One of the uniformed men handed the flag to me. I held it pressed to my bosom as Gijs and I followed the coffin out of the church, down the steps to where it was slid into a black hearse with its motor running, creating white steam in the frosty air.

We watched the Cadillac pull out of the driveway, turn onto the road, down the steep hill. It started to slide sideways on the slick, snow-covered road. The driver tried to right the car, but the hearse slid to the other side. He recovered it and continued to slip-slide all the way to the bottom of the hill where he turned it onto Route 109, toward Boston and cremation.

Vic would have liked that ending, I thought, keeping everyone in suspense. It would have tickled his ever-ready sense of humor. When we came home from the funeral, his green Chevy stood parked in our yard as it had since Vic moved into the Tripp house. Encased in snow, it looked like a frosted cake. When Gijs wanted to move it to another spot, it wouldn't start. A mechanic from the local garage was called. He couldn't budge the car either. Like its longtime owner it was stubborn and worn-out. We had it towed away. Vic would have liked that too. It had all gone the way he'd wanted.

Chapter 33
A Trip to
Holland with the Averys

The late spring of 1969 found the Averys, five of them, and the four of us Bozuwas, on a big fishing boat in Holland. We were traveling on 'Het IJsselmeer', a huge lake that until 1932 had been an inland sea. Sharing a boat made from steel and not for comfort would make or break our bond. A friend of a friend had known about the "Urker" vessel, which came with a skipper and heavy maroon-colored sails. It looked like a barge, but when the wind blew hard it could outrun any fancy yacht. Luckily, it also had a powerful diesel motor to get us into small harbors and through narrow canals. The skipper's name was Harold, a hippie in his twenties, tall, lean and bearded, his hair falling in curls to his shoulders, full of himself and proud of his boat. All five children slept in hammocks in the bow, Mary and I on beds in the main cabin, Flagg and Gijs on mattresses out on the open deck.

"Wait till I tell my men I slept on number two boiler plate on my vacation!" Flagg chuckled. "His men" welded stainless steel together with the utmost precision to form vessels for nuclear power plants.

On the windy days, the stiff canvas sails billowed out, straining the ropes and wooden pulleys, while seagulls followed in our wide wake hoping for parts of a catch. They recognized the tub like hull of a fishing boat. With a good wind the boat tilted and sent the dishes in the cabin sliding from one end to the other. The sound of the waves against the bow, the creaking of the wooden masts and the smell of the water brought me back to that time after the war when I'd spent the summers sailing in Friesland, the province where my mother had lived her teenage years. It boasted the largest lakes in the country, and some of the richest clay. Huge cows, the famous Friesians, dotted the flat landscape of lush green meadows. I still had relatives there. Tall, big-boned, blue-eyed, unsentimental people who viewed the world with a ready sense of humor, but who underneath their jokes hid an inflexible nature, as hard to ply as the clay they'd grown up on.

When Mary and I hatched the plan to go to Holland with both our families, I suggested a boat big enough to hold all of us, because Holland is best seen and understood from the water. Water is a Dutchmen's best friend and his worst enemy. It wrote his story over the centuries. To keep the water at bay he had to build dikes and erect windmills. Holland's location on the North Sea had opened up the world to trade. Dutch ships loaded with tea, coffee, spices and rubber had plied the oceans for centuries returning from the East and West Indies, Africa, New York, Brazil. Holland's merchants, farmers and admirals owed their fame and wealth to the water. Now its smart engineers were subduing it to create land for a burgeoning population. Portions of what once was an inland sea were encircled with dikes, the water pumped out. Thousands of acres for farming and housing had resulted. What was left was the enormous lake we were sailing on.

The towns where we anchored for the night: Staveren, Hoorn, Spakenburg and Hindeloopen, were monuments to the days when vessels left the small harbors daily, except on Sundays, and set sail for the fishing grounds off Scotland for herring, or to Norway and the Baltic countries for lumber. After they got cut off from the North Sea forever, a period of steep decline followed. The stately homes built by rich merchants and sea captains still lined the narrow canals, standing proud in their brick splendor like their counterparts on the island of Nantucket. But these days, the harbors had been reduced to marinas for pleasure boats.

Some people still wore costumes typical for the town they lived in, and the churches still filled every Sunday with God-fearing people dressed in sober suits and dresses. All black, even their socks and stockings. The message from the pulpit was severe, the hold of the minister on his flock firm but slipping in the face of a rapidly changing world.

It galled the citizens that they had to make their living off frivolous pleasure instead of the honest, hard work they used to do; and they resented making their living as servants to tourists from far away, Germany even, who wore uncouth clothing on Sundays and exhibited habits the ministers had told them would lead them straight to hell. Now they were their bartenders, their chefs and their skippers. They felt reduced by it.

How could they uphold their own principles, their strict religious beliefs in the face of these baneful influences? Would the next generation be able to maintain their culture? It was the same story as we'd heard along the coast of Maine and on Cape Cod. Change comes hard, but it comes as surely as the tides and one can't hold it back.

The five children on our steel boat weren't thinking about Holland's past or future. They were living in the now of childhood, and that meant sneaking off to buy candy, fight over the best seat on deck and, for the two older Avery boys, jockeying for position. The position was Joan. Paul Avery was her age, Linc two years older, and as kids will do, Joan looked up to the eldest in the group. He took advantage of this fact of life, which didn't please his brother Paul. Some innocent experimenting was probably going on under the bow of "Willempje", our wonderful, unlikely vacation vessel. The Avery boys, who didn't have a sister, now had a girl in their bedroom! Eruptions of laughter, secretive giggling, bickering and cries of fighting came from their quarters. Linc knew he was winning Joan and he was playing it cool. Joan knew she had all four boys in her pocket, and she was very content.

Mary and I were the cooks. Armed with big canvas shopping bags we went on shore, in and out of small, immaculately clean stores: the butcher, the baker, the fresh-vegetable farmer, the grocer who hadn't been overtaken by the supermarket yet. Mary wanted to know about everything that was displayed in the stores, being a naturally curious person and a stickler for detail. She was as amazed at the different cuts of meat as I had been when I first came to the States.

While Mary and I tried to throw a meal together in a space about one tenth the size of our kitchens back home, Gijs and Flagg relaxed on deck with a beer, and the kids played ball on little meadows next to the harbor. In Spakenburg, some local kids on wooden shoes came to watch from the sidelines. They quickly concluded that our kids were foreigners and that they didn't know how to play soccer. Well-aimed pieces of rotted fish sailed through the air and hit Paul Avery in the face. He exploded with anger and came back to our ship—reeking of herring way beyond its prime—to wash his face and put on a clean shirt.

The other four children were luckier in ducking the foul-smelling fish. Harold, our skipper, interfered and invited the rascals to play with them. On their wooden shoes they outran our sneakered kids, but at least the fish throwing stopped.

The Averys helped us align the two countries at opposite ends of the Atlantic Ocean. We had carefully encapsulated our memories of Holland. As we compared Holland to America, we always thought of the two countries as being very different. Sailing through the Dutch landscape with American friends on board opened up a new premise. Maybe it was time to think about the various ways these countries resembled each other. After all, both were part of the same Western civilization and our mainstream religions rooted in the same Bible. Furthermore, the struggle to be free from foreign domination had shaped America as much as it had shaped Holland.

This soggy plot of meadows behind the dunes, called the Netherlands, with its fickle weather and water all around, had created a national character that could be labeled as industrious and inventive. It was not as easy to peg the American national character, because it entailed such a vast area. The obstacles faced by mountain people were not the same as the ones faced by fishermen in small boats on an angry sea. Walls of snow and bitter cold shaped a man differently than a balmy trade wind. An American living in the deserts of Nevada had to be a very different American from a farmer on the plains of Kansas. Yet foreigners labeled them all the same. It would be better to compare New England to the Netherlands and to see what the two regions had in common: a demanding climate that fosters a silent tenacity in its inhabitants.

When Gijs and I first immigrated, practically everything we saw was new to us and different from what we had learned as children and young adults. The small aspects of daily life didn't feel familiar. That was the key word. It didn't feel familiar to us to take a car instead of a bicycle to get to the grocery store. It didn't feel familiar to exchange big gifts, wrapped up in expensive paper and done up with a shiny bow, at Christmas. It seemed strange to see people we visited open the refrigerator and make a sandwich on the counter instead of waiting to have lunch with the rest of the family at the dining room table. It was bizarre to have the TV on all day with hardly looking at it, and to see children in their pajamas watching cartoons on Saturday mornings.

But was Holland in 1969 the same country we'd left in 1957?

On the few visits back, Gijs and I had sought out the old villages, the traditional farms sitting in green polders and the fishing boats moored in quaint harbors. The recognition of these familiar places had been balm for our souls, reinforcing our treasured memories. Flagg Avery, without setting out to do so, pointed up what had changed. He noticed the rows upon rows of apartment buildings that spilled into the meadows beyond the city walls. Marx blocks, he called them. Traditional costumes were a rarity in the streets. The shop windows displayed the fancy non-essential stuff that hadn't been there during and following the war. Holland had climbed from austerity into consumerism. In conversations with our hippie skipper, Flagg quickly pinpointed an attitude among the young people they expected to be coddled from cradle to grave. Artists were supported whether they produced art or junk. Where was that toughness the people had displayed during the war, and what had happened to religion? The biggest church in my hometown had been reduced to rubble. Not by the Nazis during the war, but afterward, by developers who replaced it with a shopping mall.

While Gijs and I struggled to grasp the shift from an austere post-war society to a self-confident, self-indulging one that embraced a sort of socialistic capitalism, Mary and Flagg allowed our Dutch relatives and friends to focus on similarities between themselves and Americans. It had always been easier to see the differences. Dutch perceptions of Americans had been shaped by Hollywood movies and GI's stationed in Germany, who spent lavishly with their strong dollars. Americans were loud, sex-obsessed, not very erudite, dressed like clowns and generally lacked good taste. Everything American was king-sized, shiny and gaudy. But the Averys didn't fit that mold, our relatives had to admit. It was something of a revelation to them.

After our sailing adventure we stayed with my parents in Breda. The country house couldn't hold all nine of us, but it was great weather and we set up a tent for the boys to sleep in. Flagg took charge of the operation. He didn't know beans about setting up a tent, but he did know how to motivate people. The kids were divided into camps and thus the chore was turned into a competition. The instructions that came with the tent were in German, but Flagg figured it all out on the go, and after a lot of hustle and bustle, an orange-colored tent graced my parents' immaculate lawn. Gijs looked on in amazement. He would have read the instructions before he started, found all the parts, laid them out carefully and then instructed whoever he could find to put it together under his tutelage. Who knows, it might have been quicker that way, but it wasn't the way Flagg did things.

Setting up the tent

June was asparagus month in Breda, the specialty crop of the region because of its sandy soil. Mammie wanted to surprise her American guests with white asparagus, and had asked the neighboring farmer to pick a fresh load. She put on her apron, stationed herself on a bench in the garden with a bucket, a sharp kitchen knife and a platter. Mary watched as my mother peeled each stalk carefully from the fibrous bottom to the purplish bud. It took her over an hour. The kids came and sat at her feet on the lawn. What was she doing and why were these asparagus white? For an answer, Mammie told me to take them to the farmer. We walked through rows of miniature dykes that had been shaped in the previous fall. There were no asparagus to be seen. They hid in the sand, out of sight from the sun. The farmer told us to look for star-like cracks in the soil. We found several. With his fingers he exposed the buds and gingerly dug farther down along the stalk. A tool with a prong cut the asparagus off at the base. After two months of harvesting he would level the dykes, he told us, and let the plants shoot up so their root systems could expand for next year's crop. We ate them that evening with our fingers – a Dutch tradition, but only for white asparagus – dipping them in mashed hardboiled eggs with melted butter and ground nutmeg.

Mammie took Mary and Flagg on a little sightseeing tour of Breda. She'd learned to drive at the age of sixty and bought a car made in Holland, called a DAF, that was so simple even she could operate it. All you had to do, she explained to Flagg, who was an avid car buff, was pull the shift-stick up to go forward and backward for reverse. She invited her guests into her little shoebox and drove off to show them where my father's pharmacy had been. It was now a Chinese restaurant. She drove from the market square into a side street, the one I'd walked every day to grade school with my two brothers. What she didn't know, since she didn't live in the heart of the city anymore, was that the sidewalks had been done away with. Granite posts stood between the cobblestones at regular intervals. Mammie paid no attention to a round sign with a car drawn on it and a diagonal black line through it. To my mother's annoyance pedestrians were walking all over the street. She jerked her steering wheel from left to right to avoid the granite posts that stuck like fingers through the pavement, and treated them like flags on a slalom course and the pedestrians as spectators at a ski race. Flagg described how she just grinned when he pointed out that maybe they shouldn't venture farther. She winked and drove her golden carriage, as she called it, to the very end of the street. Mary and Flagg stepped out of the car with both a sense of relief and awe for this undaunted woman.

One Saturday afternoon two carriages, drawn by matched pairs of black Friesians in shiny tack and driven by coachmen in blue livery, appeared at our doorstep. The children went in the landau, the adults in the surrey with a fringe on top. Everyone had emerged in party dress. The boys wore dark suits, white shirts and neckties. Joan was in a chiffon dress with white knee stockings and white patent leather shoes. All of them were painfully aware of their own transformations. The youngest three boys giggled, but Joan and Linc stole sideways glances at each other. On the boat they had gingerly stepped over the threshold between childhood and puberty without any outward sign of change, though we hadn't been fooled as much as Linc and Joan thought. Tonight they would be in the company of adults. We had practically begged them to behave. This was not going to be a rowdy birthday party at MacDonald's. So here they were, looking like miniature adults.

The hooves of the horses clattered over the pavement in the steady rhythm of a trot. When we arrived at our destination, the coachmen offered their white-gloved hands to lean on. The big villa where we'd stopped was where we'd celebrated our wedding.

"How appropriate for your twelve-and-a-halfth!" Mary said, referring to what we call in Holland *de koperen bruiloft*, the brass anniversary, the one important anniversary before the silver one, a halfway point.

The same owner greeted us at the door as he'd done on that splendid day in June of 1956. Even the landau the children had traveled in was the same one we had stepped out of then; Gijs in black morning coat, a white rose in his lapel and I in a floor length satin dress with a long train. But the composition of our guests was not the same. Some faces were missing, like Vader Bozuwa's. Other faces had been added, like the ones of the many Dutchmen who'd visited us in Wakefield. The Averys were the only Americans in the group.

We were welcomed by song. Moeder Bozuwa had written a poem for Joan and Paul to recite in Dutch. They pulled it off with an American accent, the best illustration of where our life had led us.

My father was a gifted speaker. Poetic and witty, he knew how to move his audience to tears through laughter and sincerity. Our contemporaries were more into roasting. They had gathered lots of ammunition, and gleefully loaded their guns with skits and a narrated movie that Bob Koumans had taken during a picnic at Cooks Pond in Brookfield, which made Flagg Avery, who recognized his own property by the lake, stand up and pull our leg about not being invited to a party at his own house.

Gijs whirled me around on the dance floor with a protective arm around my back. In step with the music of the trio that played a waltz at his request, he led me without hesitation. He was a great dancer, a great partner.

"Are you ready for the next twelve-and-a-half years?" he asked while he made an elegant pass over the shiny hardwood floor. I didn't really have to think about the answer.

"Yes."

When he'd asked me to marry him, in 1954, I'd said yes also. But when I woke up the next morning I thought, "I don't even know this man." When he came back a few days later I said, "Sorry, but this is too hasty for me." I handed him a diary I'd written while I was a governess in London for four months. This might tell you something about me, I told him, but now I have to study for my college finals. Gijs left and spent the afternoon on a terrace in Amsterdam, drinking beer and reading my thoughts. His proposal to get married right away and go to America had overwhelmed me. The fact that he had been awarded a Fulbright scholarship and could earn money as an intern wasn't enough to convince me to jump into his boat and sail away. In my heart I knew I would eventually, but it took me two months to say so. Gijs had such persuasive powers that, over the years, I had learned to say no first to his plans and then consider what they entailed. He had been patient. He wouldn't always be, but we usually worked out this fundamental difference between us.

We had shared a good part of the fifties and all of the sixties out of the way of hippies, drugs, the Beatles, long hair for men, short skirts for women and disdain for authority. In Wakefield we'd stepped back into an old world, which had been brand new to us. The sixties, the way they would be historically remembered, had bypassed us.

What would the seventies bring? Joan and Paul would become teenagers, go to college and leave us. Our Dutch friends had already left us. At the end of this party, they would return to their familiar nests.

On the dance floor, Gijs did one of his fancy passes in which he made me step beside him, backward, while he moved forward with sure strides. Then he switched me around. Now I strode forward and he took the steps backward. It felt elegant and easy to execute. His sense of rhythm was uncanny. As I twirled in his arms, I couldn't help thinking that he'd done this to me in more ways than one. He'd taken me to America, and it had felt like being backed into the unknown. After twelve years I'd switched around. I was moving forward. The new world had become familiar. After this party and this trip we would also return to a familiar nest. I had been made an American citizen and I would never apologize for that. It had been a struggle, but now I was committed. While I stepped forward, with the seventies stretching before me like a rich promise, I felt hesitation in Gijs as he stepped backward. The emigration had been an adventure. Was it time for something else? A whole new adventure, or maybe back to where all these good friends lived?

Chapter 34

Changes

Wakefield Village was buzzing with rumors when we returned from our trip to Holland. I heard all about it when I went to the post office to pick up our bag of accumulated mail. There seemed to be a lot on the mind of our postmistress, Lois Pike, who owned the house the post office was in. She was the only clerk there and she often came from behind the wooden counter to join her customers, who could comfortably seat themselves in the green vinyl chairs she'd put out for that purpose. As she picked the wilted leaves from her array of ever blooming African violets, she listened to the scuttlebutt in town, or added to it.

New people—not a family, mind you, it looked more like one of those communes you read about in the paper—had moved into the village. To hear her tell it, these newcomers had taken down the American flag and hoisted a psychedelic cloth in its stead, smack in the middle of our Old Colonial village. She told me they came to her office on sandals cut from tires. And their clothes, you know, they look like rags. It was an outrage. What's the world coming to!

It was clear that Lois, who was a proper farmer's wife, clad in proper dresses, her hair neatly arranged in a permanent and with sensible shoes on her feet, could not stomach how these people walked with an air of superiority through the town where she'd lived all her life. What nerve! Of course, what intrigued as well as galled her was the commune style of living. There was no sign of marital arrangements. Not that she could tell. None of the residents shared a last name, she said. Lois Pike, I sensed, had wild imaginations about what went on in that place.

"What house did they move into?" I asked.

"Next door to you! The old Inn!" said Lois.

In itself that was nothing unusual. Since 1958, the Inn had changed hands many times. A few days after we moved into our house, the owner of the Elmwood Inn closed the door behind her for good because Route 16 no longer went through the village. It had been rerouted. Her business was doomed, she said. The developers who'd bought Moose Mountain were the next owners, but not for long. The ski area sucked up all their dollars. They sold it to a dreamer who told us he'd been offered the sole dealership of Volkswagen for the entire New England area, but had passed it up. This lack of foresight ate away at the man when he saw how popular the little beetles became. He tried to drink his way out of his depression, but landed in the hospital with the DT's during the winter, when the outside temperature fell precipitously and all the water pipes of the heating system he'd installed froze up for lack of oil because he hadn't paid his bills. He was declared bankrupt soon afterward. A man with a hump-back, a wife and two young children bought the three-story inn for a song, but the needy building did him in as well. In desperation he rented it out. To a commune, according to Mrs. Pike.

Joan and Paul spied from the windows of the Tripp house and came back with strange reports. " Hippies in Wakefield, Mom, just like the ones we saw around the monument on *De Dam* in front of the palace in Amsterdam. They have long hair and wear torn jeans. You should see them, Mom."

I took their reports with a grain of salt. My desk was buried under a pile of unopened mail after our trip. I had no time to go look for myself. But one day, as I mowed the lawn of the Tripp house, one of our new neighbors—the kids had not yet determined their exact number—called me over to the white picket fence that divided our properties. I considered it only neighborly to acknowledge his presence and walked over. Joan stood beside me in a flash. At age twelve she knew she could just stand there, take it all in and say nothing.

The descriptions of Mrs. Pike and the children clicked with what I saw before me: a man with very long hair and very short shorts. He asked me for my name and played with its pronunciation as if he tasted a delicacy. The name Titia seemed to intrigue him. He asked me for the date of my birth. July 13th, I answered. What year, he asked while focusing on my face with bizarre intensity, as if I were an out-of-the-ordinary apparition in my cotton slacks and blouse. I gave him the correct answer: 1932.

Without looking at her, I knew that Joan was devouring this unusual, one-sided introduction of her mother to a stranger who casually leaned on the fence, close enough to touch.

"Do you know on what day of the week you were born?" he asked.

"No idea," I answered. This was going too far. "Does it make any difference?"

"Oh, yes, a huge difference," the man said in a slow drawl. "The course of your entire life is determined by how the stars, the sun and the moon are lined up at exactly the minute of your birth."

Get out of this, Titia, my inner voice warned, before you get in too deep. There was a hypnotic quality about the man. It filled me with a strange anxiety as if I were being X-rayed, body and soul, by probing eyes. He allowed himself the luxury of mentally undressing his neighbor without even bothering to introduce himself!

"Nice to have met you," I lied. I took Joan's hand and walked away from the white picket fence that Vic had wisely built, telling us when we bought the Tripp house that we should establish our boundaries right away. The bank, which held the mortgage of the Inn after one of its frequent bankruptcies, had sold us a strip of five feet on the Inn side.

Back in the house, Joan turned to me and said, "See, he's *weird*."

Gijs wasn't immediately aware of the drastic change in our village population. Cars were parked on both sides of our street all the daylight hours with patients coming and going. But one morning he decided he needed a breath of fresh air and walked over to the post office. He was surprised to have a stranger wearing sandals fall in step beside him. Gijs had walked on sandals for three years during his prison camp experience; on sandals and with only a loincloth to cover his body. Nothing much in the way of clothing had shocked him after that. However, in Wakefield in 1969, a man walking to the post office on rubber-tire sandals was a rarity. He said hello to the stranger and answered the usual questions of who he was and what he did.

"And how about you?" Gijs asked. "Who are you and what brought you to Wakefield?"

"I'm a writer," the man answered.

"Interesting! And what do you write about?" Gijs asked.

"Pornography," the man answered. "It pays best."

Gijs took me aside the minute he came back to the house.

"Tiets, we have new neighbors," he said, a frown on his forehead.

"Yes, I know."

"I'll tell you what you don't know." He did. "Let's take our distance. Joan is at a tender age."

"Love thy neighbor," I said, half-teasing.

"Sure, sure, but there's a limit." Gijs focused his blue eyes on me. They looked stern and scared at the same time.

"Don't worry," I said. "Joan has already pegged him. She thinks he's weird."

I didn't tell him how she'd come to that conclusion. Gijs had enough on his mind, and I didn't want to admit that I hadn't handled the over-the-fence introduction very well. Of course, I should have asked for the man's name instead of answering his invading questions.

Another building on our street had also changed hands. The Webbers had bought Rosie's store. They had two small children. She was a nurse. The man was a jack-of-all-trades who immediately involved himself with civic groups. Already he was the Boy Scouts leader.

Mrs. Pike was right. Things weren't as they used to be. The general store was a thing of the past. There were fewer farmers and more city folk. A subtle shift in the population was turning Wakefield further away from its agricultural past.

Spying on the neighbors had been fun for a week, but it was not an altogether healthy entertainment. Joan was clowning dressed up like a hippie. She'd found an old batik cloth that must have come from Gijs's Indonesian days, wrapped it around to make a long skirt and paraded barefoot for us, imitating a careless lope by swinging her hips out. And Paul came home from one of his early morning rides on his pony and reported he'd seen a creepy man coming out of the Inn, getting into an old, beaten-up station wagon with North Carolina license plates and leaving. The sun had barely come over the horizon. Now, what did *that* mean? When we asked him why he thought the man was creepy, Paul said he was black, but that wasn't really it. He seemed like he was drunk or something, dirty-looking.

It was time to distract their attention.

We enrolled both of them for a week at a horseback riding camp in Springvale, Maine, thirty minutes away by car. I had planned to call George, the owner, and ask him to bring the horses over in his big van, but Paul had a different idea.

"Let's ride over," he suggested.

"Are you crazy?" Joan asked. "That'll take all day!"

Paul persisted, a trait we would see more of. He took the large mounted topographic map off the wall in the waiting room and brought it to the dining room table. With our fingers we traced dirt roads that curved around lakes, over hills, through meadows and along old logging roads. The three of us packed into our Volkswagen to inspect what we had mapped out. Some parts we couldn't get to, but it seemed feasible to get to Springvale on horseback without going over the main roads. The kids started to prepare for our expedition the very same day. Paul had the zeal, Joan the organization.

When the day came, a warm red glow spread over the tree line behind the church. It would be a hot and humid August day. Paul was already in the barn feeding the horses and Gijs made breakfast for us.

We picked our path carefully through the woods that connected to the Tuttle field. From the end of the field, we veered from our usual course and took a right. Ah-hi, the Arabian I had bought after my first ride with Mary Avery, seemed to drift to the left, to the field she loved to gallop up. She knew we were leaving familiar territory and I had to use my whip to urge her on. Horses were like people: some eager to explore, others content to trudge the same path day after day, with a safe return to the stable as the reward. Gijs could be expected to veer off the road whenever he saw a promising clearing in the woods. Paul never hesitated to follow. Joan went along for the ride, but she would just as soon do something that was her *own* idea, and I didn't embark readily on an unmarked path, though Gijs never gave up tempting me.

We trotted by Lovell Lake, which looked like a sheet of glass, not a ripple on it, just a rowing boat here and there with a fisherman sitting like a statue, angling for bass. At the end of the lake we took a logging road and the next one and the next, until we didn't recognize where we were. There was no telling Maine and New Hampshire apart. When I used to bicycle over the heather fields in Breda, it wasn't unusual to find myself suddenly in Belgium. There the farms were built with a different type of brick, easy to recognize. Here all houses on either side of the border were clapboarded and painted white, the barns red. So far, we'd only passed three houses, tucked away in groves of maple trees, had-been farms without signs or smells of animals.

"Where are we?" Joan asked, after we'd hacked over logging roads for what seemed like hours.

I pulled up under an oak and took out the map and handed a candy bar to Joan and Paul.

"You don't know where we are, do you?" Joan said as she chewed on her Milky Way.

"Not exactly. You're right."

"We should've brought a compass," she said. I told them not to worry, I had a watch and I could tell from the position of the sun that we were heading in the right direction.

We got our horses moving again, but Ah-Hi suddenly stopped. Her foot was caught on a root that had been worked to the surface of the old logging road. Paul shouted from behind and jumped off his pony and lifted up Ah-hi's left front leg. It wasn't a pretty sight. The iron shoe was partly pulled off. Joan reached into her rucksack, produced a hoof pick and handed it to Paul, who tried to pry off the part that was still attached. The iron was stubborn and clung to the hoof.

"She can't walk on three legs," Paul said, and handed me the hoof pick. Here we were, in the middle of nowhere with this puny hoof pick. Joan rummaged in her rucksack and produced a rasp.

"Here, try this!" she said.

Paul took the pointed end and stuck it between the iron and the hoof. Reluctantly, the flat nails let go, and Paul triumphantly held the iron in the air. Then he rasped the hoof and evened it out as best he could. I wondered what I would have done if the iron hadn't let go. Have one of the children go and get help even though we didn't know exactly where we were?

The heat seemed to rise up from the ground. Leaves from years past were smothering like bay leaves in a stew, mixing with the smell of softened pine pitch. Droplets of sweat collected under my black velvet riding helmet and I could see rivulets form down Joan's blue cotton shirtShe began to sing "I have confidence in confidence alone" from *The Sound of Music*.

"Are you scared?" Paul asked her.

"No, but I wish we were there."

Finally I saw a patch of light ahead of us. A had-been farm sat at the edge of an overgrown field. Paul got off his pony and handed me the reins. Almost immediately after Paul knocked on the screen door, a man opened it, as if he had been standing watch there.

"We want to go to Springvale, Maine," Paul said.

"Where did you come from?" the man asked while he tried to take stock of what had landed in his front yard.

"From Wakefield," Paul said. "Wakefield, New Hampshire. "

"Well I'm glad it wasn't Wakefield, Massachusetts on a hot day like this!" He walked over to me. Eyes twinkling, he explained where we'd gone wrong. A real Yankee, I thought, like Irving Tuttle. That same lean body, and the same wicked charm.

"Frances," he yelled. An elderly woman came to the screen door. "Find some buckets. These horses are thirsty."

It didn't take long before we sat sprawled in the grass under the canopy of a wide maple tree. The woman had brought out a pitcher of lemonade with a few ice cubes floating on top. Joan and Paul loosened the girths of the saddles, removed the bridles and put on halters with lead ropes while I got out the sandwiches. They'd taken on strange shapes, riding on my back.

"You thought of everything, it looks like," the man said as he sat on the porch steps.

"My sister made the sandwiches," Paul said. "She puts the good stuff on it. My mother just puts a slice of cheese on. At school the other kids laugh at us."

"What's wrong with cheese?" the man asked.

"The others get peanut butter and jelly on theirs. Or marshmallow even!" Joan said eagerly. It was their pet peeve, and they loved to tease me with it.

"I grew up in Holland," I said by way of explanation. "You can't convince a Dutchman to put jelly on top of peanut butter. We don't use lettuce, or pickles, or make triple-deckers stacked so high you can't even get them into your mouth!"

"Holland? That where you come from?" the man asked in his Maine accent. "My son was there in the war, drove into Eindhoven on top of a tank. He said people climbed all over him."

"Eindhoven isn't too far from where my parents live. Where is your son now?"

"Oh, he's in the big city. You know, people his age don't want to make their living off the land these days. We had a nice little farm going here. Cows, sheep, chickens. But it all went to hell after the war." There was a mixture of anger and resignation in his voice. He'd fought his battles long ago.

We tacked up again, and our host pointed out the route to take as he stood in the middle of the road with his Frances beside him, two figures of Maine's past: tough, enduring, in some ways eternal, in others transitory. They waved as we went around the bend.

The horses picked up a good pace and we walked without talking until Joan said, "They seemed lonely, don't you think, Mom? I think the man didn't like it that his son hadn't taken up farming, the way he had."

We had transitioned to dirt roads, skirting the city, and soon we were on black top. The sun blasted over the open landscape of cornfields. The horses trudged along, their coats glistening with sweat. Gone were the eager, pricked ears and the lively tread of the early morning. We could have boiled an egg in the hot moisture of our perspiration under our black velvet helmets. I remembered how my mother's brother had referred to the sun as "the copper bastard' after enduring the tropical heat in the jungle of the Dutch East Indies. There was no hiding from the piercing rays that I could feel even through my cotton shirt, as if I stood too close to a fired-up wood stove.

The three of us rode in silence, trying to ignore the blisters that were in the making from our bums rubbing back and forth in damp underwear over a leather surface that seemed to get harder by the minute. Was this supposed to be fun? Wouldn't it have been easier to pick up the phone and say, "George, can you come over and get the horses?"

Ridgecrest Stables finally came into view. Mary Avery was waiting for us. She jumped out of her Ford station wagon when she saw us coming up the street, and even though life seemed to have flowed out of my children only minutes earlier, they sat up straight in the saddle, ready to tell tall tales about their ride. We'd been on the road from seven in the morning till three in the afternoon.

"My God, Titia," Mary said. "You look as red as a lobster. Are you all right?"

It was all I could do to dismount. I grabbed a hose and let the cold water pour over my heated scalp. The other campers crowded around Paul and Joan. Everybody wanted to hold on to the horses, cool their well-exercised legs with ice-cold water. Joan and Paul beamed. They had sore bums, but it had been well worth the attention.

As its name indicated, Ridgecrest Stables sat on top of a ridge, one in a row of declining farms. George Chamberlin had saved his family's homestead by capitalizing on the growing interest in horseback riding. Judging from the peeling paint and rope-mended fences, it provided only a marginal living.

What the kids loved, what we all loved, was the lively pulse of the place. Huge Newfoundlanders, forever drawling and panting from the heat, lingered in the shade of the ancient trees, their long fur matted with bits of hay. There was always a panic: a fence broke and the horses ran out onto the street, or rotted boards in the old stalls gave out and a horse disappeared into the dirt cellar underneath, to be pulled up minutes later with ropes and sweet coaxing.

I had ridden Ah-hi over because George had suggested we have her bred by a thoroughbred stallion that he'd picked up on one his frequent horse buying trips down south. Battle Bob, he said, was a direct descendent of the famous racehorse Man O' War, who lay buried in a grave fit for a king down in Lexington, Kentucky. He had the papers to prove it. I fell for the scheme not for want of a new horse but for the romantic aspect of living on a farm and having a foal born there. I threw all caution to the wind, and it felt good and liberating. As I would find out in the next decade of intense involvement with the equine race, the smartest thing for a horse trader who also instructs and trains, is to get a rider fixed up with a horse that is appealing to the eye but bewitched by problems that only time and professional training will fix.

Mary Avery had driven over to bring the children's luggage and take me home. We said good-bye to everybody and promised Joan and Paul we'd come and pick them up in a week.

Gijs was happy to see me. I'd looked forward to reporting on our arduous trip, but I could see his mind wandering. He prepared gin and tonics for us and took them out to the terrace. It wasn't long before he switched the subject to his own adventures of the day. Marion Doe, mother of the twins, had called to warn that the house we'd inherited from Vic Bezanson, diagonally across the road from her new home, had been broken into. Two men with a truck had pulled up that afternoon, opened the front door and took out a large clock. Did she think she could identify these men, Gijs had asked "Oh, sure," Marion Doe had said. "I watched it all. One of them is your new neighbor and the other one is a kid I've seen growing up in town. He hangs out there now."

Which neighbor? New neighbors surrounded us!

It was Mr. Bob Webber, the civic-minded plumber in Rosie's old store, the new scout leader in town. Couldn't be, Gijs had thought. He seemed so friendly and his wife was such a cheerful, competent nurse. Why would he need to steal? But Marion could swear it on a Bible. In between seeing patients, Gijs called the real estate agent who handled Vic's property. The agent said he'd given Bob Webber the keys to Vic's house to turn on the water, back in the spring.

What to do? Gijs didn't like the idea of alerting the police and getting his neighbor into trouble. He decided to check it out himself, so he went to Vic's house after office hours. The clock was gone. Then he went to Rosie's old store and saw Bob Webber.

"Gosh, I would never do such a thing, doctor," Mr. Webber said. "But," he added in a whisper, with a nod in the direction of the youth that hung around with him, "I don't know about him."

Gijs had told Bob Webber that he wouldn't alert the police if he gave the clock back. Our new neighbor maintained his innocence, and Gijs reported the theft to the police. They appeared minutes later in full force, handcuffed the duo and put them in jail. Finally they got him, they told Gijs. They were delighted he'd notified them. Mr. Webber was no sweetheart. He was suspected of many thefts in the area, but he'd been too sly to be caught. Bob Webber had a bad record in Massachusetts and they'd run him out of the state.

As the sun sank below the tree line that hemmed in our meadow, we were still sitting on the terrace, holding our empty glasses and occasionally swatting at a fly. Together we agonized over the incident. Should Gijs have gone to the police in the first place? Was it stupid to give a man a chance? Had he been responsible or naive? To me, even more surprising than having a thief for a neighbor, was the fact that Gijs had been so gullible because part of his character make-up was suspicion. He took a dim view of the neighbors in the Inn, for instance, but that probably had more to do with anxiety about the culture of drugs and his teenage daughter.

When too many bugs went for our blood, we got up and stumbled to bed. Before he fell asleep Gijs mumbled, "Tomorrow, we'll have to buy a lock for the Tripp house."

In no time—faster than the blisters on my bottom could heal—the news of the theft reached our little post office. The villagers took turns sitting in the green vinyl chairs at the post office and chewing on the report. Gossip about pornographic movies being made at Rosie's old store was added to the facts. It was even rumored that Mr. Webber was part of the Mafia. Can you imagine? Right here in Wakefield? We'd better start locking up our houses and watch out for our kids. The Bozuwas were suddenly included in the old guard, part of the "We." Unlike the new people on the block, we hadn't blatantly broken the unspoken codes that bound the old-timers together. Not everyone in town trusted us, though. One old crank, a member of the Birch Society, tried to introduce the notion that the Bozuwas were closet communists, but it didn't take a hold. It was even ridiculed. Through the mistakes of others we were drawn into the circle of our community.

Although it seemed that we had an airtight case against Mr. Webber, it got thrown out of court because Mr. Webber managed to create an alibi for himself that didn't click with the time Marion Doe said she saw him at Vic's house. He had taken advantage of Gijs's visit to him.

As promised, Mary and I picked up the children from their horseback riding camp a week later. George took me aside. Sambal was cute but lazy, too small for a growing nine-year-old. Paul really needed a bigger mount. The stubborn pony, who seemed to know that George was too big to sit on his back and make him do what Sambal really didn't want to do, had bucked Paul off more than once.

We would think about it, I told him.

Paul's reaction to George's advice forecast his career as a businessman and his penchant for independence: he thought of a way to pay for a new pony. His chickens were good layers and he expanded his egg-route. Lois Pike's husband Schuyler, a farmer from way back, gave him an egg scale to sort his eggs into medium, large and extra large. Paul gathered the eggs every other day in a wire basket and washed them in the kitchen sink. Each one was put on Schuyler's scale, its size determined and placed into a recycled carton. With his dog Jippy in tow, he made deliveries to people in the street who gave him cookies as well as money. Schuyler Pike, when he heard Paul wanted to buy his own pony, made yet another donation: a sign made of solid iron and supported by four legs. A white chicken painted on a black background with the words "Fresh Eggs" had been painted underneath it. Paul set it out in the front yard for his father's patients to notice.

His new goal gave him more incentive to care for his flock of twenty-five Rhode Island Reds. Early in the morning, he crossed the lawn to the converted milk house with a pail of fresh water. In the evening, their metal feeder got refilled with corn mash he'd paid for from his egg money. Paul had no trouble with the lesson that it takes money to make money, but understanding the need for mucking out the pen was less successful. He usually waited till the chicken manure had built up to a layer a foot high. The sickly-sweet smell of ammonia, mixed with the fermented corn mesh, was enough to drive visitors out. It needed to be chopped off the floor while the cackling chickens fluttered about. Paul tried to get Joan to give him a hand, but she was quick to point out that it was *his* egg route and its benefits were for *his* pony.

Only a few weeks into his new goal in life, Paul realized that the money he earned with eggs would not buy him a pony. He came up with another scheme: he could breed his dog. Mary Avery had found Jip, his purebred black Labrador, for his eighth birthday, so he had me call her to ask how we should go about it. Mary told us it would take a first-rate sire and that she would find us one. Jippy went on a short vacation and came back pregnant. Together with Gijs, Paul built something that looked like a sand box, which he placed next to his bed and filled with shredded newspapers. Jippy ignored the box and, instead, sat in the comfortable chair she had claimed for herself in Paul's room. One day she disappeared. Paul looked for her, whistled for her. No Jippy. Joan suggested she'd gone off to have her litter, but Paul countered that he was Jippy's best friend, she would deliver her babies in the box he built for her. Joan had her doubts and, without saying a word, went snooping around the neighborhood, up and down the street. On her way back—she'd gone as far as the post office—she heard squeaky noises just as she passed the Inn. She stood still and listened. It sounded like a small army of mice going to war. She whistled softly, but there was no response. Yet the "peep-peep-peep" was very insistent. It came from under the wide porch in front of the Inn. What about those hippies, though? What would Dad say if she rang the bell and talked to them? I better get Mom and Paul, she thought.

Together we went over to the white picket fence between the Tripp house and the inn and strained our ears, but we heard nothing.

"She wouldn't go into that dark hole," Paul said.

"Mrs. Pike says dogs hide when they're in pain. Having babies hurts!" Joan said.

There was no sign of life around the Inn. Their old car was parked in the place it always stood. The hippies lived more inside than outside.

"Okay," I said, "let's chance it. We'll go and look and we'll just tell them honestly what we're up to, if they ask."

We walked across the lawn of the Inn. Joan was right. We could hear the puppies squeal. Paul crawled into a hole at the side of the porch that looked like a freshly dug tunnel.

"What do you see?" Joan asked in a hushed voice. All *we* saw were Paul's legs sticking out of the hole. "Hurry up, or those people will come."

Moments later we saw Paul's hand emerge from the hole with a fuzzy ball in his palm. Then a second puppy, a third, a fourth! Joan took them from Paul's hand and nestled the furry balls in the basket we'd brought. When eleven puppies had emerged, Paul's leg moved backward. We could hear his muffled voice trying to calm Jip down, but she bolted out.

Jip and one of her puppies

"Quick, let's get out of here," Joan said, "before Jip starts barking."

Joan took the basket with the squirming puppies and ran as fast as she could while Paul grabbed Jip's collar and whispered soothing words at her. Shadows moved behind the windows on the second floor. I tried to propel my body over our neighbor's lawn with as much dignity as I could muster. We got away without being caught.

The puppies were sold for $100 each. The special savings account marked "PONY" had almost enough in it when George called to say he'd found a wonderful Welsh mare.

During Christmas vacation, our whole family took riding lessons from George. Paul and his new pony were like two peas in a pod, both perky and bold. He called her Nutmeg for the brown color of her coat, with just a bit lighter hair around the muzzle. She carried her little master around with patience for his lack of ability and threw her heart over any fence George put in front of them. Nutmeg was an absolute gem and Paul beamed. He didn't participate in any of the school's team sports because he couldn't see a ball coming at him until it was too late. Dr. Goodall had tugged and pulled at his eye muscles three times, but he still had some growing to do before he could feel confident to get the ball back to where he aimed it. From now on he would step off the school bus, whistle for his dog and dive into the barn. His playing field was at home.

As we were heading out the door on a winter day for one of those riding lessons, Sigrid Spalding called from Wolfeboro to ask us over for cocktails. Bring the children too, she said. Sigrid and I had met years earlier on a boat on Lake Winnipesauke while watching the Fourth of July fireworks, each with a baby in our arms. Our host had made a special point of introducing us since we both came from Europe. Never mind that the countries of our birth, Germany and Holland, had been at war in very recent memory. For the sake of social graces, we blotted out our childhood memories. All of us had been sucked into the war because of one huge ego with an appetite to swallow our entire continent. Yet, I had to admit that every time I was introduced to a German a little jab cut through my mind. Between the ages of seven and thirteen, I had loathed Germans. They had taken my bicycle away, my family's radio, put us on rationed food and made the Jewish girl who sat next to me at school disappear. She never came back. Of course I hated them. However, to carry that loathing forward from decade to decade didn't make sense. Didn't we drive a German Volkswagen, and wasn't my favorite camera a German Rolleiflex? To carry hate around was like sticking a nugget of radio-active material in your pocket for defense, and have it eventually destroy not the object of your hate but your own soul.

Sigrid and I became friends. Her husband had finished a career in the American Foreign Service and presently was a stockbroker. They brought their family up to Wolfeboro from Washington, D.C. every June. Our children played together, and Gijs and I exchanged cocktail talk with an array of people from the Washington scene. They appeared like exotic flowers in a bouquet of field daisies: people who lived miles and worlds apart from our own rural existence. So, when Sigrid called that day to invite us to meet her good friend, the wife of the American ambassador to Chili, I thought: oh well, another exotic flower that will wilt in my memory.

On the way back from Springvale, Gijs said he had a house call to make; he'd be just a minute. In his riding habit he walked toward a small house covered by tarpaper. Paul noticed that none of the windows matched. Joan speculated on what the people inside would think of Dad's riding boots. When he came back, Gijs told her that the woman who lived inside was beyond noticing details like riding boots. Not to worry, he said. She wouldn't have cared anyway, even if she'd noticed. She was a free spirit, determined to die at home. He admired her for that. The children stored this information with all the other bits they picked up from Gijs's life as a doctor.

The house call had taken more than a minute. We had the choice of going home to change and arriving too late at the Spaldings, or showing up in our riding clothes and being on time. We chose the latter. The Spalding children, Charles and David would still be in ski clothes probably, so if Paul and Joan were in riding clothes that didn't matter.

Gijs looked smashing in beige riding breeches and a herring-bone tweed jacket, and by nature he couldn't care less what anyone thought of him because of what he happened to wear. I was the one who would look and feel completely out of place. Sigrid Spalding was one of the most beautiful women I knew. She possessed an urban kind of beauty, very suited to the diplomatic life. The first thing you noticed in Sigrid was that everything about her was perfect: the texture of her skin, the essential sizes of waist and bust, the length of her legs, the size of her shoes, not a hair out of place and just the right amount of makeup. There was another kind of perfection about her: she dressed with style and, obviously, she didn't spare her husband's bank account to get the results she wanted.

As I sat in the car on the way over I felt like an absolute fool in my riding boots, breeches, turtleneck and sweater. A distinct horse aroma emanated from my clothing. Not only did I lack the impeccable taste of my hostess, I wasn't so sure I knew what to say to her guest. I had met another wife of an ambassador once at Sigrid's house, an incident memorable for its trauma. Asked to take pictures at a lawn party with lots of balloons, candies and cake for Charles Spalding's seventh birthday, I had gone inside to the relative darkness of the living room to load film into my camera. A woman rustled by in a silk dress. I thought it polite to introduce myself and said, "Hello, I'm Mrs. Bozuwa," to which the woman replied, "I am a Mrs. too, but I don't introduce myself that way." She walked on, leaving me standing there feeling like a whipped puppy. In Holland one didn't ever use first names in introductions. Where did this presumptuous woman grow up? In Australia, it turned out. Nobody had ever put me down like that since I was a child, and I was rip-roaring mad and humiliated.

By the time we drove up to the Spaldings' elegant old colonial on Main Street, which distinguished itself by a sweeping curved veranda, I had worked myself into a state of anger at the diplomatic set. These uppity people could go to hell, as far as I was concerned, and I would happily crawl back into my much more realistic cubbyhole with down-to-earth farmers and shop keepers, and all the other people who came to our house for medical care and who would just say "Hi Doc" and who didn't care if his wife wore smelly L.L.Bean boots and dungarees.

Once inside, the combined smell of a fire and Christmas greens put me at ease. Fran and Sigrid had a practiced yet sincere way of welcoming their guests. Sigrid was never at a loss for words. She could make her guests feel as if she'd been on the edge of her chair all day waiting for them. Charles and David came running out in their ski clothes, as I had predicted. They took Joan and Paul to their room to show off their Christmas presents. Gijs and I were ushered into the large living room that was remarkable for its white walls and darkly stained wood trim. It had a German feel to it, which always surprised me when I thought about the colonial aspects of the house.

In front of the wide fireplace stood a stunningly beautiful woman. In her late forties or early fifties, I estimated. Her blond hair had been gently pulled back from her face and done up in an elegant bun at the nape of her neck. She had an air of nobility about her that I recognized from Loes Hugenholtz, something innately chic that couldn't be bought or found in haute couture. She was as different from the Australian ambassadress as a Thoroughbred from a buggy horse. She was introduced to us as Jane Howe. Light blue eyes that revealed sadness dominated her fair-skinned face. Whatever the sadness was about, it lay buried under many layers of protective self-discipline. Not glossed over, but kept private and out of sight.

Gijs apologized for appearing in riding habit, but Jane Howe said she was quite used to it. She lived in Virginia and was surrounded by horses and horse-people. She spoke with a distinct English accent. Was she British?

Jane Howe

Fran Spalding mixed drinks for us, while Sigrid went to the kitchen to warm up some hors d'ouvres. They hadn't brought up their housekeeper for the Christmas holiday, she said, so she would try her best even though she wasn't very familiar with the stove. Gijs and I were left with Jane Howe in front of the roaring fire. I wondered how she could live in Virginia if her husband was the ambassador to Chili, and why her husband wasn't here with her. She lived on a farm outside of Charlottesville, she told us. A son lived on the next farm over and trained racehorses. I tried to make sense out of this information. There was a veil of mystery about her she wasn't willing to lift, and she skillfully shifted the conversation to the particulars of our life in New Hampshire.

Fran and Sigrid returned with drinks and food as Joan wandered into the room, bored with the three boys and their toys. She seated herself next to Jane on the couch and looked at her keenly. Jane responded with conversation that was attuned to a child, yet adult enough for Joan to feel appreciated and understood. I really liked this woman. She intrigued me.

Sigrid's bubbly conversation brought out some of the missing pieces of the puzzle Jane Howe presented. They talked about people they knew in Colombia where they had met before Jane's husband was appointed ambassador to Chili during the Eisenhower administration. Jane's husband had died suddenly, and recently. The subject got skirted. The wounds were too fresh to touch.

I surprised myself by inviting Sigrid and Jane to have lunch with us the next day. Gijs offered to take all the children skiing. They arrived at noon, minutes after I'd mucked out the horse stalls and kicked off my L.L. Bean boots. Sigrid looked very European in a fur coat over stretch ski pants, as if she'd just stepped off a plane from Switzerland. Jane wore a sensible but oh so beautifully cut sheepskin coat with a matching belt that accentuated her narrow waist. Panic settled in my stomach as I watched them walk toward the barn door. What kind of a fool had I been to invite them? These society women were used to a life with servants, to a style that went with being in the Foreign Service. Then I heard my mother, as if she stood next to me. "Never apologize for whom you are. You'll only make the other person uncomfortable, or hand them a wand of power over you."

These thoughts floated through my mind like leaves on a roaring brook as I bravely stepped out to greet my guests. Jane Howe sniffed the air of hay and manure and asked to see the horses. I rolled the heavy back door to the side and opened up the view of Moose Mountain in the distance and the snow-covered pastures nearby. Three horses quietly munched on a mound of hay I'd tossed them earlier. Steam rose from the manure pit, the only dark spot in the otherwise pristine snow-covered landscape. Jane asked what breed the horses were, what age. Did we ride English or Western? She was well versed on the subject of horses.

Over a cheese omelet and green salad Jane asked how we'd come to Wakefield, and she told about the small town of Litchfield, Connecticut where she'd brought up her four sons and how she couldn't have done it without the marvelous common sense and wit of the doctor there. I had no idea where Litchfield was on the map, but Jane made it sound like Wakefield. I felt understood. Sigrid's introduction of "the wife of the ambassador to Chili" had thrown me off. Jane Howe seemed like an extraordinary human being. Not because her husband had been an ambassador. As with Loes Hugenholtz, there was more to her than title.

When she left, Jane said she hoped to meet our family again. "Maybe in Virginia?" She looked like she meant it.

As I waved good-bye, I saw the hippies bundled up in shawls and sweaters lugging wood from their barn into the house. They looked cold and out of place. How different our life in Wakefield had become! For neighbors we had hippies on one side, a thief on the other, and elegant people from far away visited us. We had horses in the barn, children on skis. None of it I had imagined on the day we bought our house.

Chapter 35

Are We Going to Brazil?

We weren't any closer to understanding the hippies next door than we were on the day we discovered them. At the end of the summer we still didn't know their names. The only one who got a little closer was Gijs when one of the women came to the office, barefoot and dressed in a bikini. She had sat herself down next to the other more conventionally dressed patients. Gijs hardly ever looked in the waiting room to see who was there. His nurse did the calling. But on this hot day she alerted him to the mounting tension in the waiting room. Our neighbor was restless and the other patients, who chose presentable clothes to go and see the doctor, made no effort to hide their disdain for someone dressed in a scant bathing suit. As Gijs peeked in, the woman got up, swooned and fell into his arms. He carried her into an examining room, treated her puncture wound, gave her a tetanus shot and quickly saw her to the door.

It was a bizarre incident, one that was talked about in town, but it didn't add to our knowledge of what our neighbors did for a living besides write pornography. They were quiet, unto themselves, didn't bother anyone. The only times we saw them venture outside was when they got wood from the barn during their first winter in Wakefield. I noticed, but didn't give it much thought at the time, that they never carried logs. There seemed to be a limitless supply of odd-sized weathered pieces of lumber in the big barn behind the Inn. At times, standing in our driveway, we smelled curious aromas rising from their chimney, more acidic than wood smoke.

Then one day, two Wakefield policemen knocked on our door and asked to speak to me. Could I show them a room with a good view of the

Inn, they asked. I led them up the rickety back stairs to the old shoe shop in the Tripp house. Splendid, the uniformed men said, this would give them just the right angle.

"The right angle for what?" I asked.

"To monitor their comings and goings."

"You mean to spy?"

"Just observe. We suspect they're involved with drugs."

"I'm sorry, but I won't let my house be used for spying on my neighbors."

"No, we can't make you," the older man said.

Not long after their visit, it got very quiet next door. The three-story Inn stood as lifeless as a statue in a wax museum, as it had for most of the twelve years we'd lived here. Its inhabitants seemed to have vanished. Maybe they were looking for a warmer climate during the cold winter months like so many people in our area did. Snowbirds, we called them.

Gijs was not amused when I told him about our neighbors' activities. It was as if, by telling him, I had invited into our home everything that was deplorable about contemporary life. What we knew about drugs came from reading the newspapers. We didn't know anyone who smoked pot or who had children on drugs. If they did, they kept it very quiet. At dinner parties we discussed with like-minded people such current issues as the war in Vietnam, the decline in respect for authority, young men ducking the draft, burning of the American flag, but the time spent on it was like visiting a museum and viewing other people's lives through protective glass. You thought about it, took in the information and then went back to your own life. Were we living in a fool's paradise? The age group of people with children who could be drafted was sparsely represented in Wakefield. There was no work for them here. They'd moved away before we arrived. Nobody we knew, even indirectly, had been killed in the Vietnam War.

The violent protests against the military grated on Gijs. His own upbringing had been based on respect for authority and for a man in uniform. Vader Bozuwa had put his life on the line more than once to defend the Dutch flag. Now kids cut their country's symbol into random pieces and sewed them onto their torn jeans. It burned him up. Gijs wondered if these kids were on drugs, since they didn't seem to know what they were doing. Having the hippies vanish didn't change his mood. They had brought the rise of drug use into focus, and having Mr. Webber

steal Vic's clock hadn't helped either. Gijs felt threatened by the evil
brought to his doorstep.

"What are you really worried about?" I asked him.

"About Paul and Joan," Gijs answered.

"I don't think you have to worry about them. They'd pegged those
hippies before we had. Now they *know* they were right."

Gijs ponders his future

"What I worry about is the whole trend. Drugs will sneak their way
into schools. You wait! The GI's come home from Vietnam hooked on
them. Before you know it, it will be a way of life here."

No matter how I pooh-poohed the idea, Gijs dug into his apocalyptic
view of where the American society was headed. I was stunned. Gijs,
the optimist, where had he gone? This man who'd embraced the idea of
emigrating to the New World, and who'd made it all happen? Where was
the spirit of the eighteen-year-old who, when beaten by a Japanese guard
because he refused to give up his one and only blanket, had endured
his lashings and hung on to what was rightfully his? I wasn't despairing
that negative forces would swallow Paul and Joan. They had too much
common sense for that. What scared me was to have Gijs turn into a
pessimist. Our roles reversed. Maybe I was more optimistic because I

didn't go out of my way to inform myself about what was really going on with that war in Vietnam. The TV set was in our bedroom with strict rules on when and for what it could be turned on. Mostly, we'd watched Captain Kangaroo and Mr. Green Jeans in the mornings. Joan and Paul used to crawl under the blankets with us in our king-size bed to watch Mr. Moose drop ping-pong balls on Captain Kangaroo's wig. These days it was *Hogan Heroes* but hardly ever the news at six. No burning villages, bleeding GI's, or body bags entered our living space. At six o'clock Gijs would still be in the office, Paul feeding the horses and chickens, Joan in her own room doing homework or pretending she was, and I would be in the kitchen preparing the evening meal.

I took stock of the last thirteen years and saw that I was beginning to fit into the role of wife, mother, doctor's wife and citizen of a country other than the one I was born in. The house I'd hated at first sight had become the home I loved. Taken together with the Tripp house and the big barn it was as pliable as the sand castles I used to build on Holland's beaches. Patients, guests, horses, dogs, cats and chickens had their place in it without being in each other's way. The possibilities seemed endless and tempting. My home was my castle. Certainly, there were things I missed and maybe I was becoming provincial without much exposure to cultural events, but I was happy in my marriage and grateful for having children.

Gijs had a different perspective. Whereas I projected Joan and Paul happily riding their mounts through the meadows, bonding with each other and with the place where they were being brought up, Gijs saw dangers encroaching upon them. Riots in Chicago, students killed at Kent State University, a president assassinated, a civil rights leader murdered, all in broad daylight. These happenings weighed heavily on him.

Still, that wasn't all of it. Adventures had cemented the various pieces of Gijs's life. Some bits were bright as stars, like the crossings on luxurious ships that ferried him and his family back and forth between Holland and the Indies. Others were stark and opaque, such as the war years spent in Japanese internment camps. Only one thing had been constant in his life and that was change.

"Tiets," he said one evening in April, after the children had gone to bed, "I looked into joining the Peace Corps."

I was shocked but not totally surprised.

"I've been thinking this would be a good time to do it. Joan and Paul are just the right age."

"You mean, pick up and leave your practice? Everything?"

"It wouldn't be forever."

"Why is this a good time for Joan and Paul?" I asked. I got up from my chair in the living room and walked over to the fireplace.

"If we stay here I'm afraid they'll become spoiled. "

"If you think they have too much, then we are the ones who gave it to them," I said, and reached for a log to throw on the fire. Gijs went to the kitchen and filled the kettle to make coffee.

"Everything around them coaxes them into it. There's more to life than buying a better pair of skis!" He called this out from the kitchen.

I felt like a drop cloth had fallen on me. I couldn't see two feet ahead. My vision was limited to single words with big meaning: disease, loneliness, foreign languages, leaving and jungle. I clammed up and busied myself by fanning the fire with the bellows till sparks flew up into the wide chimney.

Something was afoot in Gijs's mind. His drive had led us to this little speck on the map, but the engine behind it was still running and it didn't want to run in place. It wanted to press on and land in the Peace Corps, away from forces that might be hard to tackle like drugs, violence, the hunt for the mighty dollar in the land of plenty; away from the lure of the Madison Avenue marketing gurus, who put sex and image ahead of other values.

I didn't want to leave what I had struggled to accept for the good of people in some outpost. Weren't we already in an outpost? Gijs felt insulted when I brought up these knee-jerk reactions and brushed them away. I was a stick-in-the-mud. He didn't say it that way, but he made me feel like one.

"But, Dad," Joan and Paul cried out, when Gijs informed them of his plans, "Who will take care of the animals? What will we do with Ah-Hi's foal?"

"Can you only think of your own things?" Gijs shot back. Joan was in tears. They tried to listen to what the Peace Corps stood for. Paul thought it over for a few days and said he would give up his new pony if it would make Dad happy. Joan wasn't quite as quick to come around, but eventually she did, more or less.

Gijs contacted the Peace Corps, set up a date for an interview in Washington, D.C. and left early one morning to take a plane from

Boston. The office was closed, the nurse and the secretary given time off. I had a rare day to myself. There were so many things I wanted to do. Curl up on the couch and read a book? I couldn't concentrate. Go shopping? That would take too much time. Stores of any size were an hour or more away.

I turned out the horses and watched them sink their hooves into the thawing ground. There wasn't much for them to munch on in a pasture that was only slowly emerging from its winter blanket. Back in the house I noticed the silver tea set had lost its luster. I got out the polish and installed myself at the dining room table. While Gijs was negotiating about the course of our life, my index finger was rubbing away the tarnish on my inherited sugar bowl and teapot. The harder I rubbed the blacker my cloth got. Perspiration beads stood on my forehead as I looked at the result. The bowl's curving surface rendered the entire room in the crazy perspective of a fish-eye lens with me in the middle. I looked like a bush, a bit crazy and sprawling. A bush transplanted from Holland. Not a seed carried on the wind. The roots had taken their time to find their bearings in foreign soil. Now that it was firmly anchored, it wouldn't blow away. Hard winds could bend it but not break it. How many times can you transplant a bush like that?

I looked up at the view of the pasture out the window. What I saw jolted me out of my reflective mood. The horses, all four of them, were galloping through the field, their tails up high. They didn't seem to be chasing each other. It looked more like a Wild West movie with a stampede of horses in flight. I walked to the window and saw them lined up at the far end of the field where the fence had stopped them. They turned around, their tails still up high, all pointing in the same direction with the intensity of a hunting dog that's cornered a partridge.

Then I heard a shot. The horses quivered, wanted to turn away but realized they were hemmed in. Nutmeg, Paul's gutsy pony, took a step forward toward the opposite end of the field, away from the Inn where the shots had rang out. Another shot! I bolted through the kitchen to the barn. More shots. *God, this sounds like the end of the war when German snipers shot at people from the houses they holed up in.* I looked through the wide gap of our barn door. More shots, in rapid succession as if fired from a machine gun.

A rage took hold of me. *They're not going to kill our horses!* I quickly opened the stall doors, ran down the path to the pasture and opened the gate. On the cow path that led from the Inn to a field behind ours I saw a man with long dark hair coming toward me. He carried a pistol in each hand. It was the hippie who had talked to me over the fence. The look on his face was even weirder now. His eyes burned, furtive, mad, this man was out of control! Maybe the police had been right about the drugs. What was he up to? Target practice? But not with that look on his face! Would he kill?

I called to the horses. Nutmeg took the lead and spurted toward me; the others followed. Their hooves thundered over the ground, splashed me with clods of mud, and once they reached the barn they turned around and snorted through their wide-open nostrils. With my arms spread out wide I ran as fast as my legs would carry me to keep them from running back to the field. Horses in flight do crazy things. I locked them into their box stalls, closed the barn door, ran to my car and spurted down the hill to the center of town to take Joan and Paul off the school bus, so they wouldn't be dropped off at home. My neighbor wasn't going to kill my kids *or* my horses! I nearly grabbed them by their coat sleeves and dragged them into the car. There was no need for this. They were perfectly willing to go home, but I told them that was not where we were going.

Just then the police cruiser came by. I honked my horn and gestured. The older officer who'd asked if he could spy on my neighbors listened, got back in his car and sped up the hill. Paul and Joan were all excited. What were we going to do now, they asked. Joan suggested that since the police was there we were safe and might as well go home. We did.

In front of the Inn, the older policeman was leaning over the car that was parked in front of the Inn. Joan and Paul recognized the hippies in it. I drove into our yard. Moments later we saw the officer leave in his car. The hippies' car left also, in the opposite direction.

Still seated in our car we heard another car pull up to the Inn. Had they come back?

But it was the state trooper. He walked into our driveway and asked me for my story. I took him to the end of the pasture and there we found bullets in and around an old apple tree. Paul and Joan were fascinated and inspected every hole in the trunk.

When I asked the trooper what this was all about he told me that our neighbors were serious drug dealers and made LSD on the side. He had no idea why they'd fired all those shots into the apple tree; probably wanted to get rid of their bullets. The police had spotted their car. They'd been waiting for them to come back because they knew they had a solid case against them, but first the trooper had to go to court to get a warrant to arrest them.

"When I came back they were gone," the trooper said.

I told him I had alerted the local police because I'd been concerned, to say the least. I thought it was the right thing to do since I knew they'd wanted to spy on them. I apologized for having foiled his plan.

"Not your fault, lady," the trooper said. "They shouldn't have stuck their nose into it. It wasn't their case. It was ours."

Even though the state troopers were on the lookout all over the state, they never caught them. Happenings over the past year began to fall into place: the beat-up car from North Carolina, the funny smell from the Inn's chimney, the secretiveness. And when the fields dried up and we could ride again in the ring behind the Inn, we discovered that the whole backside of the Inn's barn had been taken down. It looked like a skeleton. So that's where all those odd pieces of lumber had come from. They'd stoked up the barn of their rented abode to make LSD. The next owners of the Inn told us they'd had to spend weeks cleaning up the place, and the worst part had been the many fireplaces. Not because of the ashes, but because the inhabitants had chosen them as the perfect place to defecate.

When Gijs returned from Washington, the Peace Corps was not the hot topic. The Inn was.

At the Peace Corps Headquarters in Washington D.C., Gijs had been placed number one on the list for South America. Brazil would probably be the first opening.

"Where would we live?" I asked.

"In the capital."

"Not in the country?"

"No. They need a doctor to care for their volunteers. Part of the time I would be traveling, of course."

"What language do they speak in Brazil? Spanish or Portuguese?" I knew that one of the reasons Gijs thought this move would be good for the children was to learn Spanish.

"Portuguese," he said, and I could tell this was a disappointment.

It would be a two-and-a-half year stint, starting sometime this fall. He would find someone to take care of his practice.

So that was it! Leaving this year! Gijs would be working only indirectly with the people the Peace Corps was set up to help. I didn't ask for any details, like how that schedule would jibe with Joan and Paul going to school and what kind of school they would go to, or where he would find a doctor willing to live in a rural area like Wakefield. The very posing of the questions would sound as if I was barricading myself against his plans to join the Peace Corps. I was sure Gijs sensed my discomfort with the prospect of being uprooted again, and I was equally sure that my reluctance angered him. Important decisions, especially life-changing decisions, shouldn't be made in a contentious atmosphere, I thought. Better to let the pot simmer down. No action needed to be taken anyway until we heard from the people in Washington, so I put the Peace Corps plans on the back burner and moved the imminent birth of Ah-Hi's foal to the front of the stove.

My horse looked like a white balloon tethered by four legs. Her due date was around Joan's birthday, the 29th of April. That day came and went. I decided to sleep in the hayloft on a camp bed, positioned across from Ah-Hi's stall and above Nutmeg and Liz's stalls.

Gijs and the children asked if I was really going to do that, sleep in the barn? Did all horse owners with pregnant mares sleep in their barn? Didn't foals just get born by themselves? Mother Nature would take care!

Maybe, but I wasn't taking any chances. My ears were always tuned to noises in the barn that carried through the timbers, and many a night I slid out of bed, tiptoed through the house and went to check. I had a sixth sense for trouble. If the car made a suspicious noise, or a child was listless, or a horse had ever so slight a limp, I was sure to spot it first. When everyone had gone to bed, I mounted the hay ladder and pulled the sleeping bag around me. The barn cats whose mission was to keep mice away from grain, curled up at the foot of my sleeping bag. Overhead hundreds of nail ends peeked through the roofing planks, holding down the asphalt shingles on the side of the sky. The wood had darkened to rich amber from exposure for a hundred and eighty years. Through two windows, one at each end, faint light entered and the stars were framed in their small rectangular panes. From my camp bed, next to an opening in the floor, I saw Nutmeg's nostrils sniffing at the hay and her supple lips grabbing the blades she liked and avoiding the prickly wild rose stems that got mixed in. I heard the intimate sounds of their steady munching and their droppings hitting the floor. They dozed standing up, resting in the hammocks of their own joints. Deeper into the safety of the night they laid down, lowering their big bellies onto the shavings with a thud.

After five nights of this routine, Paul joined me, bringing his own camp bed and sleeping bag. He had picked the right night. It was the fifth of May, twenty-five years to the day that Hitler's army had capitulated in Holland. I told Paul that sleeping on the hayloft reminded me of the day the war started and my family had to flee from our home. After a very long march while German fighter planes flew overhead, diving and shooting at us, we'd ended up somewhere near the Belgian border. A farmer was talked into letting us, and a hundred other people it seemed, sleep in his cow stalls on fresh straw.

We heard the pitter-patter of raindrops on the roof. It lulled us to sleep, though not for long. A storm approached the ridge we lived on. Rumblings sounded from the east. I gratefully thought of the three lightning rods on top of the barn. The church across the street, a landmark for well over a century, had burned to the ground in a violent storm the year before we moved here. Its stately structure was still mourned. The claps of thunder came closer, and every other minute or so the interior of the barn lit up like a stage, as if we were sleeping on the set of a horror movie. Paul was awake, I could tell, but he pretended not to be. The rain lashed the roof. In the book about equine medicine that we'd acquired for this occasion, I had read that noise could either stimulate or depress the first phase of a foal's birth. I lifted my head from the pillow. In the midst of the clattering rain, which had a certain rhythm to it, I heard a sound like the breaking of a dam. I looked over to Ah-Hi's box stall and saw her standing up with a quizzical look in her eyes. The amniotic fluid! I poked Paul and told him to go and get Dad.

"Wake Joan up too!" I called after him as he climbed down the steep ladder from the loft. Gijs was used to being aroused in the middle of deep sleep, though he never moved fast. He used the time it takes to get dressed to gather his wits before going out on a night call, aware that he would be asked to act decisively. Joan would take a little longer to put things into perspective.

Ah-Hi moved about and bent her head to look at her belly as if to figure out what she felt there that she'd never felt before. A human female goes into labor anticipating the birth of the fetus she's carried, but an animal? While I pondered that question, Paul returned with his father.

A little later Joan came. Gijs examined Ah-Hi and determined that labor had begun.

"Let's observe her from the hayloft," he said. " She's not going to deliver that foal with us standing around her."

Paul folded the camp beds and replaced them with hay bales in a row for the four of us to sit on while we watched what happened in Ah-Hi's stall below. Beneath us, Liz and Nutmeg munched on their hay, totally unconcerned about what was happening in the stall across from them.

Ah-Hi laid herself down on the soft bed of fresh shavings with her legs extended. The contractions were more violent now and we saw something emerge. We'd instructed Joan and Paul not to talk, so Joan took my hand and squeezed it. The tension was mounting and our bodies lost their midnight slump as if our muscles contracted in sympathy.

Ah-Hi was working hard, but nothing more than a little stick was visible from her behind. I saw a frown form on Gijs's forehead.

"Stay here," he said to the kids, and then to me, "Let's go down."

He looked at the one leg sticking out and told me to call the vet. It was one a.m.

Dr. Burns said he'd be right over, but he had to come from Rochester, a half-hour ride.

Back in the barn things hadn't progressed. Suddenly, Ah-Hi stood up. This was not according to the textbook. A mare normally delivers lying down, and the fetus comes head first with forelimbs, head and neck fully extended. We were looking at only one leg. Ah-Hi got restless and I was afraid she would break that little leg against the stable wall.

"I don't know a lot about this, but we shouldn't let her be in distress too long. I know that much," Gijs whispered.

"Can we do something for her?" I asked, while holding on to Ah-Hi and stroking her neck in an effort to reassure her.

Gijs pulled up his shirt sleeves and stuck his right hand into Ah-Hi's birth canal. His whole arm disappeared up to his elbow. The shapes felt unfamiliar. He made a guess and carefully tugged at what must be the missing leg. Moments later a muzzle resting on the two legs Gijs was holding onto appeared, then a rump, and two outstretched hind legs. Through all of this Ah-Hi was standing, and Gijs caught her foal in his arms, like he'd caught Joan from my womb.

Joan and Paul shrieked. They lowered themselves down the steep ladder with the ease of cats. Together we watched Ah-Hi lick her foal. Not a word was spoken. The children sat down in the shavings and took in this blob of slimy fur with moving legs and wide-open eyes, two hundred times bigger than any of Jip's puppies had been, this heap of flesh and bones that had been summoned to life by mysterious forces. Their eyes reflected awe for how creatures come to be, and for their father who had known what to do.

The barn door opened and Dr. Burns walked in.

"How are we doing?"

Gijs explained in medical shorthand what had happened and apologized for having called him out in the night.

"No problem! You did this for my mother, more than once!"

"Your mother?"

"Yes, do you remember Anna Burns? She lived on the road to Province Lake. You took care of her. She died of cancer ten years ago."

"I remember her well, but I hadn't realized the family connection."

Dr. Burns said we had a healthy filly, with white stockings and a white blaze on her forehead. He gave Ah-Hi a shot and told us to go to bed, that the mare could take care of the foal, make her stand up and drink that very important first milk.

"What shall we call her?" I asked.

"Thunder!" Joan said.

"Stormy," Paul suggested. "She was born during a storm."

"Thunder sounds so violent, don't you think? How about Rainbow?" I asked.

They agreed.

Ah-hi and her foal

Chapter 36
A Family Outing

Our homestead seemed like a paradise. The view from the dining room window resembled an eighteenth-century painting of a mare and her foal roaming in a field of dandelions. Our backyard held cackling chickens, two handsome dogs, a vegetable garden with lush plants that forecast a promising harvest: strawberries as big as pebbles, potatoes, onions, ruby red beets, tomatoes the size of a man's fist. On the street side of our home, patients came and went. Gijs's practice was flourishing.

A Dutch immigrant doctor contacted Gijs to see if she could help out in his practice for a month during the summer. She was in her second year of a psychiatry residency, had been recently widowed and had to face the world alone with four children ranging in age from seven to sixteen. Gijs had started the Netherlands-American Medical Society for just that kind of situation. Of course she could! She would live in the Tripp house and help Gijs part-time. The two girls, who were the oldest, would take care of the two boys while she worked.

It seemed like an ideal situation. She was a likeable woman and the children were well behaved. But the doctor, it turned out after she got here, couldn't work independently from Gijs because of license and insurance issues. Besides, it had been a while since she'd done general practice. Joan and Paul involved the girls with the care and riding of the horses, but that left their small brothers out. I took them under my wing. One followed me around like my shadow. After three weeks of this—Gijs double-checking everything his assistant did and me keeping a household with six children going—it was time for a break.

Gijs had the solution: we would go camping for a night on an uninhabited island in the middle of Cooks Pond, the same lake where the Averys had their cottage. The very idea transported Gijs back to his late teenage years in prison camp where he learned to survive from day to day. He gathered the tools for our outing, determined to teach his children survival techniques. Flagg Avery raised his eyebrows at his friend's idea of relaxation, but he didn't doubt that Gijs would pull it off, having slept on the steel deck of a fishing boat in Holland with him. He wondered how the rest of us would enjoy it. Flagg chuckled, made some wisecracks but never discouraged his friend from living out his dreams.

With tent gear, sleeping bags, a hatchet, lots of bug spray, matches and food we arrived at the Averys on a very hot Saturday afternoon. Mary Avery took us over to the island in her motorboat. To get on land we had to jump into the water. Gijs went first and climbed onto the banking. Tangled roots from tall pine trees greeted his bare feet. We threw him our gear. Joan and Paul dove off the boat and swam ashore while Mary helped me down from the bow and handed me the cooler with food.

"Well, have fun," she said with a trace of doubt in her voice, as I set my feet among the elder bushes. "We'll come by and see if you need anything."

Gijs was already laying out the parts of the tent on a clearing in the woods. Paul and Joan were told which part to pick up, where to place it, how to fasten it. They didn't challenge their father's instructions. No sense having a better idea. Dad had a plan and objecting to it would set him on edge. One wrong word might make the bucket of this summer's tensions overflow. We created a campsite in no time. Paul and Gijs built a barbecue pit with the rocks that popped up all around us. Joan arranged our sleeping gear inside the tent and helped me look for ways to prepare a meal without the taken-for-granted conveniences of a kitchen such as a stable surface to cut the onion and carrots on.

The fun was in finding the things we needed: kindling wood to start a fire with, pine bows to sit on. When everything that was possible to do had been done, we sat around the crackling fire to keep the bugs away. It was time to talk. It didn't take long for the Peace Corps to emerge as the topic. Washington had contacted Gijs. The position in Brazil would open up soon. Contemplating the prospect was like looking at a crystal: we got lost searching for its most defining facet. Paul liked the adventure and trusted he would get back to Wakefield. Joan wasn't so sure. She would miss the new friends she'd just made. I wasn't convinced that Gijs would be satisfied in the long run, and, on a personal level, I cringed at having to leave our home.

But Gijs wanted to do it. That was obvious. So was his inner conflict. His summer assistant had demonstrated that leaving his patients for two years was not doing them a favor, and weren't his solo practice in a small town, the farm with animals and vegetable gardens, his children and wife involved in it all, exactly what he had always dreamed of?

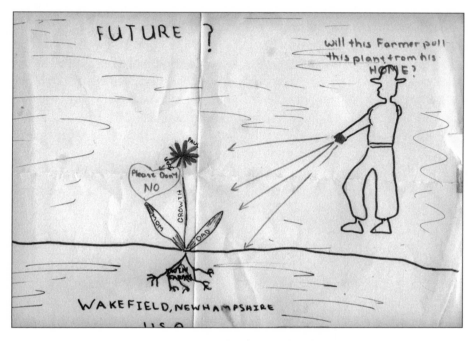

Joan made her point with a drawing

Gijs was a master in the art of debating. That evening, on the island in Cooks Pond, he met his match. After he had explained where we would be going and the good reasons why we might all give up some of the things we loved and enjoyed so we could help the people who were terribly disadvantaged in this life, Joan said, "I don't think you're doing it for those people. You're doing it for the adventure." Her arrow hit its mark.

"What do you mean? The Peace Corps hasn't been organized to create little adventures!" His eyes went dark with a rising anger.

"I know," Joan said. "It's to do good. But you said yourself, we will be living in the capital of Brazil, probably in a nice house, and you'll take care of the workers, not the people." Exactly what I'd been thinking.

"That's just as important! " Gijs got up and started pacing around our small campsite. He looked like a threatening bull, but Joan didn't back off.

"I don't see the difference between taking care of poor people here and those in Brazil," she said. Her father looked at her in disbelief. How dare she?

"The difference is that here they have access to the most advanced health care in the world, poor or not. " Gijs was trying to sound rational.

"But Dad, when you came back from Honduras, you said that people got sick and died because they walked in dirty streets and that the rich didn't care. You said they needed a different system, and plumbers. Not doctors!" Joan was putting his words to him.

"That doesn't happen overnight. In the meantime, the people suffer." Our little matador had put the arrows in the bull's neck and he was bleeding, but there was plenty of vigor left in him. It was a frightening sight. I shrank. Paul watched as his father paced around the small patch of living area we had created.

Joan

"You're leaving your patients here. They suffer too. It's just more glamorous to go to Brazil," Joan dared to say. This arrow was a big one and the blood gushed out. Gijs's eyes turned black with anger and his fists balled up. To say to a doctor that he's abandoning his patients is a serious accusation, the kind that gets him into court. Joan probably didn't realize this. I wondered what I could do to keep father and daughter from destroying each other. What had been said within just a few minutes would loom large over time and couldn't be undone. All I could hope to do was blunt their tools.

"Let's lighten up!" I said. "A doctor who wants a career change isn't abandoning his patients, Joan. Come on, let's go for a swim and get ready to make dinner."

It was very quiet around the smoldering fire. Gijs was still pacing around. Paul, who hadn't said a word, was poking the fire with a twig. I got up and walked toward the edge of the lake. Maybe the others would follow.

With a few quick strokes I gained distance from the island. The spring-fed water washed away the film of sweat that had built up over my entire body while sitting around the fire on this hot summer afternoon. From my new perspective, the island looked serenely peaceful, as if nothing in this world could tip it out of balance, and the spring-fed water of Cooks Pond held me like a mother. I relaxed, floating in its embrace.

Gijs and Joan were still locked in their contrarian moods, Paul still the observer. They hadn't come to the waterside. I felt guilty. I had let Joan do the hard work for me. She'd taken the hot, underlying issues out of hiding. Nobody, including myself, had dared to point out to Gijs that his ideal of serving in the Peace Corps might be influenced by his penchant for adventure and, equally important, by a desire to be loved and admired. She had been blunt in her youthful feeling of righteousness. As I floated around the island with enough backstrokes to keep from sinking, I reflected that for all the ease in our marriage there were a few times when I'd rather stay silent than speak my mind to Gijs. Around the edges of his good humor and common sense loomed the possibility of an explosion, and I wasn't so sure that I knew how to handle the fireworks. Besides, maybe he was right that joining the Peace Corps was a good thing for the children. Maybe he was right that I was a stick in the mud. Other wives packed up at a moment's notice and happily, or dutifully, followed in the wake of the mobile society that today's world had become.

I knew the reason why I hadn't spoken out against it. I was brought up to follow. But I silently cheered Joan because I was also selfish.

I had circled the island, back to where I started. The only way to break out of it was to clamber back on shore. I was soaked and hoped we'd not forgotten to bring towels. The debating club had broken up. Paul and Gijs were gathering wood. Joan handed me a towel and went swimming herself.

The evening was spent cooking, eating and preparing for bed. All three activities absorbed our energy, but sleep required peace of mind. Paul seemed to be the only one who had it. After a night of tossing around in a sleeping bag that was too hot for this summer night, and feeling every lump and bump through the thin tent floor, we happily greeted the sun and dove into the water. Gijs tied a red handkerchief to a branch of a tree that was in full sight of the Avery cottage. It was a relief to see Mary's boat motoring toward us, and to set foot on the mainland that offered many distractions from the oppressive single-mindedness of the island.

A few weeks after this outing, an old friend came over from Holland with his wife and son. Hans Sandkuyl had come back on the same boat from Indonesia with Gijs when they were repatriated after the war. Hans had also studied medicine and now, like Gijs, had a solo general practice in a small town. They had a lot in common, except that Hans had evaded to Chili when the Hungarian revolt broke out in the fall of 1956 and it looked like a third world war was brewing. But after a year or two, he decided to return to Holland.

Hans was smart, observant and outspoken. It didn't take him long to convince Gijs that here in Wakefield he had the world by the tail. Hans knew what South America was like and he knew what Gijs was like. He made it perfectly clear that he would give his left arm to step into what Gijs had created and practice in this wonderful little town with an excellent hospital nearby where he was even on the staff. (In Holland GP's were barred.) When Hans left, Gijs was in doubt. The next visitor was Alex ter Weele, a consultant who'd recently finished an exhaustive study of the Peace Corps. He advised Gijs against joining.

His good plan didn't look so good anymore. After a long summer of hard work and emotional upheaval, Gijs slumped. His car slumped with him and needed an overhaul or replacement. Flagg Avery took charge. Over dinner in Portsmouth they discussed the Peace Corps plans. After dinner they bought a brand new Mercedes with white paint on the outside, blue leather on the inside. I rubbed my eyes when I saw Gijs drive it into the yard with an impish smile on his face. It was a stretch to go from material sacrifice for the good of the suffering to the status of a Mercedes, even the smallest model, in the driveway.

"Will we take this to Brazil?" I asked.

"No. We'll keep it right here," Gijs said.

Chapter 37
Thanksgiving in Virginia

Jane Howe invited our family to celebrate Thanksgiving in Barboursville, Virginia. "Bring your riding clothes," she wrote. "My son Peter will take you on the foxhunt."

I accepted the invitation by return mail. Thanksgiving in Virginia sounded romantic and a foxhunt was an added attraction, but most exciting was the opportunity to reconnect with the extraordinary woman we'd met around Christmas the previous year. The image of her standing by the fireplace in the Spalding's vacation home had stayed with me. I'd recognized in her facets of my mother, Loes Hugenholtz and some of the women I had met in England. It was my mother's love of children, Loes's intelligence and bearing, the British speech and looks that had immediately attracted me, but her position as an ambassador's wife didn't make it likely, in my view, that I would meet her again, and I had counted that as a loss.

"The earth is red in Virginia," the kids shrieked when we entered the state. "What did they do to make the earth look red?"

"Nothing," we told them. "Red earth is God-given."

The landscape reminded us of New England with its rolling hills, although it exuded a different feeling. The Greek column-fronted homes bespoke the self-confidence of landed gentry, quite different from the unassuming architecture of the Puritans with their sober outlook on life. Jane's house struck a balance between the two. At the end of a circular driveway stood a home made of white-painted brick, proportioned like an Old Colonial. In spite of being set in a wide landscape, it felt cozy and loved.

As I peered into the side window of the door, I noticed the long oriental runner in the hall and the small table with a cheerful bouquet of flowers. My mind flashed back to our own abode with dog hair clinging to the worn fabric of a couch that should have been replaced many years ago—a symbol of our thrown-together-anything-goes kind of lifestyle.

Jane opened the door and threw her arms around Joan and Paul, and I felt as though we'd gone to visit family. Our suitcases went upstairs by elevator, and Joan immediately started unpacking while Paul sauntered into our room to tell about the four-poster bed he was going to share with his sister.

Over the traditional mantle in the living room hung a painting that raised my curiosity. Mountains dominated the canvas, but it didn't bring Connecticut to mind, or the Blue Mountains we saw through the back windows. Was it Chili? When I asked, Jane answered that it was where she was born: Colorado.

"Colorado?"

"Yes," Jane said. "I was raised on a ranch."

I almost said, "I'll be darned," because I'd assumed Jane came from England. This was true of her father, Jane told us. He'd come as a young man and had raised hop for the breweries in the Midwest. A British governess had schooled her at the ranch.

A South American woman brought in a tray that held everything that goes with an English tea, like small sandwiches, cookies and a fan of neatly arranged lemon slices. Paul, feeling no barriers, had all but curled up in Jane's lap, sitting in a children's chair between the fireplace and Jane's wingchair, and Joan helped serve the tea around.

Jane's husband, even in his absence, was a palpable presence. The answer to most questions led back to him. Like her father, he'd been a giant of a man, and I sensed these two men had dominated her life and influenced her whole being. Walter Howe had been a professor in history, Speaker of the House in Connecticut, served in WW II, was sent to Colombia to head AID (American International Development) and finished his career with an appointment as US ambassador to Chili. I think she would have loved and adored him even if he'd had a less illustrious career. Sigrid Spalding lamented how she wished Jane would remarry. Such an attractive woman, wealthy to boot, shouldn't have to stay single. But Jane was still in love, and always would be, with Walter Howe. It was the part about her I understood best.

At the dinner table the plans for Thanksgiving Day were laid out.

Her son Peter would have a pony for Paul and a Thoroughbred for Gijs for the foxhunt. Joan and I would hunt the following day. Peter would meet us at the Episcopal Church for the "Blessing of the Hounds," and his family would join us for the Thanksgiving meal.

Paul was up at the crack of dawn and came into our room in his riding outfit. He took stock of himself in the full-length mirror and obviously admired his new tweed jacket with the fancy split in the back. After breakfast, we drove over to the stone church; the field next to it was blanketed with horse trailers. Joan spotted Peter's blue van with the red letters "Red Horse Farm" painted on its side. A black stableman was busy braiding the horses' tails. The scene repeated itself: large vans, shiny horses, black men grooming and tacking them up for their employers who arrived in separate cars and were handed their mounts.

Blessing of the hounds

Our experience with horses was modest. Black grooms were not part of the New England horse scene. This was the South and this was Albemarle County. The gorgeous horses under men in scarlet coats and women with silk top hats, with the rolling landscape as backdrop, created an exotic sight. I felt as if I were looking at a movie, detached and entertained. We had been plunged into a world of privilege that looked attractive from the outside, but that didn't raise envy in me. I remembered the backbiting at my father's tennis club and I imagined a good deal of conniving went on among these horse owners.

Jane, Joan and I found a place in front of the church where the Master of the Hunt was keeping order among the yelping hounds on the lawn. A priest stepped out of the church and silence fell over the yard. After a prayer, he stepped over to where the hounds were milling, raised his hand and blessed them. I couldn't help wondering if another priest somewhere else was blessing the fox. During the war I'd seen German tanks being blessed by chaplains. My father told me that across the Channel, in England, Allied tanks received the same treatment. It had baffled me that clergy could be suckered into this. Would God take sides? Would it make the hunters feel better as they trampled the fields and risked their necks over stony fences to catch that naughty fox, knowing they followed hounds that had been blessed? I did not speak these thoughts. Hunting was a sport with deeply rooted traditions. Clearly.

Paul came back from the hunt proud as a peacock. He had been "blooded."

"It means," he explained to Joan, "that I was initiated in the hunt." The fox had been caught and killed before his eyes. The Master had hacked off one paw and smeared blood over Paul's hand. He wasn't supposed to clean it off for a day. That was the tradition.

"Yak," Joan said. "Barbaric." But she was impressed.

The part of the visit I'd looked forward to the most was the Thanksgiving meal. It would be a first. No, that's not true. Gijs and I had been invited to be part of the Thanksgiving celebration of the family where I had been a governess, in Marshfield Hills, on the south shore of Massachusetts, before we were married. By the time the turkey made it to the table, all the men—except for Gijs—were drunk. As soon as the meal was over, the men sat in front of the TV, watched a football game and kept drinking. We weren't tempted to make it part of our own family's traditions if that was the way to celebrate this much heralded American holiday. Instead of turkey, we had roast beef, and we ate it at night. When everybody else in town sat down for their turkey, we went for a long walk. What was worth celebrating was that everybody was too busy eating their turkey to need a doctor; although one year, Gijs was called away because a hunter shot his friend in the woods. But sometimes, when Thanksgiving was coming around again, I wished that Norman Rockwell hadn't painted that super-happy family around a festive table with a large turkey in the middle, grandpa getting ready to carve the bird and everybody folding their hands in prayer. It was one of the certainties of our immigration that our table would never look that way.

Jane had pulled out all the stops, and the rectangular mahogany table was dressed up with a center bouquet of chrysanthemums in autumn colors, tall silver candlesticks, two large porcelain chickens and all the proper implements for eating this special meal. So this was how it's done, I thought. A family get-together to give thanks, to connect with one another, even if I sensed undercurrents of conflict between Jane and her daughter-in-law. Maybe not every family had a South American couple to cook, serve and clean up, but that was Jane's good luck and she wore her privileges with grace. There was nothing ostentatious about her. She knew how to ask and how to give. Thirty-four years later we attended her ninetieth birthday party—a sit-down dinner affair—to which she'd invited her immediate family, a handful of friends and all the African-American people with their families who had cared for her over the years. They were proud to be there. As equals.

On the morning we were to leave, I found Paul sitting at Jane's feet, listening to a story she read from *Wind in the Willows*. She had captured his imagination, as she had all of ours. Standing in the library, she would pull out a book and ask if I'd read it. Most of the time I hadn't, and the way she described the book made me wish to get it. The bookcases that lined the walls were no mere decoration.

For a few days we were taken up in a world that was as different from Wakefield as a crisp Macintosh apple from a juicy Georgia peach. Yet we'd felt completely at home and at ease with our hostess. I wondered how Gijs felt in this lap of luxury after his Peace Corps dreams, but why ask and wake sleeping dogs? Certainly, his new Mercedes fitted in well, as though we belonged here. At times it was tempting to think we did. There was enough here to remind us of where we came from. Vader Bozuwa, like Walter Howe, had known the life of pomp and circumstance, of moving up in rank. When they lived in the Dutch East Indies there had been no shortage of servants. As a young boy Gijs wasn't a bit surprised to see a *katjong* clip the grass in their yard, a *baboe* pick up after him, a *kokkie* cook their meals. In the home I grew up in, books were on every table. My parents collected paintings. My mother played the piano, my father the violin. Their home, like this one, had an air of gentility.

Our own horizons were broadened for each of us in different ways. For Paul it was Peter who seemed to be good at everything he did. Gijs felt transported back to the days before WW II, when his life was elegant and orderly. Joan had found a role model for her own sense of style and other qualities she didn't have a name for but admired in Jane.

Myself?

Quite aside from the feeling that I had met a woman who understood me because she also tried to blend two cultures, and apart from my delight with her gift of friendship, the visit gave me much food for thought. Jane was twenty years younger than my mother and thirteen years older than I. These older women ran their households like CEOs, feared and loved by their staff, setting the tone on every front except the domain of their husbands. Their style of leadership was rooted in a sense of entitlement. WW II and the sixties had rearranged my own generation's priorities. The tasks were the same, the means very different. We didn't have maids, governesses and gardeners. What we did have were machines. Gadgets like dishwashers, vacuum cleaners, riding lawn mowers that empowered and emancipated us to the point that many of my peers didn't see much need to take the second-in-command position in their homes. Our lifestyle was informal out of necessity. Here, in Jane's home, I was confronted with the sacrifices as well as the progress of that development. We lost a good bit of style in our day-to-day lives, as well as time to read and reflect while we ran our time-saving machines. What we gained was independence.

I pondered about these differences for days and months. My time was today. Theirs was yesterday. The spirit of the times in which Gijs and I lived and raised our children opened up new avenues, like careers for women. Jane and Mammie's tasks had been adjunct to their husband's careers. I felt myself straddled on a fence because I saw virtue on both sides.

A quality that overarches the generations, though, that one either possesses or doesn't, is grace. It was what Joan saw in Jane but didn't yet know how to name. They sensed it in each other. Jane carried the wound of Walter's premature and sudden death without bitterness or self-pity. In this she reminded me of Loes Hugenholtz. Joan was lucky to have these two women in her life during her growing years.

Chapter 38
Wakefield Forever?

When we married, Gijs was like a spirited horse that charged ahead, kicking up a cloud of dust, thundering toward new horizons. Now, as we drove back from our visit to Jane Howe, he seemed more like a volcano that rumbled with doubts and worries.

"What would you think of moving back to Holland?" he asked while negotiating the New Jersey Turnpike.

Joan and Paul, having Virginia on their minds and feeling far away from home, thought it was a great idea. They were suspended between worlds.

"Move? Wouldn't that be fun?" they said. " Where would we live? Close to Opa and Oma, or Tante Janneke and Oom Dick? We could see the Hugenholtzes again, and the Cehas, and all those people."

"Why would you want to move back, Gijs?" I asked. "You once convinced me that we left Holland for good reasons," and I ticked off the surplus of doctors, the national health care system.

"We have Medicare here now!" Gijs shot back. "I just think that this country is headed for trouble. It's like a civil war. Look at Kent State! The Vietnam War is dividing this country. It's the same with the race problems. The drugs! It's a mess. Besides, I miss my friends."

Gijs met many people in his work, but he had forged very few meaningful friendships with Americans.

Joan and Paul piped in with their own grievances. Joan said she didn't feel close to any of her classmates, even though they'd done her the favor of voting her "most beautiful girl" of the class.

"They're just into fads. All they can talk about is boys." She giggled.

"Or girls of course." She paused for a moment. "They all want to dress the same, paint their fingernails, it's so stupid! I like Cassandra Curtis. She's the only one I see outside of school. I don't know, maybe it's because we live in another town."

"How about you, Paul?" I asked.

"I like Holland. I love the farms, and the cows, and the people." He chuckled. "And the food, of course! I sort of like school, but I don't play baseball. The boys in my class don't know anything about horseback riding and I don't know anything about baseball."

The oil storage tanks beside the turnpike appeared like mushrooms sprung out of the ground after a heavy rain. The landscape was dull and uninspiring. I couldn't find anything in the stretches of brown grass to lift my spirits. We were close to the Long Island Sound, which had seen many ships ply its waters to bring immigrants from Europe. In 1955, I had stood on the deck of the *ss Nieuw Amsterdam* as the tugboats piloted our colossal ocean liner by the Statue of Liberty. My friends and I had cheered and waved at her as if she were alive and would wave back. Gijs had met me in Hoboken with his Chevy from before the war. My luggage barely fit in the trunk because he had several boxes with bottles of motor oil stacked in there. His car was addicted to oil, he said. He drove me straight from the boat along this coast to Atlantic City, where the American Medical Association held its annual meeting. We were young, in love, a whole new world before us to explore.

Now, fifteen years later, we were driving on the same turnpike with two children in the backseat, and we were thinking of returning. How many immigrants who came from Ireland, from Italy and Sweden, from Russia had thought about going back to their homeland? They'd come with a one-way ticket. Most of them had burned their bridges, didn't have anything to go back to and had no choices. We had choices. I felt like a rich kid with a trust fund who can afford to quit his job if he doesn't like his boss. We'd become American citizens only six years ago. Would we desert the country that had adopted us because it was in trouble? Put on the old comfortable shoes because the new ones pinched a bit and caused blisters? I didn't say it out loud. It wouldn't be fair to greet plans that weren't really plans yet, just flights of fancy, with a closed mind.

When we reached our home, Joan and Paul jumped out of the car and ran to the barn. The sweet smell of hay and manure greeted us and we saw the horses sticking their heads out over the stall doors. They greeted us with loud whinnies. Paul opened Nutmeg's stall and threw his arms around her neck.

"Why don't you go to Holland?" I suggested to Gijs. "Check it out. Your mother and Janneke can use your help." His two aunts had recently died. Gijs and his sister were the only heirs. Their estate needed to be settled, their house emptied.

Gijs went, and his own mother and mine talked him out of his plans. Don't do it, they said. We may not have a Vietnam War going on in this country, but our society is becoming just as materialistic. Hardly anyone your age goes to church anymore. The old taboos about sex have been thrown out. If you think America has a permissive society, turn on the TV here and you won't believe your eyes! There are no limits to what they dare to show on the screen.

The mothers told Gijs that students dressed like street beggars and the difference between a boy and a girl was hard to tell these days. There were drugs. Holland was only a few years behind America. Wakefield is a paradise you won't be able to recreate here, they said. Your wife and children are happy. You have built a successful practice. Why give it up? The Holland you remember is fading fast. Stay where you are!

Gijs came back riddled with doubts. He hated himself for it.

Right after Christmas it was my turn to go to Holland. My father had been diagnosed with prostate cancer. My mother had bronchitis. "Go over," Gijs said. "We'll manage."

A taxi drove me up to the front door of the apartment building. Mammie was waiting in the big hall downstairs. I hadn't expected her. The connecting flight from London had been delayed. She'd sat herself on a couch in the hall with a view of the street and waited for me to come home as she'd done so may times when I was a teenager, out for a late night. Her embrace, the warm body gathering me up, broke my contained emotions. This loyalty, this unconditional love; where do we find it after we leave home? Was this part of what Gijs was missing? Not my mother's embrace, but the intense familiarity?

My father looked pale. I drove him to his doctor's appointment. After he was seen, I spoke with Dr. Wierdack alone. I asked him what the prognosis was.

"That's impossible to say," Dr Wierdack said. "It can be in remission for years, but then again, it could rear up sooner. Your father doesn't know he has cancer, but I think he suspects it. He hasn't asked and I haven't volunteered. We'll play it by ear. I think he's better off not knowing." The healer went by his gut feeling that my father would be better served this way. Besides, he had no cures to offer. My father lived another thirteen years.

It was like falling back into a soft cushion to live my parents' life for a few weeks. I had forgotten how late the sun came up in the dead of winter, and how early it set. From my bedroom window I saw people going to work on their bikes in the pitch dark, and it was already past eight in the morning. The weather was mostly wet and windy, the lawns still green. The occasional frost hadn't bitten hard enough yet to turn it yellow. I took my mother's large leather shopping bag and walked to the butcher and the baker around the corner. Both stores sparkled with cleanliness, just as I remembered. I couldn't sleep at night. This was such a sweet place. Why didn't I want to go back to it? Was I stubborn, couldn't admit life in America had its pitfalls? What was I defending?

It felt good to sit on the soft couch by the window and cry while my mother listened, just sitting there in her chair by the tea table, her hands folded in her lap.

"I know it's harder for Gijs and the children," I said. "I don't have to deal with patients or nasty kids on the school bus. Janneke told me that Gijs had said, 'It's the most fun for Titia to live in Wakefield.'" This is where I had started to cry. "Dammit. I don't play. I work hard."

"I know you do," my mother said. It was enough encouragement to kick over my bucket of confusion and spill it all.

I received two letters from Joan, three letters from Paul and numerous telephone calls from Gijs. When I came home, my side of the bed was turned down. A chocolate wrapped in gold foil sat on the pillow, a glass of water on the table next to it, just as Joan had seen it done at Jane's house. She had set the table, placed a vase with fresh white mums in the middle. Gijs had bought steaks, which he grilled in the open fireplace. I put my presents for them on the counter between the dining room and kitchen: cigars for Gijs, sweets for the children, a saddle pad for Paul, a leather pocket book for Joan. It was already dark outside. The melted fat from the steaks made the fire flare up with sizzling sounds. The shadows of the flames danced on the white walls, and the dark paneling between the beams in the ceiling sat over us like a warm tent. We felt cozy. We knew we were an entity.

In bed, I curled up in Gijs's arms, my head fitting perfectly in the crook of his arms. I told him why I thought we should stay in Wakefield.

"You know, Gijs, it was wonderful of course in Holland, great to see my parents. I had one of the best visits with your mother. She knows you well! And she was so sweet to make a lunch with everything she knows I love, like fresh herring. It was fun to go shopping, to go to the farmers' market in front of my parents' old house. But you know what? I missed the adventure. Living here is an adventure and it keeps being an adventure. After a while I felt stifled in Holland. I don't know how to say it, but I felt like I couldn't be myself. Isn't that strange? I love my family, but they sure have a way of telling you what to do. If you have a plan they either take it over and start remaking it for you or they tell you it's a crazy idea. I'm not used to that anymore! Here people let you be, if you want to experiment. 'Go ahead, do it your own way!'"

"I know what you mean," Gijs mumbled.

"Here it's a challenge to try to blend our 'Dutchness' with what's typically American, although I wouldn't be able to say what it is exactly that makes something typically Dutch or typically American. If we've learned anything in Holland and believe in it, we should be able to pass that on to our children. If we find the balance, we'll have created something unique. I think the clue is that we have to really believe in what we want to pass on and be positive about that   American values as well as Dutch values, the best of both worlds. Paul and Joan will have to decide for themselves, later on, what they want to pass on to their own kids."

We talked some more. The spaciousness of America, the climate, the friendliness of the people around us, the endless possibilities, these were the themes we kept coming back to. After we had exhausted ourselves, we made love. We melded together in a bond that needs no explanations.

I dreamed of a heron with feathers the color of steel, like the sky on an overcast day. It stood in shallow water at the edge of a lake, staring down into the water at the micro world of fishes below. It took what it needed and was content. It stood there for a long time, its two feet firmly planted in the sandy soil. Then it flew up, neck curved and long legs stretched, a gray line against the sky. With sure strokes of its wide wings it flew away over the ocean and landed near the dike that contained a wide river. Filled up on fish again, it flew back over the wide ocean, landed in the marshy edge of the lake and blended in with the tall grasses. It stayed there.

When I woke up, I knew that bird was me.

Epilogue

The next day, Gijs came back from Wolfeboro with a big bouquet of red roses.

"Let's stay here," he said.

I remember that bright bouquet well, and the warm embrace that went with it, yet it looks different in my memory from the actual moment. I wasn't so sure then that the words "let's stay here" would mean just that, but I now know that it was the beginning of the tenuous process of putting our roots down. Writing memories has a way of reframing them. With those roses, Gijs threw a switch and backed his train onto its original track.

He celebrated his decision by calling his patient Marshall Fox to see if he might have a piece of land for sale that we could ride to with our horses, tie them up, have a picnic, maybe even pitch a tent and stay overnight. Certainly, that would be the kind of thing you couldn't do in Holland where there wasn't a square inch of land left for that kind of extravagant purpose. Marshall said we could buy the Kimball Lot in Brookfield, named after the man who once ran a sawmill on it. A flat piece on a hill was suitable for building a paddock. A nearby brook meandered through a marshy meadow that grew the type of coarse grass the settlers had fed their cattle until they'd worked the woods into new pastureland. A summer meadow, they called it.

When the four of us walked the Kimball lot in the snow after the deed was signed, I thought of the early settlers who drove a stake into the ground after they had claimed it as their own; a symbol of their commitment to till and work that land, and eventually to belong to it.

A compromise was made for Joan. She attended the American High School in The Hague where she lived with Paul and Loes Hugenholtz for two years. Our own Paul had no wish to follow in her footsteps. Holland was a nice country to visit, but he projected his future on this side of the Atlantic. He told us he wanted to go to Holderness. Gijs and I had never heard of a boarding school in Holderness, but Paul had and he was determined to go there.

The seventies turned out distinctly different from the sixties. Gradually, the profile of Gijs's patients changed. The old farmers were disappearing and a different type of people bought their land. The young and idealistic wanted to get away from urban or suburban life, and the older ones had family roots in the area and came here to retire. The town lost its worn look. His new patients were more sophisticated and took an active part in their own health care. Natural childbirth was now "in," and younger women especially sought alternative ways of healing. Gijs applauded this trend, though he had deeply respected the plucky elders who stoically accepted their fate.

When Joan and Paul left home, I was forty-three years old. Like every mother who sees the young flee the nest, I had to adjust. Before the children left, I had started a Pony Club. We called it the Twin Ridge Pony Club. Every weekend ten trailers drove up with horses or ponies and their young riders. They slept in the Tripp house, made their own breakfast and lunch and were instructed in the art of riding as well as caring for their mounts over the course of two days. The parents provided the evening meals. It was a glorious time of horsy activity, young people around, building fences and cross-country courses together, putting on horse shows and events. But by 1980, it was time to stop. Without Paul and Joan present, it didn't serve its original purpose of making new friends and learning about organization and responsibility.

But it was through serving on several local boards that I became more attuned to the American way of life and to the people in our town. I gained deep respect for both. As a trustee for the local libraries and as deaconess of the Congregational Church, I learned how a true democracy governs and what majority rule means in practice. I was impressed with the seriousness with which people of various walks of life approached these civic duties.

Yet it took a tragedy to fully experience that we had been made a part of this town. When Joan died six weeks after her twenty-ninth birthday

– of breast cancer – Wakefield closed itself around us the way a family would. Americans have a marvelous quality of acting on their charitable feelings when they perceive a need. That quality had shown itself in 1958 when the selectmen organized a reception for the new doctor. We experienced it again as an avalanche of letters, flowers, pies and various forms of warm food flowed to our doorstep.

Loes Hugenholtz came over from Holland to be with Joan for that last week of her life. Peter Howe brought his mother over for what turned out to be her last night. While he took care of the horses for me, Jane read to Joan from one of her favorite books. Diana Hopewell fed Joan chicken bouillon, spoon for spoon, while Bob mowed the neglected lawn. Mary Avery stayed close by and suffered as much as we did.

Over five hundred people attended Joan's funeral. It was in those heartbreaking days that we knew we had become Americans. All four of us.

About the Author

Titia Bozuwa emigrated from Holland with her husband, Gijs, in 1957. They settled in Wakefield, New Hampshire where Gijs established his medical practice. They raised two children, Joan and Paul.

At age 29, Joan passed away after battling cancer for a little over a year. Titia's first book, *Joan - A Mother's Memoir*, explores this loss. The book earned her the 2001 Klive Knowles/Jimmy Yates Award.

The first chapter of *Wings of Change* is based on her short story, "Crossing the Atlantic," published by *Garden Lane* magazine in 2001.

In the Shadow of the Cathedral, published in 2004, recounts Titia's childhood experiencs growing up in Nazi occupied Holland during World War II.

Titia and Gijs still live in their original Wakefield residence where she conducts the Twin Farms Writers Workshops.